D0855899

BLOOM'S

HOW TO WRITE ABOUT

J.D. Salinger

CHRISTINE KERR

Introduction by Harold Bloom

BLOOM'S
LITERARY CRITICISM
An imprint of Infobase Publishing

Bloom's How to Write about J. D. Salinger

Copyright © 2008 by Christine Kerr

All rights reserved. No part of this book may be reproduced or utilized in any form or by any means, electronic or mechanical, including photocopying, recording, or by any information storage or retrieval systems, without permission in writing from the publisher. For information contact:

Bloom's Literary Criticism
An imprint of Infobase Publishing
132 West 31st Street
New York NY 10001

Library of Congress Cataloging-in-Publication Data

Kerr, Christine.
  Bloom's how to write about J. D. Salinger / Christine Kerr; introduction by Harold Bloom.
    p. cm.
  Includes bibliographical references and index.
  ISBN 978-0-7910-9483-9 (alk. paper)
  1. Salinger, J. D. (Jerome David), 1919—Criticism and interpretation. 2. Criticism—Authorship. 3. Report writing. I. Bloom, Harold. II. Title. III. Title: How to write about J. D. Salinger.
PS3537.A426Z675 2008
813'.54—dc22   2006100570

Bloom's Literary Criticism books are available at special discounts when purchased in bulk quantities for businesses, associations, institutions, or sales promotions. Please call our Special Sales Department in New York at (212) 967-8800 or (800) 322-8755.

You can find Bloom's Literary Criticism on the World Wide Web at http://www. chelseahouse.com

Text design by Annie O'Donnell
Cover design by Ben Peterson

Printed in the United States of America

Bang CGI 10 9 8 7 6 5 4 3 2 1

This book is printed on acid-free paper.

CONTENTS

SERIES
INTRODUCTION

BLOOM'S How to Write about Literature series is designed to inspire students to write fine essays on great writers and their works. Each volume in the series begins with an introduction by Harold Bloom, meditating on the challenges and rewards of writing about the volume's subject author. The first chapter then provides detailed instructions on how to write a good essay, including how to find a thesis; how to develop an outline; how to write a good introduction, body text, and conclusions; how to cite sources; and more. The second chapter provides a brief overview of the issues involved in writing about the subject author and then a number of suggestions for paper topics, with accompanying strategies for addressing each topic. Succeeding chapters cover the author's major works.

The paper topics suggested within this book are open ended, and the brief strategies provided are designed to give students a push forward on the writing process rather than a road map to success. The aim of the book is to pose questions, not answer them. Many different kinds of papers could result from each topic. As always, the success of each paper will depend completely on the writer's skill and imagination.

INTRODUCTION
by Harold Bloom

HOW TO WRITE ABOUT J. D. SALINGER

I T IS both a burden and a help in writing about J. D. Salinger's major creation, Holden Caulfield, to follow critical precedent and invoke Huck
Finn. Huck is now American mythology, and Holden hovers in the outer
shadows of the American Dream, which he may not embody as much as
does Jay Gatsby. So dimmed is the American Dream in 2007 that it may
now be just another study of the nostalgias, in our third Gilded Age.
Mark Twain fought his era's Gilded Age, as did Sinclair Lewis the next
one. Our current Gilded Age of Dubya, or Shrub (to honor the late Molly
Ivins), will be of shorter duration than the first two, since the age of
information moves with instantaneous speed, which may be why we do
not yet have an adequate literary satirist among us to skewer the ongoing
reign of Bush the Second.

Even if the American Dream fades away forever, Holden may emu-
late Gatsby as a permanent protagonist in American literature, though
neither is likely to join Huck Finn as an American legend. Huck's fictive
persuasiveness is so enormous that he is as legendary as "Walt Whitman," the persona of *Leaves of Grass,* or Captain Ahab in *Moby-Dick.* The
demarcations between the American Dream and the American mythology are ghostly, and they shift with our socioeconomic political fortunes.
But *The Great Gatsby* is clearly not a Period Piece, and after more than
five decades, *The Catcher in the Rye* (1951) possibly is not one either. It
is an irony that J. D. Salinger personally now seems to be a Period Piece.
Born in 1919, he maintains his reclusive authorial silence. His stories of

the Glass siblings have faded away (at least for me) because there is no Holden among their protagonists.

You cannot write well about any author if you begin with an inflated estimate of her or his eminence. Holden is a legitimate descendant of Huck Finn, in that lineage that stems both from Huck's evasion of those who would deceive him and from his tough idealism. This varied group includes Hemingway's Nick Adams, who is too finely prosed not to outshine Holden's more wavering narrative voice, since Holden is a kind of borderline hysteric though always a vivacious one.

Huck's knowing innocence, his other crucial attribute, is a kind of beautiful nostalgia for an America that never was, yet at the start wanted to be. Emerson's American Adam was incarnated in "Walt Whitman," in the fictive Thoreau of *Walden* (fed dinner nightly by Mrs. Emerson), and in the visionary company of Hemingway's Jake Barnes in *The Sun Also Rises* and in Fitzgerald's Nick Carraway in *The Great Gatsby.* I think also, in a darker register, of Darl Bundren in Faulkner's masterpiece, *As I Lay Dying,* and of Nathanael West's Miss Lonelyhearts and Thomas Pynchon's Oedipa Maas in *The Crying of Lot 49.* All of these characters are ultimately wiser than Holden, and the stories they tell are larger and more intellectually challenging than his. And yet, like all of them, Holden Caulfield has some share in the superb aesthetic dignity of Mark Twain's Huckleberry Finn. I know of few better ways to begin writing about Holden than by going back to Huck. "Start with the sun and the rest will follow," D. H. Lawrence observed. Start with Huck in writing about Holden, and then see what will follow.

HOW TO WRITE
A GOOD ESSAY

WHILE THERE are many ways to write about literature, most assignments for high school and college English classes call for analytical papers. In these assignments, you are presenting your interpretation of a text to your reader. Your objective is to interpret the text's meaning in order to enhance your reader's understanding and enjoyment of the work. Without exception, strong papers about the meaning of a literary work are built upon a careful, close reading of the text or texts. Careful, analytical reading should always be the first step in your writing process. This volume provides models of such close, analytical reading, and these should help you develop your own skills as a reader and as a writer.

As the examples throughout this book demonstrate, attentive reading entails thinking about and evaluating the formal (textual) aspects of the author's works: theme, character, form, and language. In addition, when writing about a work, many readers choose to move beyond the text itself to consider the work's cultural context. In these instances, writers might explore the historical circumstances of the time period in which the work was written. Alternatively, they might examine the philosophies and ideas that a work addresses. Even in cases where writers explore a work's cultural context, though, papers must still address the more formal aspects of the work itself. A good interpretative essay that evaluates Charles Dickens's use of the philosophy of utilitarianism in his novel *Hard Times*, for example, cannot adequately address the author's treatment of the philosophy without firmly grounding this discussion in the book itself. In other words, any analytical paper about a text, even

1

one that seeks to evaluate the work's cultural context, must also have a firm handle on the work's themes, characters, and language. You must look for and evaluate these aspects of a work, then, as you read a text and as you prepare to write about it.

WRITING ABOUT THEMES

Literary themes are more than just topics or subjects treated in a work; they are attitudes or points about these topics that often structure other elements in a work. Writing about theme requires that you not just identify a topic that a literary work addresses but also discuss what that work says about that topic. For example, if you were writing about the culture of the American South in William Faulkner's famous story "A Rose for Emily," you would need to discuss what Faulkner says, argues, or implies about that culture and its passing.

When you prepare to write about thematic concerns in a work of literature, you will probably discover that, like most works of literature, your text touches upon other themes in addition to its central theme. These secondary themes also provide rich ground for paper topics. A thematic paper on "A Rose for Emily" might consider gender or race in the story. While neither of these could be said to be the central theme of the story, they are clearly related to the passing of the "Old South" and could provide plenty of good material for papers.

As you prepare to write about themes in literature, you might find a number of strategies helpful. After you identify a theme or themes in the story, you should begin by evaluating how other elements of the story—such as character, point of view, imagery, and symbolism—help develop the theme. You might ask yourself what your own responses are to the author's treatment of the subject matter. Do not neglect the obvious, either: What expectations does the title set up? How does the title help develop thematic concerns? Clearly, the title "A Rose for Emily" says something about the narrator's attitude toward the title character, Emily Grierson, and all she represents.

WRITING ABOUT CHARACTER

Generally, characters are essential components of fiction and drama. (This is not always the case, though; Ray Bradbury's "August 2026: There

Will Come Soft Rains" is technically a story without characters, at least any human characters.) Often, you can discuss character in poetry, as in T. S. Eliot's "The Love Song of J. Alfred Prufrock" or Robert Browning's "My Last Duchess." Many writers find that analyzing character is one of the most interesting and engaging ways to work with a piece of literature and to shape a paper. After all, characters generally are human, and we all know something about being human and living in the world. While it is always important to remember that these figures are not real people but creations of the writer's imagination, it can be fruitful to begin evaluating them as you might evaluate a real person. Often you can start with your own response to a character. Did you like or dislike the character? Did you sympathize with the character? Why or why not?

Keep in mind, though, that emotional responses like these are just starting places. To truly explore and evaluate literary characters, you need to return to the formal aspects of the text and evaluate how the author has drawn these characters. The 20th-century writer E. M. Forster coined the terms *flat characters* and *round characters*. Flat characters are static, one-dimensional characters who frequently represent a particular concept or idea. In contrast, round characters are fully drawn and much more realistic characters who frequently change and develop over the course of a work. Are the characters you are studying flat or round? What elements of the characters lead you to this conclusion? Why might the author have drawn characters like this? How does their development affect the meaning of the work? Similarly, you should explore the techniques the author uses to develop characters. Do we hear a character's own words, or do we hear only other characters' assessments of him or her? Or, does the author use an omniscient or limited omniscient narrator to allow us access to the workings of the characters' minds? If so, how does that help develop the characterization? Often you can even evaluate the narrator as a character. How trustworthy are the opinions and assessments of the narrator? You should also think about characters' names. Do they mean anything? If you encounter a heroine named Sophia or Sophie, you should probably think about her wisdom (or lack thereof), since the word *sophia* means "wisdom" in Greek. Similarly, since the name *Sylvia* is derived from the word *sylvan*, meaning "of the wood," you might want to evaluate that character's relationship with nature. Once again, you might look to the title of the work. Does Herman Melville's

"Bartleby the Scrivener" signal anything about Bartleby himself? Is Bartleby adequately defined by his job as scrivener? Is this part of Melville's point? Pursuing questions like these can help you develop thorough papers about characters from psychological, sociological, or more formalistic perspectives.

WRITING ABOUT FORM AND GENRE

Genre, a word derived from French, means "type" or "class." Literary genres are distinctive classes or categories of literary composition. On the most general level, literary works can be divided into the genres of drama, poetry, fiction, and essays—yet within those genres, there are classifications that are also referred to as genres. Tragedy and comedy, for example, are genres of drama. Epic, lyric, and pastoral are genres of poetry. *Form,* on the other hand, generally refers to the shape or structure of a work. There are many clearly defined forms of poetry that follow specific patterns of meter, rhyme, and stanza. Sonnets, for example, are poems that follow a fixed form of 14 lines. Sonnets generally follow one of two basic sonnet forms, each with its own distinct rhyme scheme. Haiku is another example of poetic form, traditionally consisting of three unrhymed lines of five, seven, and five syllables.

While you might think that writing about form or genre might leave little room for argument, many of these forms and genres are very fluid. Remember that literature is evolving and ever changing, and so are its forms. As you study poetry, you may find that poets, especially more modern poets, play with traditional poetic forms, bringing about new effects. Similarly, dramatic tragedy was once quite narrowly defined, but over the centuries playwrights have broadened and challenged traditional definitions, changing the shape of tragedy. When Arthur Miller wrote *Death of a Salesman,* many critics challenged the idea that tragic drama could encompass a common man like Willy Loman.

Evaluating how a work of literature fits into or challenges the boundaries of its form or genre can provide you with fruitful avenues of investigation. You might find it helpful to ask why the work does or does not fit into traditional categories. Why might Miller have thought it fitting to write a tragedy of the common man? Similarly, you might compare the content or theme of a work with its form. How well do they work together? Many of Emily Dickinson's poems, for instance, follow the meter of traditional hymns. While some of her poems seem to express traditional religious doctrines, many seem to challenge or strain against traditional conceptions of God and theology. What is the effect, then, of her use of traditional hymn meter?

WRITING ABOUT LANGUAGE, SYMBOLS, AND IMAGERY

No matter what the genre, writers use words as their most basic tool. Language is the most fundamental building block of literature. It is essential that you pay careful attention to the author's language and word choice as you read, reread, and analyze a text. Imagery is language that appeals to the senses. Most commonly, imagery appeals to our sense of vision, creating a mental picture, but authors also use language that appeals to our other senses. Images can be literal or figurative. Literal images use sensory language to describe an actual thing. In the broadest terms, figurative language uses one thing to speak about something else. For example, if I call my boss a snake, I am not saying that he is literally a reptile. Instead, I am using figurative language to communicate my opinions about him. Since we think of snakes as sneaky, slimy, and sinister, I am using the concrete image of a snake to communicate these abstract opinions and impressions.

The two most common figures of speech are similes and metaphors. Both are comparisons between two apparently dissimilar things. Similes are explicit comparisons using the word *like* or *as,* and metaphors are implicit comparisons. To return to the previous example, if I say, "My boss, Bob, was waiting for me when I showed up to work five minutes late today—the snake!," I have constructed a metaphor. Writing about his experiences fighting in World War I, Wilfred Owen begins his poem "Dulce Et Decorum Est," with a string of similes: "Bent double, like old beggars under sacks, / Knock-kneed, coughing like hags, we cursed through sludge." Owen's goal was to undercut clichéd notions that war and dying in battle were glorious. Certainly, comparing soldiers to coughing hags and to beggars underscores his point.

"Fog," a short poem by Carl Sandburg provides clear example of a metaphor. Sandburg's poem reads:

The fog comes
on little cat feet.

It sits looking
over harbor and city
on silent haunches
and then moves on.

Notice how effectively Sandburg conveys surprising impressions of the fog by comparing two seemingly disparate things—the fog and a cat.

Symbols, by contrast, are things that stand for, or represent, other things. Often they represent something intangible, such as concepts or ideas. In everyday life we use and understand symbols easily. Babies at christenings and brides at weddings wear white to represent purity. Think, too, of a dollar bill. The paper itself has no value in and of itself. Instead, that paper bill is a symbol of something else, the precious metal in a nation's coffers. Symbols in literature work similarly. Authors use symbols to evoke more than a simple, straightforward, literal meaning. Characters, objects, and places can all function as symbols. Famous literary examples of symbols include Moby-Dick, the white whale of Herman Melville's novel, and the scarlet *A* of Nathaniel Hawthorne's *The Scarlet Letter.* As both of these symbols suggest, a literary symbol cannot be adequately defined or explained by any one meaning. Hester Prynne's Puritan community clearly intends her scarlet *A* as a symbol of her adultery, but as the novel progresses, even her own community reads the letter as representing not just *adultery,* but *able, angel,* and a host of other meanings.

Writing about imagery and symbols requires close attention to the author's language. To prepare a paper on symbolism or imagery in a work, identify and trace the images and symbols and then try to draw some conclusions about how they function. Ask yourself how any symbols or images help contribute to the themes or meanings of the work. What connotations do they carry? How do they affect your reception of the work? Do they shed light on characters or settings? A strong paper on imagery or symbolism will thoroughly consider the use of figures in the text and will try to reach some conclusions about how or why the author uses them.

WRITING ABOUT HISTORY AND CONTEXT

As noted above, it is possible to write an analytical paper that also considers the work's context. After all, the text was not created in a vacuum. The author lived and wrote in a specific time period and in a specific cultural context and, like all of us, was shaped by his or her environment. Learning more about the historical and cultural circumstances that surround the author and the work can help illuminate a text and provide you with productive material for a paper. Remember, though, that when you write analytical papers, you should use the context to illuminate the text. Do not lose sight of your goal—to interpret the meaning of the literary work. Use historical or philosophical research as a tool to develop your textual evaluation.

Thoughtful readers often consider how history and culture affected the author's choice and treatment of his or her subject matter. Investigations into the history and context of a work could examine the work's relation to specific historical events, such as the Salem Witch Trials in 17th-century Massachusetts or the restoration of Charles to the British throne in 1660. Bear in mind that historical context is not limited to politics and world events. While knowing about the Vietnam War is certainly helpful in interpreting much of Tim O'Brien's fiction, and some knowledge of the French Revolution clearly illuminates the dynamics of Charles Dickens's *A Tale of Two Cities,* historical context also entails the fabric of daily life. Examining a text in light of gender roles, race relations, class boundaries, or working conditions can give rise to thoughtful and compelling papers. Exploring the conditions of the working class in 19th-century England, for example, can provide a particularly effective avenue for writing about Dickens's *Hard Times.*

You can begin thinking about these issues by asking broad questions at first. What do you know about the time period and about the author? What does the editorial apparatus in your text tell you? These might be starting places. Similarly, when specific historical events or dynamics are particularly important to understanding a work but might be somewhat obscure to modern readers, textbooks usually provide notes to explain historical background. These are a good place to start. With this information, ask yourself how these historical facts and circumstances might have affected the author, the presentation of theme, and the presentation

of character. How does knowing more about the work's specific historical context illuminate the work? To take a well-known example, understanding the complex attitudes toward slavery during the time Mark
Twain wrote *Adventures of Huckleberry Finn* should help you begin to
examine issues of race in the text. Additionally, you might compare these
attitudes to those of the time in which the novel was set. How might this
comparison affect your interpretation of a work written after the aboli-
tion of slavery but set before the Civil War?

WRITING ABOUT PHILOSOPHY AND IDEAS

Philosophical concerns are closely related to both historical context and
thematic issues. Like historical investigation, philosophical research
can provide a useful tool as you analyze a text. For example, an investigation into the working class in Dickens's England might lead you to
a topic on the philosophical doctrine of utilitarianism in *Hard Times*.
Many other works explore philosophies and ideas quite explicitly. Mary
Shelley's famous novel *Frankenstein,* for example, explores John Locke's
tabula rasa theory of human knowledge as she portrays the intellectual
and emotional development of Victor Frankenstein's creature. As this
example indicates, philosophical issues are somewhat more abstract
than investigations of theme or historical context. Some other examples
of philosophical issues include human free will, the formation of human
identity, the nature of sin, or questions of ethics.

Writing about philosophy and ideas might require some outside
research, but usually the notes or other material in your text will provide you with basic information and often footnotes and bibliographies
suggest places you can go to read further about the subject. If you have
identified a philosophical theme that runs through a text, you might ask
yourself how the author develops this theme. Look at character development and the interactions of characters, for example. Similarly, you
might examine whether the narrative voice in a work of fiction addresses
the philosophical concerns of the text.

WRITING COMPARISON AND CONTRAST ESSAYS

Finally, you might find that comparing and contrasting the works or techniques of an author provides a useful tool for literary analysis. A com-

parison and contrast essay might compare two characters or themes in a single work, or it might compare the author's treatment of a theme in two works. It might also contrast methods of character development or analyze an author's differing treatment of a philosophical concern in two works. Writing comparison and contrast essays, though, requires some special consideration. While they generally provide you with plenty of material to use, they also come with a built-in trap: the laundry list. These papers often become mere lists of connections between the works. As this chapter will discuss, a strong thesis must make an assertion that you want to prove or validate. A strong comparison/contrast thesis, then, needs to comment on the significance of the similarities and differences you observe. It is not enough merely to assert that the works contain similarities and differences. You might, for example, assert why the similarities and differences are important and explain how they illuminate the works' treatment of theme. Remember, too, that a thesis should not be a statement of the obvious. A comparison/contrast paper that focuses only on very obvious similarities or differences does little to illuminate the connections between the works. Often, an effective method of shaping a strong thesis and argument is to begin your paper by noting the similarities between the works but then to develop a thesis that asserts how these apparently similar elements are different. If, for example, you observe that Emily Dickinson wrote a number of poems about spiders, you might analyze how she uses spider imagery differently in two poems. Similarly, many scholars have noted that Hawthorne created many "mad scientist" characters, men who are so devoted to their science or their art that they lose perspective on all else. A good thesis comparing two of these characters—Aylmer of "The Birth-mark" and Dr. Rappaccini of "Rappaccini's Daughter," for example—might initially identify both characters as examples of Hawthorne's mad scientist type but then argue that their motivations for scientific experimentation differ. If you strive to analyze the similarities or differences, discuss significances, and move beyond the obvious, your paper should move beyond the laundry list trap.

PREPARING TO WRITE

Armed with a clear sense of your task—illuminating the text—and with an understanding of theme, character, language, history, and philosophy, you are ready to approach the writing process. Remember that good writing is grounded in good reading and that close reading takes time, attention, and more than one reading of your text. Read for comprehension first. As you go back and review the work, mark the text to chart the details of the work as well as your reactions. Highlight important passages, repeated words, and image patterns. "Converse" with the text through marginal notes. Mark turns in the plot, ask questions, and make observations about characters, themes, and language. If you are reading from a book that does not belong to you, keep a record of your reactions in a journal or notebook. If you have read a work of literature carefully, paying attention to both the text and the context of the work, you have a leg up on the writing process. Admittedly, at this point, your ideas are probably very broad and undefined, but you have taken an important first step toward writing a strong paper.

Your next step is to focus, to take a broad, perhaps fuzzy, topic and define it more clearly. Even a topic provided by your instructor will need to be focused appropriately. Remember that good writers make the topic their own. There are a number of strategies—often called "invention"—that you can use to develop your own focus. In one such strategy, *freewriting*, you spend 10 minutes or so just writing about your topic without referring back to the text or your notes. Write whatever comes to mind; the important thing is that you just keep writing. Often this process allows you to develop fresh ideas or approaches to your subject matter. You could also try *brainstorming*. Write down your topic and then list all the related points or ideas you can think of. Include questions, comments, words, important passages or events, and anything else that comes to mind. Let one idea lead to another. In the related technique of *clustering*, or *mapping*, write your topic on a sheet of paper and write related ideas around it. Then list related subpoints under each of these main ideas. Many people then draw arrows to show connections between points. This technique helps you narrow your topic and can also help you organize your ideas. Similarly, asking journalistic questions— Who? What? Where? When? Why? and How?—can develop ideas for topic development.

Thesis Statements

Once you have developed a focused topic, you can begin to think about your thesis statement, the main point or purpose of your paper. It is imperative that you craft a strong thesis; otherwise, your paper will likely be little more than random, disorganized observations about the text. Think of your thesis statement as a kind of road map for your paper. It tells your reader where you are going and how you are going to get there.

To craft a good thesis, you must keep a number of things in mind. First, as the title of this subsection indicates, your paper's thesis should be a statement, an assertion about the text that you want to prove or validate. Beginning writers often formulate a question that they attempt to use as a thesis. For example, a writer exploring the character of Sergeant X in Salinger's "For Esmé—with Love and Squalor" might ask, How does Esmé's interaction with Sergeant X help the troubled soldier overcome his war trauma? While a question like this is a good strategy to use in the invention process to help narrow your topic and find your thesis, it cannot serve as the thesis statement because it does not tell your reader what you want to assert about Sergeant X. You might shape this question into a thesis by instead proposing an answer to that question: X's feelings of depression and alienation caused by war trauma prove impossible to surmount alone. However, the power of love and compassion shown by another human being can be the determining factor in overcoming the aftermath of war and regaining a sense of connection with the rest of humanity. Note that this thesis provides an initial plan or structure for the rest of the paper, and note, too, that the thesis statement does not necessarily have to fit into one sentence. After establishing the negative emotions that Sergeant X is experiencing, you could examine the ways in which X tries to withstand the depression that is engulfing him and then continue to show how Salinger casts Esmé's loving gesture to Sergeant X as the event that has the power to heal the despondent man.

Second, remember that a good thesis makes an assertion that you need to support. In other words, a good thesis does not state the obvious. If you tried to formulate a thesis about Sergeant X by simply saying, Salinger's Sergeant X in "For Esmé—with Love and Squalor" is a man who has been traumatized by war, you have done nothing but state the obvious. Since the central section of the short story describes in detail Sergeant X's combat stress symptoms, there would be no point in using three to five pages to support that asser-tion. You might try to develop a thesis by asking yourself some further questions: Why was Sergeant X affected so badly by the war? Does the story validate Sergeant X and his attitudes toward the war and the war environment, or does it criticize him? How does Sergeant X differ from characters who are not traumatized by the war? What event allows Ser-geant X to start the process of healing from war trauma? Such a line of questioning might lead you to a more viable thesis, like the one in the preceding paragraph.

As the comparison with the road map also suggests, your thesis should appear near the beginning of the paper. In relatively short papers (three to six pages), the thesis almost always appears in the first para-graph. Some writers fall into the trap of saving their thesis for the end, trying to provide a surprise or a big moment of revelation, as if to say, "TA-DA! I've just proved that in "The Laughing Man," Salinger shows how a child's innocence is fragile and can easily be blighted by confron-tation with adult realities." Placing a thesis at the end of an essay can seriously mar the essay's effectiveness. If you fail to define your essay's point and purpose clearly at the beginning, your reader will find it dif-ficult to assess the clarity of your argument and understand the points you are making. When your argument comes as a surprise at the end, you force your reader to re-read your essay in order to assess its logic and effectiveness.

Finally, you should avoid using the first person ("I") as you present your thesis. Though it is not strictly wrong to write in the first person, it is difficult to do so gracefully. While writing in the first person, begin-ning writers often fall into the trap of writing self-reflexive prose (writing about their paper in their paper). Often this leads to the most dreaded of opening lines: "In this paper I am going to discuss. . . ." Not only does this self-reflexive voice make for very awkward prose, it frequently allows writers to announce a topic boldly while completely avoiding a thesis statement. An example might be a paper that begins as follows: *The Catcher in the Rye*, Salinger's most famous novel, follows a few days in the life of Holden Caulfield who, during his travels around New York City, wonders what happens to the ducks in the Central Park lagoon during winter. In this paper I am going to discuss the significance of the ducks in the novel. The author of this paper has done little more than announce a topic for the paper (the significance of the ducks). While the last sentence might be intended as a thesis, the writer fails to present an opinion about the significance of the ducks. To improve this thesis, the writer would need to back up a couple of steps. First, the writer should consider the functions of the ducks within Salinger's text. From here, he or she could select the function that seems most engaging and then begin to craft a specific thesis. A writer who chooses to explore the relationship between Holden and the ducks might, for example, craft a thesis that reads, Holden's preoccupation with the ducks in Central Park is a projection of his psychological anxiety about his own survival in a heartless world. This is revealed through his constant questions about the ducks, his awareness of other people's indifference to the ducks, and his final visit to the Central Park lagoon, which parallels Holden's and the ducks' situations.

Outlines

While developing a strong, thoughtful thesis early in your writing process should help focus your paper, outlining provides an essential tool for logically shaping that paper. A good outline helps you see—and develop—the relationships among the points in your argument and assures you that your paper flows logically and coherently. Outlining not only helps place your points in a logical order but also helps you subordinate supporting points, weed out any irrelevant points, and decide if there are any necessary points that are missing from your argument. Most of us are familiar with formal outlines that use numerical and letter designations for each point. However, there are different types of outlines; you may find that an informal outline is a more useful tool for you. What is important, though, is that you spend the time to develop some sort of outline—formal or informal.

Remember that an outline is a tool to help you shape and write a strong paper. If you do not spend sufficient time planning your supporting points and shaping the arrangement of those points, you will most likely construct a vague, unfocused outline that provides little, if any, help with the writing of the paper. Consider the following example.

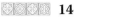

Thesis: Holden's preoccupation with the ducks in Central Park is a projection of his psychological anxiety about his own survival in a heartless world. This
is revealed through his constant questions about the
ducks, his awareness of other people's indifference to
the ducks, and his visit to the Central Park lagoon,
which parallels Holden's and the ducks' situations.

    I. Introduction and thesis

   II. Holden
        A. Questions about ducks
        B. Other people's responses
        C. Visit to Central Park
        D. The ducks

  III. New York City
        A. The lagoon

   IV. Holden's psychological anxiety
        A. Fears of future
        B. Fears of other people
        C. Choice to live or die

    V. Phoebe

   VI. Conclusion
        A. Holden unconsciously projects his anxiety
           about his own future in his concern for
           the ducks

This outline has a number of flaws. First, the major topics labeled with
the Roman numerals are not arranged in a logical order. If the paper's
aim is to show how Holden's psychological anxiety is projected into concern for the Central Park ducks, the writer should define that anxiety
before discussing Holden's pivotal visit to the lagoon. Similarly, the thesis makes no reference to Phoebe, but the writer includes her as a major
section of this outline. As Holden's beloved sister, she may well have a

place in this paper, but the writer fails to provide detail about her place in the argument. Third, the writer includes the ducks as one of the lettered items in section II. Letters A, B, and C all refer to ways Holden unwittingly reveals his obsession with the ducks; the ducks themselves do not belong in this list as a separate item. A fourth problem is the inclusion of a letter A in sections III and VI. An outline should not include an A without a B, a 1 without a 2, and so forth. The final problem with this outline is the overall lack of detail. None of the sections provide much information about the content of the argument, and it seems likely that the writer has not given sufficient thought to the content of the paper.

A better start to this outline might be the following:

Thesis: Holden's preoccupation with the ducks in Central Park is a projection of his psychological anxiety about his own survival in a heartless world. This is revealed through his constant questions about the ducks, his awareness of other people's indifference to the ducks, and his visit to the Central Park lagoon, which parallels Holden's and the ducks' situations.

I. Introduction and thesis

II. Holden's doubts and questions about his future
    A. Fears of future
    B. Questions he asks about ducks
    C. New York City versus the lagoon

III. Holden and other people
    A. Fears and doubts about other people
    B. Other people's responses to his duck questions

IV. Holden's crisis point
    A. Visit to Central Park
    B. Choice to live or die

V. Conclusion

This new outline would prove much more helpful when it came time to write the paper.

An outline like this could be shaped into an even more useful tool if the writer fleshed out the argument by providing specific examples from the text to support each point. Once you have listed your main point and your supporting ideas, develop this raw material by listing related supporting ideas and material under each of those main headings. From there, arrange the material in subsections and order the material logically.

For example, you might begin with one of the theses cited above: X's feelings of depression and alienation caused by war trauma prove impossible to surmount alone. However, the power of love and compassion shown by another human being can be the determining factor in overcoming the aftermath of war and regaining a sense of connection with the rest of humanity. As noted above, this thesis already gives you the beginning of an organization: Start by proving the notion that Sergeant X is suffering from feelings of depression and alienation, move on to a discussion of his own unsuccessful attempts to save himself, and then explain how Salinger casts X's relationship with Esmé as offering redemption through love and compassion. You might begin your outline, then, with three topic headings: (1) X's attempts to save himself from alienation and depression, (2) Sergeant X's intensification of depression and alienation brought on by combat, and (3) the redemptive power of X's relationship with Esmé. Under each of those headings you could list ideas that support the particular point. Be sure to include references to parts of the text that help build your case.

An informal outline might look like this:

Thesis: X's feelings of depression and alienation caused by war trauma prove impossible to surmount alone. However, the power of love and compassion shown by another human being can be the determining factor in overcoming the aftermath of war and regaining a sense of connection with the rest of humanity.

1. X's attempts to save himself from alienation and depression

- At beginning of war, X wanders around the town of Devon in search of connection.
  - Note Esmé's comment: "I purely came over because I thought you looked extremely lonely. You have an extremely sensitive face."
- Positive response to Esmé
  - X is "more than willing to hold up his end of the conversation"
  - Accepts offer to write
- Connection with Esmé counteracted by war
- Marginalia in Goebbels's book
  - "Dear God, life is hell"
  - Dostoevski quotation from *The Brothers Karamazov.* Ability to love and be loved allows identity.
  - X's writing is illegible

2. Sergeant X's intensification of depression and alienation brought on by combat
  - Name "X" associated with loss of identity
  - Description of physical symptoms: bleeding gums and self-inflicted pain
  - Vomits on letter from brother
  - Dialogue with Clay
    - Derisive tone
    - Refusal to participate in other soldiers' activities
    - Loretta's judgment of his nervous breakdown

3. The redemptive power of X's relationship with Esmé
  - Symbolism of Esmé's wristwatch
    - Relationship to time
    - Broken in transit
    - X doesn't wind it up

- Shifting narrative point of view:
    - First person used in America and Devon
    - Third person limited used for narration of "squalid" part of story
    - Second person used after receiving watch: "You take a really sleepy man, Esmé, and he *always* stands a chance of again becoming a man with all his fac— with all his f-a-c-u-l-t-i-e-s intact."
- Writing of story for Esmé indicates X's healing and desire for communication with the girl

Conclusion:
- Esmé's compassionate gesture allows Sergeant X to sleep.
- Human interaction and communication is the key to overcoming depression, alienation, and isolation.
- A moment of love, if it is recognized and accepted, gives a human being the capacity to reclaim identity. Love awakens a sense of self in unity with others.

You would set about writing a formal outline with a similar process, though in the final stages you would label the headings differently. A formal outline for a paper that argues the thesis about "The Laughing Man" cited above—that Salinger illustrates how a child's innocence is fragile and can easily be blighted by confrontation with adult realities—might look like this:

Thesis: In "The Laughing Man," Salinger illustrates how a child's innocence is fragile and can easily be blighted by confrontation with adult realities.

I. Introduction and thesis

II. Children's innocent world
   A. The function of the Comanche Club
      1. Gedsudski as Chief of a tribe
      2. An all-male world with no conflict
   B. Gedsudski as their hero
      1. Gedsudski's physical appearance irrelevant to children
      2. Narrator waits in park to be found
      3. Boys as descendants of the Laughing Man
   C. First-person narration reinforces an innocent worldview

III. The adult world, which the boys do not fully understand
   A. Gedsudski's fantasies and failings acted out through the Laughing Man serial narrative:
      1. Fantasies
         a. Adored by small entourage
         b. Animals do not find him ugly
         c. Fights enemies successfully as a superhero
         d. Able to transgress borders and boundaries with ease
         e. Wealthy
      2. Failings
         a. Ugliness (has to be hidden behind a poppy petal mask)
         b. Loneliness
         c. The Dufarges are his "bitterest enemies"
         d. Compassion
         e. "Family" do not accept him and try to destroy him because of his success

    B. Mary Hudson
       1. Her photograph
          a. "I asked him what he had her picture in the *bus* for, though"
          b. "we Comanches got used to it"
       2. Playing baseball
          a. "some-girls-just-don't-know-when-to-go-home" look
          b. Chief's "incompetence" in stopping her from playing
          c. Mary gets to third base on first hit
       3. Final meeting in the park
          a. she refuses to play baseball - crying
          b. narrator invites her to dinner
          c. Chief tells narrator to "tuck his shirt in" when he asks whether he'd had a fight with Mary

IV. The confrontation of children's innocence and adult realities
    A. The Laughing Man serial narrative's final installment
       1. The Dufarges' trap
          a. the Dufarges' revulsion toward the Laughing Man's ugliness
          b. the death of the Dufarges
       2. The death of the Laughing Man
          a. the death of Black Wing
          b. Laughing Man chooses to die
          c. story is "never to be revived"
    B. The poppy petal mask
       1. Literal meaning as a covering for ugliness
       2. Symbolic significance

       a. Omba replaces the mask as an "act of mercy"

       b. The Laughing Man's last act is to remove mask

       c. Red tissue paper blowing past the narrator's house

V. Conclusion

   A. Reactions of boys on bus to the end of the Laughing Man serial

      a. Billy Walsh "burst into tears"

      b. Narrator's "knees were shaking"

   B. Narrator's retrospective awareness of importance of the story to his childhood: innocence blighted by Gedsudski's adult problems

As with the previous example, the thesis provided the seeds of a structure, and the writer was careful to arrange the supporting points in a logical manner, showing the relationships among the ideas in the paper.

Body Paragraphs

Once your outline is complete, you can begin drafting your paper. Paragraphs, units of related sentences, are the building blocks of a good paper, and as you draft you should keep in mind both the function and the qualities of good paragraphs. Paragraphs help you chart and control the shape and content of your essay, and they help the reader see your organization and your logic. You should begin a new paragraph whenever you move from one major point to another. In longer, more complex essays you might use a group of related paragraphs to support major points. Remember that in addition to being adequately developed, a good paragraph is both unified and coherent.

Unified Paragraphs

Each paragraph must be centralized around one idea or point, and a unified paragraph carefully focuses on and develops this central idea without including extraneous ideas or tangents. For beginning writers, the best way to ensure that you are constructing unified paragraphs is to include a topic sentence in each paragraph. This topic sentence should convey the main point of the paragraph, and every sentence in the paragraph should relate to that topic sentence. Any sentence that strays from the central topic does not belong in the paragraph and needs to be revised or deleted. Consider the following paragraph about Sergeant X's attempts to connect with his society even though war trauma has caused him to feel isolated and alienated. Notice how the paragraph veers away from the main point that X's solo efforts to pull himself out of his depression and isolation are not totally successful.

> Some of the story's action takes place in Devon, England, in 1944, where the American soldier, Sergeant X, has been stationed to undergo a specialized pre-Invasion training course. X feels lonely because the other soldiers do not socialize or interact with him. The only reason for the soldiers to communicate is "usually to ask somebody if he had any ink he wasn't using." This lack of interaction leaves X with nothing to do, prompting him to wander around alone and explore the town. His inclination to wander represents his search for a connection to his surroundings. He meets Esmé in a tearoom, where she engages him in a conversation. X is astounded at how a thirteen-year-old girl could be so mature for her age, taking care of her brother, with both parents dead. Not only has Esmé overcome her past, but she is also extremely self-assured. She appears to know exactly where she is going. For example, she is convinced that she is "going to be a professional singer." Regardless of whether she achieves her goals or not, the ones she has set prove that she knows who she is. When she speaks to X, she uses a sophisticated vocabulary. However, she occasionally makes mistakes in her word choice. X identifies hope in the demeanor of the girl and a willingness to carry on with life, qualities that he is starting to lose himself because of the isolation he feels. When Esmé asks him if he would like

her to write to him after he is sent into combat, he replies that "[he]'d love it." Esmé innocently provides a prime example of the possibilities awaiting X if only he lets them unfold.

The paragraph begins without a valid topic sentence, and only in the fifth sentence does it start to move toward the central argument of the paragraph. Later on, the author goes on a tangent. If the purpose of the paragraph is to demonstrate that Sergeant X needs compassionate human interaction to overcome alienation and isolation, the sentences about Esmé's vocabulary are tangential here and should be deleted from this paragraph.

Coherent Paragraphs

In addition to shaping unified paragraphs, you must also craft coherent paragraphs, paragraphs that develop their points logically with sentences that flow smoothly into one another. Coherence depends on the order of your sentences, but it is not strictly the order of the sentences that is important to paragraph coherence. You also need to craft your prose to help the reader see the relationship among the sentences.

Consider the following paragraph about X's attempts to connect with his world. Notice how the writer uses the same ideas as the paragraph above yet fails to help the reader see the relationships among the points.

Some of the story's action takes place in Devon, England, in 1944. The soldier, Sergeant X, is undergoing a specialized pre-Invasion training course. The soldier feels rather lonely. When the soldiers communicate, it is "usually to ask somebody if he had any ink he wasn't using." X wanders around alone and explores the town. He meets Esmé in a tearoom, and she engages him in a conversation. X is astounded at how a thirteen-year-old girl could be so mature for her age, taking care of her brother, with both parents dead. Esmé is extremely self-assured. She appears to know exactly where she is going. She is convinced that she is "going to be a professional singer." She may or may not achieve her goals.

```
X identifies hope in the demeanor of the girl and a
willingness to carry on with life. When Esmé asks him
if he would like her to write to him after he is sent
into combat, he replies that "[he]'d love it." X is "more
than willing to hold up [his] end of [the] conversa-
tion." Esmé's innocence provides a prime example of the
possibilities of life.
```

This paragraph demonstrates that unity alone does not guarantee paragraph effectiveness. The argument is hard to follow because the author fails both to show connections between the sentences and to indicate how they work to support the overall point.

A number of techniques are available to aid paragraph coherence. Careful use of transitional words and phrases is essential. You can use transitional flags to introduce an example or an illustration (*for example, for instance*), to amplify a point or add another phase of the same idea (*additionally, furthermore, next, similarly, finally, then*), to indicate a conclusion or result (*therefore, as a result, thus, in other words*), to signal a contrast or a qualification (*on the other hand, nevertheless, despite this, on the contrary, still, however, conversely*), to signal a comparison (*likewise, in comparison, similarly*), and to indicate a movement in time (*afterward, earlier, eventually, finally, later, subsequently, until*).

In addition to transitional flags, careful use of pronouns aids coherence and flow. If you were writing about *The Wizard of Oz*, you would not want to keep repeating the phrase *the witch* or the name *Dorothy*. Careful substitution of the pronoun *she* in these instances can aid coherence. A word of warning, though: when you substitute pronouns for proper names, always be sure that your pronoun reference is clear. In a paragraph that discusses both Dorothy and the witch, substituting *she* could lead to confusion. Make sure that it is clear to whom the pronoun refers. Generally, the pronoun refers to the last proper noun you have used.

While repeating the same name over and over again can lead to awkward, boring prose, it is possible to use repetition to help your paragraph's coherence. Careful repetition of important words or phrases can lend coherence to your paragraph by reminding readers of your key points.

Admittedly, it takes some practice to use this technique effectively. You may find that reading your prose aloud can help you develop an ear for effective use of repetition.

To see how helpful transitional aids are, compare the paragraph below to the preceding paragraph about how Sergeant X's efforts to help overcome his depression and alienation are limited because he needs to embrace compassionate human interaction. Notice how the author works with the same ideas and quotations but shapes them into a much more coherent paragraph whose point is clearer and easier to follow.

As a response to his distressing involvement in war, Sergeant X searches for some form of connection with others. However, his initial efforts to engage in communication that transcends the trivial are not completely successful. Some of the story's action takes place in Devon, England, in 1944, where the American soldier is undergoing a specialized pre-Invasion training course. X feels lonely because the only reason the soldiers communicate is "usually to ask somebody if he had any ink he wasn't using" (88). This lack of interaction prompts X to wander around alone and explore the English town. His inclination to wander represents his search for a connection to his surroundings. He meets Esmé in a tearoom, where she initiates a conversation with him. She is a thirteen-year-old orphan, having lost both parents in the war, who has been burdened with the responsibility of taking care of her young brother. Esmé's readiness to approach the lonely soldier and strike up a conversation with him exposes X's sensitivity regarding his detachment from others. His being "more than willing to hold up [his] end of [the] conversation" (93) with Esmé indicates that he is aware of his loneliness and need for communication. X identifies hope in the demeanor of the girl, a determination to face life's hardships, and an ability to reach out to others even in the midst of her own trauma. When Esmé asks him if he would like her to write to him after he is sent into combat, he replies that "[he]'d love it" (102). Esmé innocently provides a prime example of the possibilities awaiting X if only he lets them unfold. However, X's efforts at connecting to his environment are not completely successful at this stage, because he allows the darkness of war to override the counteractive force of Esmé's love and compassion. Sergeant X has not fully recognized the moment of love that has transpired between the young girl and him.

Similarly, the following paragraph from a paper on the conflict between the innocence of children and the harsh realities of adult life in "The Laughing Man" demonstrates both unity and coherence. In it, the author argues that Salinger illustrates how a child's innocence is fragile and can easily be blighted by confrontation with adult realities:

The red poppy petal mask is used to show how the world is viewed through innocent eyes and through eyes whose innocent perspective has been tainted. The Laughing Man's bandit foster parents oblige him to wear a mask to conceal his hideous facial features. Rejected by strangers and acquaintances alike for his ugliness, the Laughing Man is allowed to stay in the bandits' headquarters if his deformities are concealed behind the mask. This clearly represents the exaggerated reality of John Gedsudski's daily life. He feels defined by his physical shortcomings and tolerated only so long as he makes every effort to mask his limitations. On the other hand, when the Laughing Man goes to a nearby forest, he removes his mask and revels in the animals' unequivocal acceptance of him. The trust that he feels toward the animals for their refusal to judge him is not extended to anyone else. Even his four loyal confederates are never allowed to see his face. One of these loyal adjuncts is Omba the dwarf, who replaces the Laughing Man's mask after it has blown off his face during his final showdown with the evil Dufarges. Omba's reinstatement of the mask is described as "an act of mercy." Omba, who had never before seen the Laughing Man's ugliness, covers the "hideous features" of his master in a pitiful attempt to regain his innocent perception of his master. However, the Laughing Man decisively removes the mask again before he dies. Because of the parallels between the Laughing Man and Gedsudski, this definitive unmasking of the superhero equates with Gedsudski's revealing of his troubled emotional life to his young charges. The mask cannot be replaced on either the Laughing Man or Gedsudski because the story is "[n]ever to be revived." The appearance of red tissue paper, reminiscent of the poppy petal mask, suggests the intrusion of adult realities into the young narrator's life. The unmasking and death of the Laughing Man has changed the boy's innocent view of both his heroes and the idealized world they both represented. His glimpse of the sadness of adult life, symbolized by the discarded red tissue paper, leaves him physically shaken, and he has to go straight to bed to recover.

Introductions

Introductions present particular challenges for writers. Generally, your introduction should do two things: capture your reader's attention and explain the main point of your essay. In other words, while your introduction should contain your thesis, it needs to do a bit more work than that. You are likely to find that starting that first paragraph is one of the most difficult parts of the paper. It is hard to face that blank page or screen, and as a result, many beginning writers, in desperation to start somewhere, start with overly broad, general statements. While it is often a good strategy to start with more general subject matter and narrow your focus, do not begin with broad sweeping statements such as `War affects everyone,` or `Throughout the history of literature, many authors have depicted the relationship between adults and children.` Such sentences are nothing but empty filler. They begin to fill the blank page, but they do nothing to advance your argument. Instead, you might try to gain your reader's interest. Some writers like to begin with a pertinent quotation or with a relevant question. Or, you might begin with an introduction of the topic you will discuss. If you are writing about Salinger's discussion of innocence in "The Laughing Man," for instance, you might begin by talking about the powerful effect of telling stories to children. Another common trap to avoid is depending on your title to introduce the author and the text you are writing about. Always include the work's author and title in your opening paragraph.

Compare the effectiveness of the following introductions.

1. `Throughout the history of literature, writers have depicted the relationship between children and adults. In this short story, Salinger places a story within a story to illustrate how a child's innocence is fragile and can easily be blighted by confrontation with adult realities.`

2. `Telling a story to a child has many possible goals. A story may be used to entertain, to convey moral messages, or to instruct children about their culture or society. Through the process of creative narration, the storyteller can insert himself in the plot and the characters of the story. The construction of the story becomes linked to the construction of identity for both the storyteller and the audience. In J. D. Salinger's "The Laughing Man," Comanche Club Chief, John Gedsudski, dramatizes his own life struggles in the antics of his fictional superhero. His young audience participates in those struggles through their mental association with the superhero`

character. The boys idolize both Gedsudski and the
Laughing Man and have total confidence in their
heroes' abilities to triumph over life. When Gedsudski impulsively decides to kill off his superhero
after a conflict with his girlfriend, the Comanche
Club boys feel devastated and betrayed. Their naïve
and idealized perspective on the world has been shattered. Salinger illustrates how a child's innocence
is fragile and can easily be blighted by confrontation with adult realities.

The first introduction begins with a vague, overly broad sentence and
then moves abruptly to the thesis. Notice, too, how a reader deprived
of the paper's title does not know the title of the story that the paper
will analyze. The second introduction works with the same material and
thesis but provides more detail and is consequently much more interesting. It begins by discussing the possible functions of telling stories to
children and then speaks about the relationships among the storyteller,
his audience, and his material, giving specific examples. The author and
the title of the work to be discussed are woven into the middle of the
introduction. The paragraph ends with the thesis.

The paragraph below provides another example of an opening strategy. It begins by introducing the author and the text it will analyze, and
then it moves on by briefly introducing relevant details of the story in
order to set up its thesis.

J. D. Salinger's "For Esmé—with Love and Squalor" chronicles the deterioration and recuperation of a man's
mental and physical states before and after combat in
World War II. The war environment creates a dearth of
meaningful interpersonal interaction for this American soldier serving in Europe. Sergeant X, as the man
refers to himself, ultimately disconnects from other
human beings and society because of his war experiences. Before his departure for the front line, a chance
encounter at an English tearoom momentarily relieves X

of his loneliness and isolation. Surprisingly, X's conversation with thirteen-year-old Esmé in the tearoom
becomes the starting point for a consequential friendship with the young girl. Later, her generous gift to
him of her father's watch gives him hope in face of
the depredation of Nazi Germany and restores his faith
in the goodness of humanity. X's feelings of depression and alienation caused by war trauma prove impossible to surmount alone. However, the power of love
and compassion shown by another human being can be the
determining factor in overcoming the aftermath of war
and regaining a sense of connection with the rest of
humanity.

Conclusions

Conclusions present another series of challenges for writers. No doubt you have heard the old adage about writing papers: "Tell us what you are going to say, say it, and then tell us what you've said." While this formula does not necessarily result in bad papers, it does not necessarily result in good ones, either. It will almost certainly result in boring papers (especially boring conclusions). If you have done a good job establishing your points in the body of the paper, the reader already knows and understands your argument. There is no need to merely reiterate. Do not just summarize your main points in your conclusion. Such a boring and mechanical conclusion does nothing to advance your argument or interest your reader. Consider the following conclusion to the paper about innocence in "The Laughing Man."

In conclusion, Salinger shows that there are events
that make us grow and change. Salinger uses the point
of view of a nine-year-old child, the symbolism of the
poppy petal mask, and the significance of the Laughing
Man's death to demonstrate the stages human beings go
through as they become adults.

Besides starting with a mechanical and obvious transitional device, this conclusion does little more than summarize the main points of the outline (and it does not even touch on all of them). It is incomplete and uninteresting.

Instead, your conclusion should add something to your paper. A good tactic is to build upon the points you have been arguing. Asking "why?" often helps you draw further conclusions. For example, in the paper on "The Laughing Man," you might explain how the conflict between innocence and experience is effectively portrayed. Another method of successfully concluding a paper is to speculate on other directions in which to take your topic, that is, by tying it into larger issues. You might do this by envisioning your paper as just one section of a larger paper. Having established your points in this paper, how would you build upon this argument? Where would you go next? In the following conclusion to the paper on "The Laughing Man," the author reiterates some of the main points of the paper but does so in order to amplify the discussion of the story's coming-of-age message.

There are momentous events in everybody's life that cause growth in understanding and changes in levels of maturity. Sometimes the challenge to an innocent mindset can be hard to accept for a child, but Salinger shows the impossibility of resisting the slide into the adult world. Children often attach themselves to possessions or beliefs more readily and with more fervor than adults. Therefore, it is harder for children to move on and forget about what had importance. Gedsudski and his superhero creation, the Laughing Man, served as role models in the lives of the young Comanche Club boys. The time in the Club represented an ideal, timeless, all-male world, which seemed exempt from conflict and life's problems. Gedsudski's storytelling allowed the boys to follow him into his world of fantasy and possibility. The intrusion of Mary Hudson into their world and the unmasking of their superheroes' weaknesses and failings chipped away at their innocent outlook on Gedsudski, the Comanche Club, and life.

Similarly, in the following conclusion to the paper on Sergeant X's troubled character, the author draws a conclusion about what can be learned from X's war trauma experience. Notice, too, how the author moved some material from its original place in the outline. Instead of discussing X's response to the marginalia he found in the Goebbels book in a body paragraph, the writer moves that material to the conclusion, using it as transitional material.

Salinger's depiction of the sensitive subject of war and the victims it claims implies that a person's recovery from the psychological battering that war can inflict is much harder without the assistance of other human beings. Sergeant X's identity slips from his grasp as he becomes more involved in the war; this is indicated by the variations in the narrative point of view. The condition of his body and soul worsen despite his attempts to resolve his problems on his own. His failure to bond with any of the other soldiers exacerbates his feelings of alienation. The marginalia—"Dear God, life is hell" (105)—that X reads in the Joseph Goebbels book he finds in Germany spells out X's precarious position as he hovers on the brink of succumbing to depression, even though his instinct is to overwrite this proclamation of despair with words of love. Unfortunately, the quotation from Dostoyevsky asserting the primacy of love that X tries to write in the book, is illegible. Esmé is the character who ties everything together for X, allowing him to regain pieces of his old self. The example she sets for him, by sending him her treasured memento of her father, impresses upon him that all hope for humanity is not lost. His writing of the story that she had requested about love and squalor indicates his desire to communicate with her. The dialogue between love and squalor that was "illegible" in Nazi Germany can take place in the presence of Esmé's love. For X, love defeats the demons of war and awakens a sense of self in unity with others.

Citations and Formatting

Using Primary Sources

As the examples included in this chapter indicate, strong papers on literary texts incorporate quotations from the text in order to support their points. It is not enough for you to assert your interpretation without providing support or evidence from the text. Without well-chosen quotations to support your argument you are, in effect, saying to the reader, "Take my word for it." It is important to use quotations thoughtfully and selectively. Remember that the paper presents *your* argument, so choose quotations that support *your* assertions. Do not let the author's voice overwhelm your own. With that caution in mind, there are some guidelines you should follow to ensure that you use quotations clearly and effectively.

Integrate Quotations:

Quotations should always be integrated into your own prose. Do not just drop them into your paper without introduction or comment. Otherwise, it is unlikely that your reader will see their function. You can integrate textual support easily and clearly with identifying tags, short phrases that identify the speaker. For example:

> When the boys hear about the Laughing Man's death, the narrator explains how "Billy Walsh, who was the youngest of all the Comanches, burst into tears."

While this tag appears before the quotation, you can also use tags after or in the middle of the quoted text, as the following examples demonstrate:

> "I do, too, want to play!" Mary Hudson insists.

> "I don't care," Mary Hudson informs the Chief when he explains to her that baseball is not a suitable game for women. "I came all the way to New York—to the dentist and everything—and I'm gonna play."

You can also use a colon to formally introduce a quotation:

> Sergeant X's crude words to Clay underscore his desire
> for solitude: "Leave me alone now, God damn it!"

Longer quotations (more than four lines of prose) should be set off from the rest of your paper in a block quotation. Double-space before you begin the passage, indent it 10 spaces from your left-hand margin, and double-space the passage itself. Because the indentation signals the inclusion of a quotation, do not use quotation marks around the cited passage. Use a colon to introduce the passage:

> Sergeant X is unable to add his message to the book's
> margins:
>
> > [H]e picked up a pencil stub and wrote down under
> > the inscription, in English, "Fathers and teach-
> > ers, I ponder, 'What is hell?' I maintain that
> > it is the suffering of being unable to love."
> > He started to write Dostoyevsky's name under the
> > inscription, but saw—with fright that ran through
> > his whole body—that what he had written was almost
> > entirely illegible.
>
> His estrangement from literature and love is indicated
> by his failure to write legibly.

It is also important to interpret quotations after you introduce them and explain how they help advance your point. You cannot assume that your reader will interpret the quotations the same way that you do.

Quote Accurately:

Always quote accurately. Anything within quotations marks must be the author's exact words. There are, however, some rules to follow if you need to modify the quotation to fit into your prose.

1. Use brackets to indicate any material that might have been added to the author's exact wording. For example, if you need to add any words to the quotation or alter it grammatically to allow it to fit into your prose, indicate your changes in brackets:

```
The unmasking of both his heroes terrifies the
narrator. He recalls that "[his] knees were
shaking" as a reaction to this harsh insight
into life's realities.
```

2. Conversely, if you choose to omit any words from the quotation, use ellipses (three spaced periods) to indicate missing words or phrases:

```
X acknowledges the possibility that he may heal
from his war trauma: "You take a really sleepy
man, Esmé, and he always stands a chance of
again becoming a man . . . with all his f-a-c-
u-l-t-i-e-s intact."
```

3. If you delete a sentence or more, use the ellipses after a period:

```
The descriptions of the Laughing Man hint at
some of Gedsudski's desires, fantasies, and
insecurities:
```

```
[T]he Laughing Man had amassed the largest
personal fortune in the world. Most of it
he contributed anonymously to the monks
of a local monastery. . . . [He] issued
his orders to the crew through a black
silk screen. Not even Omba, the lovable
dwarf, was permitted to see his face.
```

Punctuate Properly:

Punctuation of quotations often causes more trouble than it should. Once again, you just need to keep these simple rules in mind.

1. Periods and commas should be placed inside quotation marks, even if they are not part of the original quotation:

```
Sergeant X feels "his mind dislodge itself and
teeter."
```

The only exception to this rule is when the quotation is followed by a parenthetical reference. In this case, the period or comma goes after the citation (more on these later in this chapter):

```
Sergeant X feels "his mind dislodge itself and
teeter" (104).
```

2. Other marks of punctuation—colons, semicolons, question marks, and exclamation points—go outside the quotation marks unless they are part of the original quotation:

```
Why does the narrator ask Mary Hudson "if she
wanted to come up to [his] house for dinner
sometime"?
```

```
Sergeant X's crude words to Clay underscore his
desire for solitude: "Leave me alone now, God
damn it!"
```

Documenting Primary Sources

Unless you are instructed otherwise, you should provide sufficient information for your reader to locate material you quote. Generally, literature papers follow the rules set forth by the Modern Language Association (MLA). These can be found in the *MLA Handbook for Writers of Research Papers* (sixth edition). You should be able to find this book in the reference section of your library. Additionally, its rules for citing both primary and secondary sources are widely available from reputable online sources. One of these is the Online Writing Lab (OWL) at Purdue University. OWL's guide to MLA style is available at http://owl.english.purdue .edu/owl/resource/557/01/. The Modern Language Association also offers answers to frequently asked questions about MLA style on this helpful Web page: http://www.mla.org/style_faq. Generally, when you are citing from literary works in papers, you should keep a few guidelines in mind.

Parenthetical Citations:

MLA asks for parenthetical references in your text after quotations. When you are working with prose (short stories, novels, or essays) include page numbers in the parentheses:

Sergeant X feels "his mind dislodge itself and teeter" (104).

Works Cited Page:

These parenthetical citations are linked to a separate works cited page at the end of the paper. The works cited page lists works alphabetically by the authors' last name. An entry for the above reference to Salinger's "For Esmé—with Love and Squalor" would read:

Salinger, J. D. "For Esmé—with Love and Squalor." *Nine Stories.* New York: Little, Brown, 1991. 87-114.

The *MLA Handbook* includes a full listing of sample entries, as do many of the online explanations of MLA style.

Documenting Secondary Sources

To ensure that your paper is built entirely upon your own ideas and analysis, instructors often ask that you write interpretative papers without any outside research. If, on the other hand, your paper requires research, you must document any secondary sources you use. You need to document direct quotations, summaries, or paraphrases of others' ideas, and factual information that is not common knowledge. Follow the guidelines above for quoting primary sources when you use direct quotations from secondary sources. Keep in mind that MLA style also includes specific guidelines for citing electronic sources. OWL's Web site provides a good summary: http://owl.english.purdue.edu/owl/resource/557/09/.

Parenthetical Citations:

As with the documentation of primary sources, described above, MLA guidelines require in-text parenthetical references to your secondary sources. Unlike the research papers you might write for a history class, literary research papers following MLA style do not use footnotes as a means of documenting sources. Instead, after a quotation, you should cite the author's last name and the page number:

The narrator "can review the childhood idyll in all its escapist splendor; he can perceive its dissolution as necessary for (rather than inimical to) one's sane adaptation to a postadolescent world" (Wenke 46).

If you include the name of the author in your prose, then you would include only the page number in your citation. For example:

According to John Wenke, the narrator "can review the childhood idyll in all its escapist splendor; he can perceive its dissolution as necessary for (rather than inimical to) one's sane adaptation to a postadolescent world" (46).

If you are including more than one work by the same author, the parenthetical citation should include a shortened yet identifiable version of the title in order to indicate which of the author's works you cite. For example:

According to Warren French, Gedsudski gives "his young charges a startling object lesson in not expecting too much from life" (*Revisited* 74).

Similarly, and just as important, if you summarize or paraphrase the particular ideas of your source, you must provide documentation:

Questions arise as to whether Gedsudski deliberately chooses to undermine the boys' innocent view of their world. However, it is more likely that he does not have the goal of causing them pain. He is used to articulating his inner emotional life through his story, and the death of the Laughing Man is merely a continuation of this process (Wenke 46).

Works Cited Page:

Like the primary sources discussed above, the parenthetical references to secondary sources are keyed to a separate works cited page at the end of the your paper. Here is an example of a works cited page that uses the examples cited above. Note that when two or more works by the same author are listed, you should use three hyphens followed by a period in the subsequent entries. You can find a complete list of sample entries in the *MLA Handbook* or from a reputable online summary of MLA style.

WORKS CITED

Alexander, Paul. *Salinger: A Biography.* Los Angeles: Renaissance, 1999.

French, Warren. *J. D. Salinger.* Boston: Twayne, 1963.

———. *J. D. Salinger Revisited.* Boston: Twayne, 1988.

Gwynn, Frederick L., and Joseph L. Blotner. *The Fiction of J. D. Salinger.* Pittsburgh: U of Pittsburgh P, 1958.

Wenke, John. *J. D. Salinger: A Study of the Short Fiction.* Boston: Twayne, 1991.

Plagiarism

Failure to document carefully and thoroughly can leave you open to charges of stealing the ideas of others, which is known as plagiarism, and this is a very serious matter. Remember that it is important to use quotation marks when you use language used by your source, even if you use just one or two words. For example, if you wrote, The narrator in "The Laughing Man" can look back at his childhood in all its escapist splendor, you would be guilty of plagiarism, since you used Wenke's distinct language without acknowledging him as the source. Instead, you should write, The narrator in "The Laughing Man" can look back at his childhood in all its "escapist splendor" (Wenke 46). In this case, you have properly credited Wenke.

Similarly, neither summarizing the ideas of an author nor changing or omitting just a few words means that you can omit a citation. Paul Alexander's biography of Salinger contains the following passage about the resonance of the theme of phoniness in the 1950s:

Salinger spoke to a generation in the same way that Presley and Dean did, and he used as the vehicle for that communication a six-teen-year-old boy named Holden Caulfield. When Salinger's initial audience encountered Holden, they instantly identified with what Holden was saying: Society was full of hypocritical people who held false beliefs and stood for nothing—"phonies," to quote Holden. This theme of phoniness resonated with Salinger's readers, especially those who came to the novel later in the decade. For they could look at the figures on the national scene at the time—McCarthy, J. Edgar Hoover, and others—and know that what these figures were saying was not even genuine, much less true. Because Holden Caulfield so passionately articulated the phoniness represented by these men, *The Catcher in the Rye* would become a seminal document for the generation that came of age in the 1950s.

Below are two examples of plagiarized passages:

Holden Caulfield and his denunciation of phoniness rang true for the generation of readers who were growing up in the 1950s because they could look at many of their prominent politicians at that time, such as Joseph McCarthy or J. Edgar Hoover, with the knowledge that many of their pronouncements were not truthful.

Readers in the 1950s identified with Holden Caulfield's assertion that society was full of hypocritical people who held false beliefs and stood for nothing. The idea that people were phonies seemed valid considering that figures on the national scene at the time, such as McCarthy and J. Edgar Hoover, were making claims that were neither genuine nor true (Alexander 28–29).

Although the first passage does not use Alexander's exact language, it does borrow a main idea of the passage without citing his work. Since comparing the phoniness of Holden's world with the phoniness of America's 1950s political scene is his distinct idea, this constitutes plagiarism. The second example has simplified Alexander's passage, changed some wording, and included a citation, but some of the phrasing is Alexander's. The first passage could be fixed with a parenthetical citation. Because some of the wording in the second passage remains the same, though, it would require the use of quotation marks, in addition to a parenthetical citation. The passage below represents an honestly and adequately documented use of the original passage:

> According to Paul Alexander, the generation who read *The Catcher in the Rye* in the 1950s could personally relate to Holden's assertion that "[s]ociety was full of hypocritical people who held false beliefs and stood for nothing." When readers evaluated prominent national politicians of the time period, such as Joseph McCarthy and J. Edgar Hoover, Holden "passionately articulated the phoniness represented by these men" (28-29).

This passage acknowledges that the idea of the parallel between Holden's world and American politics in the 1950s is derived from Alexander, while appropriately using quotations to indicate his precise language.

While it is not necessary to document well-known facts, often referred to as "common knowledge," any ideas or language that you take from someone else must be properly documented. Common knowledge generally includes the birth and death dates of authors or other well-documented facts of their lives. An often-cited guideline is that if you can find the information in three sources, it is common knowledge. Despite this guideline, it is, admittedly, often difficult to know if the facts you uncover are common knowledge or not. When in doubt, document your source.

Sample Essay

Jess Adams
Ms. J. Qiu
English 102
April 11, 2007

OVERCOMING THE TRAUMA OF WAR IN
J. D. SALINGER'S "FOR ESMÉ—WITH LOVE AND SQUALOR"

J. D. Salinger's "For Esmé—with Love and Squalor" chronicles the deterioration and recuperation of a man's mental and physical states before and after combat in

World War II. The war environment creates a dearth of meaningful interpersonal interaction for this American soldier serving in Europe. Sergeant X, as the man refers to himself, ultimately disconnects from other human beings and society because of his war experiences. Before his departure for the front line, a chance encounter at an English tearoom momentarily relieves X of his loneliness and isolation. Surprisingly, X's conversation with thirteen-year-old Esmé in the tearoom becomes the starting point for a consequential friendship with the young girl. Later, her generous gift to him of her father's watch gives him hope in face of the depredation of Nazi Germany and restores his faith in the goodness of humanity. X's feelings of depression and alienation caused by war trauma prove impossible to surmount alone. However, the power of love and compassion shown by another human being can be the determining factor in overcoming the aftermath of war and regaining a sense of connection with the rest of humanity.

As a response to his distressing involvement in war, Sergeant X searches for some form of connection with others. However, his initial efforts to engage in communication that transcends the trivial are not completely successful. Some of the story's action takes place in Devon, England, in 1944, where the American soldier is undergoing a specialized pre-Invasion training course. X feels lonely because the only reason the soldiers communicate is "usually to ask somebody if he had any ink he wasn't using" (88). This lack of interaction prompts X to wander around alone and explore the English town. His inclination to wander represents his search for a connection to his surroundings. He meets Esmé in a tearoom, where she initiates a conversation with him. She is a thirteen-year-old orphan, having lost both parents in the war, who has been burdened with the responsibility of taking care of her young brother. Esmé's readiness to approach the lonely soldier and strike up a conversation with him exposes X's sensitivity regarding his detachment from others. His being "more than willing to hold up [his] end of [the] conversation" (93) with Esmé indicates that he is aware of his loneliness and need for communication. X identifies hope in the demeanor of the girl, a determination to face life's hardships, and an ability to reach out to others even in the midst of her own trauma. When Esmé asks him if he would like her to write to him after he is sent into combat, he replies that "[he]'d love it" (102). Esmé innocently provides a prime example of the possibilities awaiting X if only he lets them unfold. However, X's efforts at connecting to his environment are not completely successful at this stage, because he allows the darkness of war to override the counteractive force of Esmé's love and compassion. Sergeant X has not fully recognized the moment of love that has transpired between the young girl and him.

After combat experience, Sergeant X becomes increasingly depressed and alienated from society. The letter *X* is commonly associated with a variable or an unknown element. Sergeant X, operating as but a tiny part of a massive war machine, becomes the unknown variable of the story. By the time he is billeted in Germany after a period of intense fighting, his physical and mental states have deteriorated to the point that he is unable to communicate with others in a socially acceptable way. A tasteless letter sent to him by his brother, stating that since the "g.d. war is over and [X] probably [has] a lot of time over there, [he should send] the kids a couple of bayonets or swastikas" (106) disgusts X. He rips the letter to shreds, discards it, and later vomits on it, showing his revulsion for the insensitivity of mainstream society toward war. X has turned to chain-smoking to help assuage his depressed and fragile mental state. The incessant smoking has contributed to making his gums sensitive. He continually prods his hypersensitive gums with his tongue, making them bleed. This self-inflicted physical pain offsets the mental numbness he has retreated into as a result of war trauma. His military comrades provide him with no relief from his alienated state, and he refuses to participate in any of their social activities. When his jeep partner, Clay, visits him in his room, X's derisive tone throughout the conversation shows his disdain for Clay's seeming acceptance of the appalling conditions of war. It is Clay's "mindless insensitivity to horror that allows him to pass through the war psychologically unscathed" (Wenke 51). Clay parrots the voice of mainstream American society when he explains that his girlfriend Loretta, a psychology student, claims that no one has a nervous breakdown simply because of war and she believes that X has probably always been unhinged. Sergeant X, alone and psychologically hurting in an uncompassionate world, is starved of love and hope. He is battling to retain a remnant of faith in humanity.

At the end of the story, Esmé's father's wristwatch, which she sends to Sergeant X in Germany, symbolizes the soldier's breakdown and hints at his potential to recover. The hands on the watch have stopped, showing how X's normal life has been put on hold in order to fight overseas. Like Sergeant X, the wristwatch has not survived the war unaffected. The watch's broken crystal mirrors the way war has broken X's spirit and destroyed his ability to function effectively. Its malfunction also connotes the physical signs of X's trauma: trembling fingers, facial tics, insomnia, and constant migraines. X's reluctance to wind up the wristwatch reveals his dread that he may never completely recover from his breakdown. He knows that the watch may still function even though its crystal is broken, but he fears that the damage inflicted on him may run deeper. The winding up of the watch would signify X's reintegration back into society and normal life in the United States. The fact that the watch remains unwound at the end of the story shows that X is still wary of reconnecting with his society, even after reading the touching letter from Esmé that accompanied her gift. Nonetheless, his capacity for improvement is signaled by the shifting narrative point of view that the watch triggers. At the beginning of X's war experience, he refers to himself using the first-person pronoun *I*. When the narrative shifts to Germany at the end of the war, X has been completely shaken by what he has seen and experienced. At this point, a third-person limited narrative point of view is used, even though X is still writing about himself. This choice of point of view emphasizes X's imposition of distance from the horror of war and his disconnection from a coherent sense of self. However, after X has read Esmé's letter and is contemplating her gift, he writes:

> [X] just sat with [the watch] in his hand for another long period. Then, suddenly, almost ecstatically, he felt sleepy.
>
> You take a really sleepy man, Esmé, and he *always* stands a chance of again becoming a man with all his fac—with all his f-a-c-u-l-t-i-e-s intact. (114)

This transition from a third-person to a second-person pronoun is caused by X's inching back to a more inclusive definition of himself in relationship with others. The critic Warren French suggests that Esmé's "unexpected demonstration of unadulterated affection redeems the sergeant from his private hell and allows him to go to sleep (the usual signal of the resolution of a problem in the Glass family stories), feeling that he may yet come through the war with all his 'faculties intact'" (78). The use of the pronoun *you* and the suggestion that finally the traumatized solder will be able to sleep point toward the potential Esmé's compassionate gesture has to reconnect X to others and to a nonfragmented identity.

Salinger's depiction of the sensitive subject of war and the victims it claims implies that a person's recovery from the psychological battering that war can inflict is much harder without the assistance of other human beings. Sergeant X's identity slips from his grasp as he becomes more involved in the war; this is indicated by the variations in the narrative point of view. The condition of his body and soul worsen despite his attempts to resolve his problems on his own. His failure to bond with any of the other soldiers exacerbates his feelings of alienation. The marginalia—"Dear God, life is hell" (105)—that X reads in the Joseph Goebbels book he finds in Germany spells out X's precarious position as he hovers on the brink of succumbing to depression, even though his instinct is to overwrite this proclamation of despair with words of love. Unfortunately, the quotation from Dostoyevsky asserting the primacy of love, which X tries to write in the book, is illegible. Esmé is the character who ties everything together for X, allowing him to regain pieces of his old self. The example she sets for him, by sending him her treasured memento of her father, impresses upon him that all hope for humanity is not lost. His writing of the story that she had requested about love and squalor indicates his desire to communicate with her. The dialogue between love and squalor that was "illegible" in Nazi Germany can take place in the presence of Esmé's love. For X, love defeats the demons of war and awakens a sense of self in unity with others.

WORKS CITED

French, Warren. *J. D. Salinger Revisited*. Boston: Twayne, 1988.

Salinger, J. D. "For Esmé—with Love and Squalor." *Nine Stories*. New York: Little, Brown, 1991. 87-114.

Wenke, John. *J. D. Salinger: A Study of the Short Fiction*. Boston: Twayne, 1991.

HOW TO WRITE ABOUT
J. D. SALINGER

AN OVERVIEW

J. D. Salinger's canonical status has largely evolved out of the success and celebrity of one novel: *The Catcher in the Rye.* Despite being published in 1951, this novel still has not divested itself of its controversial reputation. In the 1950s, it was banned in some places because of its profane language and overt sexuality. The novel was also darkly associated with the death of John Lennon, whose murderer, apparently glorifying Holden's position as an outcast, was carrying a copy of the novel at the time of his 1980 arrest and made allusions to it in his police statement. The hype surrounding the novel has been further fueled by Salinger's reclusiveness. Judgments on Salinger as a writer are often made on the basis of *The Catcher in the Rye* alone, assuming that Holden speaks for the writer and that Holden's escapades replicate events in the young Salinger's life. However, Salinger nominated Buddy Glass as his alter ego on the original dust jacket of *Franny and Zooey.* Even when Salinger's entire oeuvre is taken into consideration, associating Salinger's actions or opinions with those of any of his protagonists can be an uncertain proposition because of Salinger's reticence about his life and his control over access to his personal information. Salinger's biographer, Paul Alexander, argues that the writer's legendary status has been carefully maintained over the years by Salinger himself, who releases just enough information to keep his myth alive in the minds of the American reading public. Salinger's choice to withdraw from public life has possibly prompted ongoing attention because many people are fascinated by the eccentricities that a reclusive lifestyle seems to foster. Despite the limitations as to what is known about the writer, knowledge about Salinger's life can be helpful in approaching his works, since some of his personal experiences seem to share common ground with the experiences of some of his characters. Thus, a consideration of key events in Salinger's life may be pertinent in a discussion of some of his works.

Jerome David Salinger was born in 1919, in New York City, to a Jewish father and an Irish-Scottish Christian mother. Salinger also chose to make the father (Les) and mother (Bessie) of his famous fictional Glass family Jewish and Irish, respectively. Anti-Semitism was widespread in the United States during the time when Salinger was growing up, and he dealt with the damage inflicted by racists comments in the short story "Down at the Dinghy." By 1932, business success allowed Salinger's father to move his family to Park Avenue, a wealthy WASP neighborhood in New York. This WASP world became the target of Salinger's scathing critique throughout much of his work. After the move, Salinger attended exclusive private schools, such as McBurney School, but his performance was considered lackluster by his teachers. Eventually, his grades were too poor for him to continue as a student in these elite schools.

In 1934, Salinger's father sent his son to Valley Forge Military Academy in rural Pennsylvania, hoping it would instill a sense of purpose in him. Many parallels have been drawn between Salinger's life at Valley Forge and Holden's account of life at Pencey. Unlike Holden, Salinger did manage to graduate from Valley Forge, though his grades were average. His classmates recall that he started to write during his time at Valley Forge, supposedly using a flashlight under his bedcovers to pursue this interest. In contrast to Holden's time at Pencey, Valley Forge appears to have been a mostly positive experience for Salinger.

His academic performance deteriorated once again when he started to attend college in New York. By 1937, he was trying to learn his father's import/export business, but the only thing a long trip to Europe taught him was that he would never pursue his father's profession. This abortive attempt at the meat business pushed the young man to return to college in 1938. His time at Ursinus College, also in Pennsylvania, was when Salinger started to tell his classmates that he wanted to be a writer. He did not feel that the writing courses at Ursinus were helpful in developing his craft, so again he dropped out of college. He enrolled in a creative writing course at Columbia University. The instructor was Whit Burnett, who was instrumental in helping Salinger get his first short story, "The Young Folks," published in 1940.

In 1941, Salinger tried to enlist in the military but was rejected for a minor heart condition. However, when the United States entered the war after the bombing of Pearl Harbor, the Army modified its regulations, allowing Salinger to join up. He continued to write throughout the early 1940s when he was stationed in various parts of the United States. In 1944, he was transferred overseas to Devon, in England, where he was trained in counterintelligence activities in preparation for the Allied D-Day offensive. During the Allied advance through France, according to Alexander, Salinger was responsible for sabotaging the German forces' channels of communication and detecting local enemy agents. Throughout 1944, Salinger participated in fierce fighting across France, witnessing significant casualties and injuries. Salinger's unit crossed into Germany in 1945, by which time Salinger's state of mind was noticeably depressed. Eventually, military doctors diagnosed him with a breakdown brought on by his protracted proximity to combat. His condition required a few weeks of hospitalization. Salinger's depiction of Sergeant X's breakdown in "For Esmé—with Love and Squalor" is assumed to fictionalize Salinger's own experience of combat stress. While Salinger clearly had firsthand knowledge of Devon, combat, and post-traumatic stress disorder, the extent to which Sergeant X's story is autobiographical cannot be known.

Salinger returned to New York in 1946 and continued writing and trying to publish his work. At this time, he developed an interest in Zen Buddhism, which was to influence so much of his work. Salinger received his fair share of publishers' rejection slips until the completion of a short story that came to be called "A Perfect Day for Bananafish," which was bought by the *New Yorker* magazine in 1948. Salinger's writing career started to take off; in 1950 the critically acclaimed "For Esmé—with Love and Squalor" was published. The writer's masterpiece, *The Catcher in the Rye,* was published in 1951; it made the American best-seller list. However, as Salinger achieved a degree of critical and financial success with his work, his mounting skepticism toward editors, publishers, and anyone associated with Hollywood became evident. He also felt that his growing fame was causing him to lose privacy and solitude, so in 1953 he purchased a plot of land in Cornish, New Hampshire, where he could live in relative seclusion. The last major work published after his relocation to New Hampshire was *Raise High the Roof Beam, Carpenters and Seymour: An Introduction* in 1963. It is widely believed that he has been working on many other manuscripts since his withdrawal from public life.

Only with unrestricted access to Salinger's papers and documents will a clearer picture of the enigmatic writer emerge. Although his work can be readily contextualized, for example, in terms of World War II or the social conformity of 1950s America, Salinger's work must essentially speak for itself, without much additional commentary from the author. Speculation about Salinger's relationships with and attitudes toward women has been rife, but even the number of times he has been married is disputed. However, his work provides fertile ground for analyzing the recurring female character types that populate his texts. From these character types, conclusions can be drawn about Salinger's representation of women, and authorial perspectives can be inferred though not corroborated. Similarly, his work engages with themes and philosophical ideas that are reiterated throughout multiple texts. Thus, disdain for phoniness and conformity; the importance of love for, and from, one's fellow human beings; and the spiritual emptiness of postwar America are all explored in more than one text. On the one hand, Salinger presents challenges for the writer who wants to make links between the author and his work because of his control of information; on the other hand, his attitudes, concerns, and influences are extremely accessible because of their recurrence in various works.

TOPICS AND STRATEGIES

This section will identify various topics for essays that could draw on multiple Salinger works. The topic suggestions are intended to inspire your own ideas. Many of Salinger's recurring themes, ideas, and characters appear to find their roots in autobiographical incidents. However, the writer of an essay on Salinger must be careful not to jump to conclusions about the autobiographical nature of Salinger's work or to automatically assume attitudes and concerns are direct consequences of events in Salinger's life.

Themes

Many Salinger characters are searching for meaning in their lives. They are repelled by the world they live in; they often reject society and withdraw from it. One force that can reconnect these alienated characters with the rest of humanity is the power of love. Love, for Salinger, does not refer to romantic or sexual love. Salinger's concept of love is a universal force that can provide a purpose for living. Recognizing, receiving, and giving love permit characters to transcend their hostile feelings toward the world. Despondency, depression, or a sense of superiority can be cast aside, allowing the character to participate again in the process of living. The reason so many characters reject the world they live in is because they are aware of the entrenched hypocrisy of humankind and social institutions. Some characters are marginalized because of their difference from the norms of their society. For example, a sensitive man or an unhappy mother does not conform to society's standards for masculinity or motherhood. Thus, these characters may feel themselves outcast because they are unable to don the mask required of them to be acceptable to society. With Salinger, the older a character is, the higher the likelihood that he or she lacks authenticity. Children have not usually learned to dissimulate, although some children do demonstrate latent signs of corruption. The Salinger teenager is the character who is often poised on the threshold between innocence and adult degradation. Aware of their potential fall into phoniness, these teenagers resist the call of adulthood, although it is, of course, a state that cannot be eluded. What can save an adult from the brink of insanity caused by the twisted values of society is successful communication with a like-minded person. A conversation that connects two compatible spirits can pull a character back from the edge of despair. Conversely, a meaningless dialogue can reinforce the pointlessness of human interaction and relationships, prompting a character to seek death or escape.

Sample Topics:

1. **Communication:** For Salinger, how can a conversation trigger despondency and despair? How does Salinger depict communication as having the power to save a character from despondency and despair?

   Communication, whether in the form of dialogue, letters, messages, diaries, or poetry, can have a polarizing effect on the recipient of that communication. Communication can produce either hope or hopelessness. The key to successful communication is whether the communication facilitates a true connection between the participants. An essay on the theme of communication could examine examples of successful communication and contrast them with examples of communication that fail. Works that incorporate this theme include "For Esmé—with Love and Squalor," "A Perfect Day for Bananafish," "Down at the Dinghy," and *Raise High the Roof Beam, Carpenters and Seymour: An Introduction*.

2. **Love:** In Salinger works, what is the effect of love on different characters? What are the different types of love that Salinger discusses in his novels and stories?

A quotation from Dostoyevsky's *The Brothers Karamazov*, in "For Esmé—with Love and Squalor," asserts that hell "is the suffering of being unable to love." An essay on the subject of love could analyze various Salinger works to determine if this quotation presents Salinger's position on the theme of love. If hell is being unable to love, then paradise would be the capacity to love and be loved. What kinds of relationships does Salinger portray in his works that show this capacity for love? Different examples of love relationships are present in *Franny and Zooey, Raise High the Roof Beam, Carpenters and Seymour: An Introduction*, and *The Catcher in the Rye*.

3. **Phoniness:** According to Salinger, what aspects of society have been contaminated by phoniness and dishonesty? Can any character elude the contamination of phoniness?

In *The Catcher in the Rye*, Holden decries the phoniness of many people he meets. An essay on phoniness could examine how and why Salinger shows people as dishonest, mask-wearing hypocrites. Additionally, Salinger's works can be examined to determine if any character has traits that allow him or her to evade (or partially evade) corruption. Stories such as "Uncle Wiggily in Connecticut" or "Just Before the War with the Eskimos" could prove helpful for analyses of characters who demonstrate some degree of awareness of their complicity with phoniness that lets them have moments of honesty with themselves, if not with other people.

4. **Loss of innocence:** Why do Salinger's teenage characters resist transitioning into the adult world? Since becoming an adult is unavoidable, how do the various characters learn to reconcile their hesitations with their ineluctable coming of age?

An essay on how characters respond to a loss of innocence could focus on those characters who are on the cusp of adolescence and adulthood. Holden, Franny, Jean de Daumier-Smith, and Ginnie Mannox are four young people who balk at the realities of the world they see ahead of them. However, the four characters behave very differently at their moments of crisis. All of these characters find methods of interaction with the people around them that aid in their acceptance of this difficult transition period.

Character

Of the 14 Salinger texts discussed in this book, half mention or allude to Glass family members. The two Glass parents, Bessie and Les, produced seven children: Seymour, Buddy, Boo Boo, Walt and Waker (the twins), Zooey, and Franny. Even if a Glass family member is not the focus of a story, there may still be a Glass connection. For example, in *Seymour: An Introduction*, Buddy implies that he wrote *The Catcher in the Rye* and "Teddy." What unites the Glass siblings is their intelligence and beauty. Whenever they feature in a story, Salinger's sympathy and bias toward them are apparent. They scintillate compared with the banality of the ordinary people with whom they are forced to interact. The Glass children are alienated from their society and struggle to find meaning because of other people's insincerity and superficiality. Salinger often portrays the worst that society has to offer in the figure of an adult woman. Such women are self-absorbed, yet, like sirens, they lure men away from spiritual pursuits and make them languish in the realm of the physical. Alternatively, they can reduce men to obscurity through their harping on petty concerns. Sensitive men will suffer at the hands of women. Either women will shatter these men's faith in people and love or they will prove to be unattainable, because Salinger's men do not conform to the usual standards of North American masculinity. Since Salinger adults are often bedeviled by flaws and problems, hope resides in the child characters. Children's pure and innocent interaction with their world can offer redemptive power for suffering adults.

Sample Topics:

1. **The Glass family:** What qualities do all the Glass siblings share? How does Seymour's suicide affect the other family members? How does Salinger use the Glass family to critique postwar American society?

   An essay on the Glass family could take any of several approaches. One angle would be to discuss the primary ideas that Salinger attaches to these characters. For example, several members of the Glass family are adherents of Eastern religions and advocate the concept of universal love. Another approach would be to analyze how Salinger's positive validation of the Glass family and the beliefs and attitudes with which they are associated is used to critique the average member of postwar North American society. Alternatively, looking at the five surviving Glass siblings, an essay could examine the impact of Seymour's life and death on them.

2. **Children:** How do Salinger's child characters hold redemptive power? How do the child characters compare with adult characters? How do Salinger's girl characters differ from his boy characters?

   Salinger's short stories and novels are populated by a diverse range of prepubescent characters. Charles, Teddy, Lionel, Ramona, and Sybil are just some of the precocious voices that speak to the souls of the adults they encounter. An essay could compare the presentation of the boy children with that of the girl children. In the list of children above, the two girls have far more negative traits than the three boys. What accounts for this difference? Nonetheless, girls as well as boys speak with an innocence and openness that Salinger adults have mislaid. A paper could discuss the values and qualities that Salinger associates with these childish voices, showing how those values have the power to transform the lives of adults they meet.

3. **Adult women:** What negative qualities does Salinger personify through his adult women characters? How does Salinger portray married life? Which adult women are spared Salinger's critical presentation and why?

   Joanie, Muriel, and Mrs. McArdle encapsulate Salinger's presentation of adult women. These women fixate on the physical or the trivial and are unable to respond to the spiritual or psychological needs of their husbands. An essay on the function and presentation of adult women could analyze a selection of these characters to determine what qualities Salinger attributes to them. An alternative approach would be to compare these superficial women with the adult women characters Salinger does validate, such as Franny or Boo Boo. What traits do Glass women have that elevate them above the mass of ordinary women?

4. **Sensitive men:** How do sensitive male characters react to their society, to other people they meet, and to their own psychological condition?

   The code of masculinity imposed by society excludes men who do not conform to the demands of that code. Some men will not find the image of the jock or the womanizer or the soldier appealing. They may realize that their physical and mental features automatically erect a barrier between themselves and society's dominant models. An essay could explore how these kinds of men (for example, Sergeant X, Holden, Arthur, Seymour, and Franklin) address their sense of alienation from mainstream society. Given their difference from prescriptive masculinity, another approach would be to examine how these men interact with female characters.

History and Context

All of the Salinger texts discussed here were published between 1948 and 1963. All of the works are set in the 20th century, and the majority deal with the World War II era or the years immediately following the war. Born in 1919, Salinger joined the American armed forces and was deployed in Europe in 1944 and 1945, where he participated in battles that saw many casualties. As mentioned in the brief biography, his experience of combat precipitated a nervous breakdown. His psychological problems, possibly fictionalized in the characters of Seymour and Sergeant X, could be understood as what is now referred to as post-traumatic stress disorder. In that time period, this disorder would have been labeled shell shock, combat stress, or war neurosis. Many Salinger characters have been affected by the war in a negative way, either because they fought in the war or because someone they loved was killed during the war.

Salinger treats the postwar period harshly in many of his works. The United States became increasingly prosperous after the war. However, Salinger associates this consumer-driven America with dubious values: greed, self-absorption, individualism, selfishness, banality, and superficiality, among others. His main targets for hostility are WASPs, who, as a group, epitomize for Salinger the worst that American bourgeois culture has to offer. The spectrum of Salinger's background characters works to project a distasteful image of postwar America. Only a few characters are alienated from this soul-destroying society. These special few try to stand firm in their advocacy of different values, but they are marginalized and often psychologically adrift. Characters such as Holden, Franklin Graff, Teddy, Seymour, Sergeant X, and Franny must learn to adapt to the reality of their society without succumbing to the depression or distress that interaction with their world sparks.

Sample Topics:

1. **World War II and its aftermath:** How has the war affected the various members of the Glass family? How do different characters address the legacy of the war on their personal lives?

   An essay on this topic could compare the two most important soldier characters in Salinger's work: Seymour Glass and Sergeant X. Alternatively, an essay could examine the aftermath of the war on various characters. Some characters have lost someone they loved in the war. For example, Eloise in "Uncle Wiggily in Connecticut" lost her lover, Walt Glass, whose death also affected the entire Glass family.

2. **The modern urban condition:** What are the defining features of Salinger's portrayal of 1940s and 1950s American bourgeois culture? How does the average character respond to his or her material, superficial society? How do sensitive characters handle their frustration and antipathy towards their banal environment?

   While the modern urban condition is embraced by some characters, a sensitive few reel in horror at the hypocrisy, triteness, and individualistic nature of their society. Essays on this topic could draw on all of the nine short stories and all three of the novels for supporting evidence to demonstrate how Salinger depicts modern American society in a very negative way. For him, bourgeois culture is unspiritual and propagates competition and acquisition. However, some Salinger characters persevere in their commitment to human interconnectedness and unity. How do Salinger's sensitive characters learn to live in the world? Do they all succeed?

Philosophy and Ideas

A consequence of the modern urban condition discussed in the "History and Context" section is that more sensitive characters find themselves in a state of alienation with themselves, with others, and with their society. The awareness of being an outsider, however, leads to different responses.

Some characters fall into despair when they look around at the superficiality surrounding them. This despondency may be impossible to surmount. Death may seem preferable than continuing with life. Other characters may seek alternatives, such as alcohol consumption, to numb their pain. A completely different approach for some characters is to reconnect to society through acceptance of difference or through a spiritual affirmation of unity between self and others. Several of the characters who endure the experience of being outsiders from mainstream society consider themselves spiritual in an unspiritual world. Their spiritual beliefs are drawn from the East, rather than the West. Their beliefs cause them to denounce the competitive, ego-driven norms of the West. Subscribing to ideas such as reincarnation, unity between self and other, or the ubiquity of the divine creates a rift between these adherents of Eastern religious thought systems and their Western world. Another response to alienation is the pursuit of the arts. Some characters favor writing, while others paint or tell stories. Through their art, these characters try to convey their vision of life to a largely indifferent public. However, engagement with their art form keeps these characters from behaving in a self-destructive manner. Alienated individuals who do not find an outlet for their feelings through art may find themselves undergoing mental anguish. Several Salinger characters are described as being in the process of having a mental breakdown owing to their horror at the world in which they find themselves floundering. However, some of these characters are able to overcome their mental disengagement from their world either through their own agency (Holden), through someone else's reaching out to them (Franny), or through a mystical moment that causes them to reevaluate their relationship with the world (Jean de Daumier-Smith).

Sample Topics:

1. **Alienation:** Why are some Salinger characters unable or unwilling to fully embrace their society and its values? Why are some Salinger characters unable to form meaningful relationships with others? Why are some Salinger characters blocked from developing their own sense of identity?

   An essay on alienation could discuss why so many characters feel like outsiders in their society. This essay would likely link to the "History and Context" topic on the modern urban condition. Another approach would be to analyze the different characters' responses to alienation. Is there any solution that precipitates reconnection with self, others, and society? Is any solution presented by Salinger as more effective than other solutions?

2. **Writing and the arts:** As presented in Salinger's works, what is the role of the artist in society? How does artistic expression affect the artist and any audience for his work?

Salinger described Buddy Glass as his "alter-ego and collaborator" on the original dust jacket of *Franny and Zooey*. Clearly, then, the difficulties inherent in the writing process and the dynamic among writer, audience, and material are issues with which Salinger closely identifies. Essays on writing and the arts could analyze the role of the artist in society as presented by Salinger. Another essay could consider Salinger's presentation of the relationships among writer (artist), material, audience, reception of work, and effects of the artwork.

3. **Eastern religious ideas:** How does the acceptance of Eastern spiritual ideas provide Salinger's characters with an antidote to Western attitudes toward the world?

Buddy explains in *Raise High the Roof Beam, Carpenters and Seymour: An Introduction* that Seymour's spiritual beliefs were drawn from "New and Old testaments, Advaita Vedanta and classical Taoism." The epigraph for the *Nine Stories* anthology is a Zen Buddhist koan. An essay could identify the different Eastern religious ideas that Salinger engages with and analyze how they affect theme, form, and characterization in various Salinger works. Another approach would be to push this analysis to the next stage by showing how each idea counteracts features of the Western world that Salinger (or his characters) finds abhorrent.

4. **Mental illness:** Why do some Salinger characters find themselves pushed to the brink of insanity by their society? How do the different characters surrender to, or overcome, their anxiety?

Many Salinger texts imply that withdrawing psychologically from one's society may well be a sane response to an insane world. However, if someone chooses life over death, he or she must have some form of rapprochement with society in order to continue functioning. An essay on this topic could investigate the different characters, such as Holden, Franny, Seymour, and Sergeant X, who hover on the boundary of sanity/insanity. How does each character respond to his or her situation? Which factors determine whether a character will reconnect with society or whether he or she will give up all hope?

Form and Genre

One of the features that many of Salinger's short stories share is their indeterminate ending. His ambiguous endings incite the reader to dwell on the story's multiple interpretations. As critic Wenke argues, this multiplicity is signaled by Salinger in his choice of an epigraph for the *Nine Stories* collection. The Zen Buddhist koan asks, "What is the sound of one hand clapping?" The answer to this conundrum is supposed to be considered through the process of meditation, but it defies a definitive interpretation. The goal of a koan is to prod people to break free from the constrictions of rational thought and rely on intuitive thinking to jolt the mind into awareness or an awakening. This epiphany, or satori, or moment of realization, is experienced by many of the characters in *Nine Stories*, who suddenly see life differently after a transformative event.

Another hallmark of Salinger's short stories is his use of dialogue. Dialogue is Salinger's main device in many of his short stories for advancing the plot and communicating characterization. What characters say about one another can divulge what each person is like. The style and idiosyncrasies of a character's speech can serve several additional purposes, such as situating that character in a specific time and place or indicating conflict.

Sample Topics:

1. **The open endings of *Nine Stories*:** How do the open endings of the stories link to the anthology's epigraph? How does Salinger's refusal to provide textual closure for the reader amplify many of his key themes?

Many of Salinger's short stories contain an element of uncertainty that prohibits the reader from assigning an authoritative interpretation to them. Leaving a story open-ended is obviously a deliberate choice on an author's part. An essay on this topic could discuss why Salinger favors leaving many of his short stories indeterminate. It could also be argued that the open-endedness ties in to various themes and questions that the story poses. However, the themes and questions may differ for each short story.

2. **The use of dialogue:** Why does Salinger want to establish distance between the reader and the inner thoughts of his characters by using dialogue (as opposed to description or narration)? What stylistic and language techniques does Salinger employ in order to create believable dialogue? How does Salinger's extensive use of dialogue help in conveying some of his central themes?

Salinger uses many techniques, such as having his characters repeat themselves, use slang, interrupt, trail off their sentences, and swear in order to replicate credible human speech. Essays analyzing Salinger's use of dialogue could employ various approaches. One approach could be to dissect the stylistic devices used to convey and create convincing dialogue. Diction, syntax, and level of language can communicate information about a character, but they are also used by Salinger to lambaste certain characters. How does Salinger exploit details, such as tone or the stance and gestures that supplement a character's speech, to convey additional information? Another approach would be to show how the use of dialogue embellishes Salinger's dominant and recurring themes of communication, alienation, and relationships.

Language, Symbols, and Imagery

In the 1940s and 1950s, smoking had a certain cachet, which was reinforced through the high incidence of smoking in Hollywood movies, and was socially acceptable. Although links were starting to be drawn between smoking and cancer in the 1950s, this information was not widely available. Throughout Salinger's work, the vast majority of his characters are prodigious smokers. Their style of smoking and their impetus to light up a cigarette at any given moment are revelatory of aspects of their characters. Salinger incorporates details about their smoking patterns that differentiate one character from another. Many of the characters who are smokers are undergoing some sort of spiritual or existential crisis, and the act of smoking or lighting up a cigarette is indicative of their evolving state of mind. Many of the same characters also have a spiritual awakening that alters their outlook on themselves and their world. In many cases, this epiphany is sparked by a contemplation of physical object. These epiphanic objects differ widely from text to text, but each has the capacity to generate or symbolize a change of mindset in the character.

1. **The motif of smoking:** How do a character's smoking mannerisms supplement his or her characterization? Under what circumstances do characters smoke?

   Salinger's work contains many descriptions of characters lighting up a cigarette, exhaling the smoke in a distinct way, extinguishing a cigarette, or fiddling with an ashtray. An essay could assess how Salinger uses smoking and imagery pertaining to smoking as a method to emphasize character traits and attitudes. Another approach would be to show how smoking styles and the choice to light up a cigarette (or not) reflect tensions and conflicts between characters.

2. **Epiphanic objects:** How do physical objects have the capacity to spark a spiritual or mental awakening in some of Salinger's characters?

Her daughter's glasses cause Eloise to reevaluate her life in "Uncle Wiggily in Connecticut," a young girl's watch allows Sergeant X to regain his faith in humanity in "For Esmé—with Love and Squalor," and a carrousel makes Holden understand that shielding children from the adult world is a tenuous proposition. Books, written words, piles of trusses and irrigation basins, and chicken sandwiches are just some of the other objects that become linked to specific characters to show their transitioning state of mind. Essays on these objects could analyze a selection of them to show their significance within a specific text or could look for patterns among the range of objects to argue for similarities in types of object and their effects. For example, the role of books in altering characters' relationships with their society is a possible topic.

Compare and Contrast Essays

Suggestions for comparative essays based on more than one Salinger text can be found at the end of each chapter in the "Compare and Contrast" sections.

Bibliography

Alexander, Paul. *Salinger: A Biography*. Los Angeles: Renaissance, 1999.

Alsen, Eberhard. *A Reader's Guide to J. D. Salinger*. Westport, CT: Greenwood Press, 2002.

Bloom, Harold, ed. *J. D. Salinger: Modern Critical Views*. New York: Chelsea House, 1987.

French, Warren. *J. D. Salinger, Revisited*. Boston: Twayne, 1988.

Grunwald, Henry Anatole, ed. *Salinger: A Critical and Personal Portrait*. New York: Harper & Row, 1962.

Gwynn, Frederick L., and Joseph L. Blotner. *The Fiction of J. D. Salinger*. Pittsburgh: U of Pittsburgh P, 1958.

Hamilton, Ian. *In Search of J. D. Salinger*. New York: Random House, 1988.

Lundquist, James. *J. D. Salinger*. New York: Ungar, 1979.

Maynard, Joyce. *At Home in the World: A Memoir*. New York: Picador, 1998.

Salinger, Margaret. *Dream Catcher: A Memoir*. New York: Washington Square Press, 2000.

Smith, Dominic. "Salinger's *Nine Stories*: Fifty Years Later." *Antioch Review* 61, no. 4 (Fall 2003): 639+.

Sublette, Jack R. *J. D. Salinger: An Annotated Bibliography 1938–1981.* New York: Garland, 1984.

Weaver, Brett E. *An Annotated Bibliography, 1982–2002, of J. D. Salinger.* Lewiston, NY: E. Mellen Press, 2002.

Wenke, John. *J. D. Salinger: A Study of the Short Fiction.* Boston: Twayne, 1991.

THE CATCHER
IN THE RYE

READING TO WRITE

ONE REASON *The Catcher in the Rye* is a memorable novel is the distinctive voice of its narrator, Holden Caulfield. Salinger chooses to have Holden tell his story using a first-person narrative point of view. At first glance, Holden's narration of his behavior and thoughts seems candid and unequivocal. In first-person narratives, however, questions of reliability and bias should be uppermost in a reader's mind. First-person narrators are limited by constraints on their knowledge: They are not able to read other people's thoughts, they cannot be cognizant of conversations and actions that take place when they are not present, and their point of view is compromised by their own outlook on the world and, sometimes, by their own naiveté or ignorance.

An excellent starting point for thinking about *The Catcher in the Rye* is to consider what Holden's limitations as a narrator may be. At the time he tells his story, he is a teenage boy from a wealthy family who has little experience of the world and is not very effective at communicating with other people. There is synergy between Holden as a narrator and Holden as a character. After all, most people do not like to make themselves look ridiculous when they relate stories about themselves. Appraising Holden as both a character and a narrator would be a productive way to start generating essay topics on *The Catcher in the Rye*.

The deficiencies in the way Holden presents himself are illustrated in the following excerpt, which can be found in the opening pages of the novel:

Anyway, it was the Saturday of the football game with Saxon Hall. The game with Saxon Hall was supposed to be a very big deal around Pencey. It was the last game of the year, and you were supposed to commit suicide or something if old Pencey didn't win. I remember around three o'clock that afternoon I was standing way the hell up on top of Thomsen Hill, right next to this crazy cannon that was in the Revolutionary War and all. You could see the whole field from there, and you could see the two teams bashing each other all over the place. You couldn't see the grandstand too hot, but you could hear them all yelling, deep and terrific on the Pencey side, because practically the whole school except me was there, and scrawny and faggy on the Saxon Hall side, because the visiting team hardly ever brought many people with them.

This scenario depicts the Pencey students gathered together to support their football team against a rival school. It is a community, bonding event where all the boys share the same mindset and objective: to win. Holden, however, has elected not to participate in this team activity. Instead, he is standing "way the hell up on top of Thomsen Hill." His position on top of the hill, looking down on the game, is key to understanding his character. Although he is looking down on the game because he is standing above it, the reader realizes that mentally he looks down on the game because he thinks it is beneath him. His tone confirms this notion. He sarcastically contends that "you were supposed to commit suicide" if Pencey lost, because the game "was supposed to be a very great deal." Holden presents himself as superior to the other boys because he has not succumbed to the game's inane propaganda. However, another perspective on Holden would show how alone he is. The cannon that he is standing next to is noteworthy. A cannon connotes aggression, war, and in this case, revolution. The imagery suggests that Holden is waging a lone battle against the rest of his society, a society that he looks down on. Significantly, Holden is symbolically aligned with a cannon that is described as "crazy," which prompts questions not only about Holden's mental condition but also about the state of the society with which he takes issue.

This brief passage describing Holden standing on Thomsen Hill touches on a profusion of topics that could lead to essays on *The Catcher in the Rye.* An analysis of the societal values that Holden is revolting against would make a viable essay topic. Why is Holden at war with his society? The excerpt raises questions about the role of education in a young person's life. It also makes us ponder on the concept of identity and why some people find themselves alienated from a particular group. Given Holden's age, papers related to teenage rebellion and coming-of-age are germane. Additionally, Holden can be compared with some of the other Pencey students, such as Robert Ackley or Ward Stradlater, who do—or do not—have trouble adapting to this world of aggressive competition.

Despite Holden's isolation on the hill, his desire to be understood still shines through his sarcastic and opinionated commentary. A technique in the excerpt that underscores this need is Holden's repeated use of the pronoun *you,* instead of *I.* The effect of using the second-person pronoun is to draw the reader closer and to give his experiences a more universal flavor. This tension between choosing to situate himself apart from society but also wanting to be accepted marks the character of Holden and affects his interactions with other characters. Is Holden aware of the contradictions embedded in his viewpoint? Is he lying to his readers, or is he simply too naive to have a broader and clearer perspective on life and himself? When reading *The Catcher in the Rye,* weigh up carefully what Holden claims and take into consideration any other textual evidence that may provide an alternative interpretation. In this way, a careful reader will be able to negotiate the text successfully.

TOPICS AND STRATEGIES

The remainder of this chapter will focus on potential topics for essays on *The Catcher in the Rye* and different approaches that could be deployed in writing about those topics. Remember that the topics are suggestions and should be used as springboards to aid you in devising your own original papers.

Themes

Although some of its themes are immediately apparent from a cursory read, *The Catcher in the Rye* is subtle and requires close attention to uncover its depth and complexity. One theme that is easily accessible is the idea of the lack of authenticity in adult society. Holden constantly denounces aspects of his world as "phony." For example, he pillories Ernie, a piano player, because he bows at the end of his performance as if he were humble, whereas Holden assumes that Ernie is the type of man who would only associate with fellow celebrities. Holden sets himself apart and takes pride in not participating in the hypocrisies he sees around him. Careful reading of the text, however, unearths inconsistencies in Holden's own behavior, raising doubts as to whether even he can elude phoniness completely.

His dubious behavior is exemplified when he lies to other characters with the deliberate intention of deceiving them in order to make himself feel important. Ironically, he desperately wants relationships with other people but is uncomfortable with intimate situations of all kinds. He relentlessly tries to get close to someone and then pushes him or her away. The excuses that he gives at these moments of rejection merit close attention. Is he deceiving them or is he deceiving himself?

Another aspect of the world that troubles Holden greatly is death. He has already had several close encounters with death that continue to haunt him. However, when faced with the physical and psychological violence of the adult world, he often retreats into fantasies where he is either the victim or the perpetrator of acts of violence. What Holden would really prefer to do is stay in the world of childhood, which he sees as a world of innocence. His fantasies about being a catcher in the rye and his unrealistic attitude toward his sister Phoebe show a young man who is so disgusted by the adult world that he would do anything to circumvent it altogether.

Sample Topics:

1. **Deceitfulness:** What motivates Holden to lie to other characters? What are the consequences of his lies? Does Holden ever deceive himself?

In chapter 3 of the novel, Holden brags that he is "the most terrific liar you ever saw in your life." The examples he provides indicate that his lies are motivated by various goals. In some cases, he wants to escape from a situation and feels that lying is the best way to dodge awkwardness with other people. At other times, his lies seem prompted by a desire to make himself seem more interesting and appealing. Unfortunately, his lies rarely have the effect that he hopes for because he consistently underestimates other people. Look, for example, at his conversation with Mrs. Morrow on the train to New York. Salinger provides clues that Mrs. Morrow is responding in a different manner to Holden's lies than he believes. Therefore, there is a possibility that Holden is deceiving himself more than he is deceiving anyone else. Papers on this topic would need to examine carefully the situations where Holden lies and look for discrepancies between his version of events and what may be really happening. Holden's motivations for lying and the consequences of his actions are important components for an essay on this topic.

2. **The loss of innocence:** What images and events are used by Salinger to show that Holden yearns to keep children in a state of innocence? Which characters are associated with innocence? Which characters are associated with experience and knowledge?

The period of childhood is romanticized by adults as an Edenic time when a person has no worries in the world and is free from responsibility, problems, and conflict. Holden wants to stop children from gaining knowledge of the evils of the adult world so that they do not lose their innocence. However, it is impossible to stay in a state of innocence if one lives in the real world. Holden misquotes the Robert Burns poem that provides the title for the novel. The actual line of the poem states: "gin a body meet a body / comin' thro' the rye." Thus, by changing the verb "meet" to "catch," Holden transforms a poem laden with sexual overtones into an appeal to protect children's innocence. Why does Holden want to catch the children in the rye? Why does he want to remove the obscene graffiti from the walls of Phoebe's school? Why is he obsessed by Jane Gallagher's kings in the game of checkers? What are the dangers of trying to stay trapped forever in childhood? Furthermore, believing that all children are innocent is a myth; they are often far more aware of the truth of their surroundings than they are given credit for. Essays on this topic should look closely at the character of Phoebe and determine whether she is as innocent as Holden thinks she is or whether there is textual evidence to suggest that she does not conform to Holden's image of her.

3. **Hypocrisy:** What elements of society does Holden assert are "phony"? How does Holden define phoniness? How does Holden respond to phoniness? Why does Holden believe that he is a voice of authenticity in a world that is mostly inauthentic?

Holden's narrative is peppered with the phrase "if you want to know the truth." The repeated use of this expression implies that Holden is going to tell the truth in a world where truth is rare. As was discussed in the section above on the theme of deceit, Holden is not as honest and pure as he likes to believe. In many situations, the offensive behavior that he accuses other people of, such as being superficial, pompous, or insincere, is behavior that he is implicated in himself. Essays on Holden's perception of his world could reflect on the aspects of society Holden finds affected or repulsive and contrast them with the few elements that he alleges are authentic. If Holden is unaware of his own complicity with phoniness, are other characters and situations also more complex than Holden realizes?

4. **Violence and death:** What is the significance of Allie's death in the novel? Why does Holden react to his brother's death with violence? Why does Salinger include so many incidents involving descriptions and thoughts of violence and death?

There are many possible angles from which to approach the themes of violence and death in preparation for writing a paper. At the beginning of the novel, Holden sits down to write a composition for Stradlater. He chooses to write about Allie's baseball mitt and, in the ensuing narrative, he details the love he had for his brother and the effect his death had on him. Allie's early death has left this child frozen in time as an innocent and pure boy. Paradoxically, Allie's death also shows that nothing stays constant. Chapters 18 and 20 provide critical information on Holden's attitude to Allie's death, his own death, and his fears that are linked to ideas of death. Furthermore, violent images evoking war, bombs, and shootings dominate these chapters and highlight Holden's deteriorating mental state. Death and violence are intertwined in the novel, but each theme independently could make a pertinent essay topic.

Character

The Catcher in the Rye has a first-person narrator. One important consequence is that presentations of all the other characters are filtered through the perspective and bias of the narrator. Therefore, the most straightforward way to approach character studies for this novel is to consider a character's relationship with, and significance to, Holden. Nevertheless, Salinger does provide a few clues that indicate that what characters are thinking may be at variance with the way that Holden presents them. These clues usually can be found in their dialogue, their mannerisms, or their actions.

The Catcher in the Rye traces a few days in the life of Holden and, arguably, shows his development from a boy resisting maturity to a young man who accepts life's unavoidable rites of passage. Throughout his journey, he meets many people who are crucial in compounding his confusion and disgust of the adult world while simultaneously propelling him forward in his journey toward maturity. Some characters, such as his sister, Phoebe, or D.B., his brother, may actually create ambivalence in Holden. Neither of these two characters quite live up to Holden's expectations of them, but both still embody something positive for him. Only Allie is completely pure in Holden's memory. Minor characters, such as Holden's roommate Stradlater or Maurice (the bellboy-pimp), are overtly hostile to Holden but, in the final paragraph of the novel, Holden claims to "miss" them. Why does he say this?

As a teenager searches to establish his role in society, breaking away from his parents is a natural step in asserting independence. However, the advice or concern of adults is rarely totally rejected. Holden seems to attract figures in his life, such as his two teachers Mr. Spencer and Mr. Antolini, who take a paternal interest in the boy. Holden also interacts with several mother characters, and his response toward them varies according to what he wants from them. In fact, Holden's relationships with women of all ages are complicated by sexuality and by his conflicting needs, needs that he is unable to articulate clearly to himself, let alone to the women.

Sample Topics:

1. **Holden's siblings—Phoebe, Allie, and D.B.:** How do Holden's brothers and sister influence him? What does each sibling represent to Holden?

One of Holden's brothers is dead, and the other brother is absent from his life because he lives in Hollywood and, according to Holden, has "prostituted" his writing talents for money. Only his sister, Phoebe, has regular communication with Holden. However, despite the brothers' absence, their existence has been critical in contributing to Holden's psychological problems, and memories of both brothers are still important in shaping who Holden is becoming. Essays on Holden's siblings could focus on Phoebe alone. She plays a significant role in the novel and is critical in helping Holden reevaluate his perception of the world. Another approach would be to write about the influence of the two brothers or of Allie alone. Allie's death seems to have been a pivotal event in Holden's life, and memories of Allie tend to surface at critical times during Holden's New York experience.

2. **Father figures and mother figures:** How does Holden respond to characters who take a fatherly interest in him? How does Holden depict mother figures? What is the conflict that is

inherent in Holden's dealings with both father and mother characters?

Essays analyzing the father and mother characters in the novel could focus on either only the male or only the female secondary characters, or they could deal with a comparison of both types of characters. There are some areas of overlap between the two sets of characters, but there are also some significant differences in the way Holden behaves with men as opposed to the way he interacts with women. For a novel that charts the life of a boy, one noticeable lacuna in his story is the dearth of information about his parents. It never occurs to Holden until the end of the novel to turn to them for any kind of support. Nonetheless, Holden searches for surrogate parental guidance elsewhere. In the case of men, his teachers step up and try to offer worldly advice to the troubled boy with varying degrees of success. In the case of women, sexual feelings impede honest relationships with them, as he seems more inclined to try to impress them. In all cases, Holden usually ends up running away from the dialogue he has initiated with them. What is it that makes him respond in this way? Are there any paternal or maternal figures that Holden is at ease with?

3. **A world apart—masculine men:** How does Holden perceive men who are aggressive and assertive? How does Holden respond to men who are more stereotypically masculine than he is?

Holden describes himself as scrawny and cowardly. He encounters several characters who typify traditional American ideals of masculinity more than he does. He feels vulnerable when he finds himself in confrontation with these characters. Stradlater and Maurice both present a physical challenge to Holden. Analysis of these secondary characters would be relevant in terms of their contrast with Holden or in terms of the effects they have on him. Other characters humiliate Holden verbally. The taxi driver Horwitz, for example, does not bother to conceal his irritation with Holden and makes it clear that he thinks Holden is immature. These male characters seem to have cracked the code to manhood, whereas Holden has been excluded from their group. An analysis of the presentation and function of these male characters would make a valid essay topic.

4. **Holden's relationships with women:** Why does Holden repeatedly try to invite women to spend time with him? How successful is Holden at relating to these women? Does he ever achieve a close relationship with any woman?

Holden is wary of relationships with other people. However, he is driven to try to create bonds with women in order to assuage his chronic loneliness and to satisfy the demands of his burgeoning sexuality. The fear of intimacy is constant, but there is a difference in the way Holden treats a woman he desires sexually as opposed to someone whose company he craves—although he has trouble differentiating the two types of women. Papers on the topic of his relationships with women could be linked to an analysis of the theme of intimacy. Another key question to consider is why Holden pushes women away when they could be friends to him. An analysis of the characters Sally and Jane would be relevant here. Why does Holden undermine his own efforts at intimacy? Women with whom Holden has a nonsexual relationship, such as the two nuns, could also be the focus of a paper.

History and Context

The Catcher in the Rye was published in 1951 and tapped into the budding American phenomenon of the teenager. The concept of the teenager emerged at the beginning of the 20th century, largely as a consequence of laws that stipulated mandatory high school education and abolished child labor. These laws delayed young people's entry into the adult world in a way never seen before. During the depression years and World War II, the definition of the teenager evolved. A code of conduct was associated with the term that characterized the teenager as rebellious and antiauthoritarian. Common teenage feelings of confusion, boredom, anger, and frustration turned against the very society that had granted its young people this extended period of freedom from work. The only condition that society demanded from its teenagers was that each teenager acquire an education. Education, therefore, became an obvious arena in which some teenagers acted out their subversive sentiments.

Holden's rebellion manifests itself initially by a refusal to apply himself to formal education. He has been expelled from various schools. The schools his parents send him to are elite private schools. The economic prosperity of postwar America has allowed his parents to achieve a high standard of living, and Holden has everything he could possibly want materially. In this period, there were many segments of society who were being excluded from America's growing affluence and had legitimate reasons to rebel. From this perspective, Holden can be labeled a rebel without a cause.

Nowhere was the difference between rich and poor more visible than in New York City in the late 1940s and early 1950s. At that time, New York City could claim to be the most important city in the world, and it attracted returning veterans and immigrants from Europe and elsewhere looking for fame and fortune. It provides the perfect volatile backdrop for the naïve Holden to first lose and then find himself.

Sample Topics:

1. **New York City:** How does the particularized time and place of the New York City setting contribute to the development of the characters? What do the different locations within New York City symbolize?

   New York City is a city where anything is possible. Holden travels to many neighborhoods and specific locations in New York City. Among other places, he visits Central Park, Penn Station, Fifth Avenue, Broadway, the American Museum of Natural History, Radio City Music Hall, and the now defunct Biltmore Hotel. Each of these locations prompts varying emotions and reactions in Holden. How does each setting contribute to individualizing Holden? Essays on the New York City setting could consider not only the impact of setting on character but also how the setting amplifies some of the important themes of the novel.

2. **The 1950s teenager—rebel without a cause:** Why is Holden rebelling against his society? How does the figure of a rebellious teenager encapsulate this period in American history?

As a way to assert their individuality, some teenagers may challenge authority or societal rules. In the early 1950s, teenage angst surfaced as a common theme in literature and film. The teenage rebel embodied the individualistic, youth-oriented ethos of postwar American society. Essays on this topic might look at other teenage rebel icons of the time period, such as James Dean in the 1955 film *Rebel without a Cause* or Marlon Brando in *The Wild One* (1954). One line of Brando's dialogue became widely quoted because it typified the 1950s teenage attitude. He is asked, "What are you rebelling against?" and his reply is "Whadda ya got?" Essays could examine the social values against which Holden and these other teenagers are rebelling, such as conformity, conventional gender roles, and conservative sexuality, and determine how successful and genuine their rebellions are.

3. **Rich man/poor man:** How does having, or not having, money contribute to the novel's themes and the characters' development? What is Holden's attitude toward his privileged social position? What is Salinger's attitude to the world of the WASP?

The gap between rich and poor is constantly alluded to in *The Catcher in the Rye*. Holden informs other characters that he is "loaded." What does money mean to Holden? In chapter 1, Holden claims that wealthy people are usually crooks, but later in the novel, he discloses that he is comfortable rooming with Stradlater because Stradlater comes from a comparable economic background to his own. Essays analyzing the impact of class and wealth would need to identify those characters who are desperate for money and compare them to those who take money for granted. Such an essay might also tie in with a consideration of New York City as a place of opportunity that can fulfill the American dream, legitimately or otherwise. An alternative approach to this topic is to analyze the milieu and values of the WASP (White Anglo-Saxon Protestant) world that Salinger critiques in his work. This derogatory acronym refers to the wealthy, white, powerful elite. Many of Holden's friends would be considered WASPs.

Philosophy and Ideas

Generally speaking, the influence of peers increases during adolescence, as does the need to fit in with, and be accepted by, one's peers. The concept of alienation refers to an individual's sense of distance from a group or society. Whereas Holden clearly feels alienated from his peers and his society, it is also possible to speak of him as suffering from self-alienation. Self-alienation is characterized by an absence of a clear sense of identity. Holden is uncertain about his self-image and what roles he should be adopting in life as he develops into a man.

As a consequence of the difficulties facing adolescents in this phase of development, some develop serious psychological problems such as depression or suicidal thoughts. Fluctuating emotions and a lack of emotional experience prevent some adolescents from dealing successfully with their psychological state. Although many teenagers may feel that the adult, material world is abhorrent, they cannot find consolation in spiritual beliefs. Adolescence is a time where doubts concerning faith and religious doctrine start to gather force.

During adolescence, role models such as movie actors are popular, and adolescents sometimes feel a desire to be like their chosen role model. In Holden's case, his role models are characters from other novels. Ironically, although he eschews formal education, he seems to read prolifically and finds role models in the arts but rarely in popular culture, which he mostly disparages.

Sample Topics:

1. **Religion:** In what ways is Holden conflicted about Christianity? Is it true that Holden is "a sort of an atheist" (chapter 14)?

A common part of growing up is to question the religion that is propagated by one's family and society. Holden occasionally ponders the truth or otherwise of the religious teachings that he has received. He is hostile to organized religion and any form of commercialized religion. When he witnesses the kitsch rendition of "Come All Ye Faithful" at Radio City, he aligns himself with Christ against displays of inauthentic religious worship. Essays could analyze Holden's religious positioning in the world and the nature of his spiritual crisis. It could be interesting to speculate whether Holden can be viewed as a Christ figure (since he sees himself as having similarities with Christ). Does he sacrifice anything for something greater than himself?

2. **The outsider:** Why is Holden unable to fit in with his peers? Why is he struggling to find a sense of identity?

Holden is alienated from his society and his peers, but he could also be accused of being alienated from himself. He lacks self-insight and clearly does not see himself the way that others view him. Essays on this topic should consider the factors that contribute to Holden's inability to be part of the group at Pencey School. What characteristics does he have that are alienating or that cause him to be alienated from himself? Why does he always set himself apart from other people and situations?

3. **Mental illness:** Which events indicate Holden's deteriorating mental stability? How do the contradictions in Holden's narration contribute to the suggestion of mental illness?

The contrast between Holden's commentary as he relates certain events and the information that small details offer is the place to start looking for proof as to Holden's fragile state of mind. He describes some events as if he were displaying normal behavior, whereas details let the reader know that some things are irrational. An essay on the topic of mental illness either could investigate Holden's narrative and examine the discrepancies between his version and the apparent truth or could examine the progression of Holden's breakdown and the events that cause him to deteriorate. A psychoanalytic approach could evaluate Holden's mental state and determine the causes of his condition.

4. **The importance of the arts:** Who are the literary heroes and heroines whom Holden proposes as role models? What is his attitude to the arts associated with popular culture such as films or musicals? What defines good art or bad art according to Holden?

The Catcher in the Rye is full of literary allusions, all of which are illuminating and merit further investigation. There are two main approaches to the topics of the arts. First, an essay could examine how each allusion discloses aspects of Holden's personality. For example, Holden declares that he is "crazy about" Jay Gatsby, a character from F. Scott Fitzgerald's novel *The Great Gatsby* (1925). Gatsby breaks all the rules of his society to become a successful millionaire but ends up being shot. Allusions to this novel and other books that Holden extols, such as Isak Dinesen's *Out of Africa or The Return of the Native* by Thomas Hardy, provide revealing parallels (and contrasts) between their main characters' situations and Holden's. Another approach would be to look at the arts in general and analyze which art forms Holden approves of and which he reviles. Look for contradictions, though, in Holden's critique of some art forms. He claims to hate movies, for example, but adds that he enjoys imitating them. In fact, his fantasies are often tied to film scene reenactments, and he includes movie plot summaries at odd moments in his narrative. Overall, the arts are important to Holden in helping him attempt to define and explain himself.

Form and Genre

The Catcher in the Rye is a novel, but parts of it were originally published as short stories in various magazines from 1945 onward. The short stories were not identical to their counterpart chapters in the novel, but they provided a basis for sections of the novel. This accounts for the fact that *The Catcher in the Rye* is episodic; each section of the novel could stand alone. This is why the novel can be analyzed as a picaresque novel, a genre of satiric prose fiction that recounts in a first-person narrative the realistic and droll escapades of a protagonist in low-life situations surviving by his or her wits in a corrupt society.

However, *The Catcher in the Rye* also details Holden's coming of age and thus can be considered an example of a bildungsroman. *Bildungsroman* is a German term signifying a "novel of formation" or a "novel of education." This type of novel follows the protagonist's passage from childhood or adolescence through a range of experiences and often through a spiritual crisis into maturity. One classic example of this type of novel is Charles Dickens's *David Copperfield*, a novel that Holden alludes to on the first page of *The Catcher in the Rye*.

In addition, *The Catcher in the Rye* can be analyzed as a first-person narrative, written in the form of an interior monologue. An interior monologue portrays a character's inner thoughts, feelings, and memories, without the mediation of an external narrator. Even though Holden is the novel's only narrator, other voices are still heard throughout the novel because of various techniques that Salinger applies. The overall effect is of a kaleidoscopic novel: Fragments of a puzzle are pieced together to make a whole.

One way that other voices can be incorporated into the novel is through flashback (also known as analepsis) and digression. Digression in literature is a temporary and intentional departure from one subject to another seemingly unrelated topic. The goal of a digression is usually to prove the validity of a point being made in the original subject under discussion. Digression is not only part of the form and structure of *The Catcher in the Rye*'s plot but also is a significant theme in the novel.

Sample Topics:

1. ***The Catcher in the Rye* as an interior monologue:** What are the effects of having Holden tell his story as an interior mono-

logue? Why did Salinger choose to tell the story through a teen-age boy's first-person narration? What techniques does Salinger utilize to make Holden's thoughts convincingly realistic to the reader?

Holden's voice dominates *The Catcher in the Rye;* however, Salinger is able to bring in other voices by showing Holden in dialogue with them. There is a gap between Holden's version of events and the hints and fragments that he inadvertently lets the other characters reveal, and these conflicting perspectives present an interesting topic for analysis. Holden's voice, as a storyteller, is idiosyncratic and is an important component of Salinger's success in creating a convincing interior mono-logue. Essays on this topic could analyze Holden's interior monologue to evaluate either his reliability as a narrator or his believability as a disturbed 16-year-old boy, or an essay could determine how Salinger creates sympathy on the part of the reader for his protagonist.

2. *The Catcher in the Rye* **as a digressional novel:** Why does Holden digress so often? What is the significance of Holden's anecdote about digression in chapter 24?

The novel's opening and closing pages begin and end the story in present time. Everything in between is a flashback to an earlier period when Holden's life unravelled. Within that major flashback, however, Holden occasionally describes past events and people in other analeptic accounts that also serve as digressions from the main narrative. Characters who feature in these digressions often symbolize something important to Holden. The anecdote in chapter 24 explains that, at his school, digression is a crime against coherence and clarity, but Holden affirms that he prefers digression because it is more interesting than sticking to the point. An essay could examine the significance of digression to the telling of Holden's story. Furthermore, it could connect that analysis to the theme of digression in terms of how deviation or straying from the "correct" path is related to Holden's character.

3. *The Catcher in the Rye* **as a bildungsroman:** Why is Holden reluctant to become an adult? How does he compare childhood with adulthood? Is his separation of the two life phases into good versus evil valid? Does Holden mature and resolve his quest for identity at the end of the novel?

Many of Holden's problems stem from his uncertainty about adulthood and, consequently, his desire on some levels to remain a child. At the end of the novel, Holden is forced to confront the reality of life as his sister Phoebe is reaching for the gold ring on the carrousel. At this moment, most critics believe that he has an epiphany that children must be allowed to make painful mistakes in order to learn about life. Some critics believe, though, that even at this point in the novel, Holden has not accepted life's realities because he is entranced by the ultimate symbol of childhood: Phoebe circling endlessly and unchangingly on a merry-go-round. An essay on Holden's coming-of-age could either analyze the alternative interpretations or focus on only one and argue for its validity.

4. *The Catcher in the Rye* **as a picaresque novel:** What are the targets of Salinger's satire? What aspects of Holden's society are corrupt? Does Holden successfully survive by his wits in this corrupt world?

Although all the novel's episodes contribute to Holden's development, the order of many of the episodes is not relevant to the unfolding of the novel. However, each event unveils a different aspect of society that is corrupt and that becomes the target of Holden's sarcasm and venom. An essay could investigate how Salinger uses Holden's insights to mock the shortcomings of humankind. Another approach would be to analyze to what extent *The Catcher in the Rye* does conform to the criteria of a picaresque novel. After all, Holden is a poor little rich boy, only choosing to immerse himself in "low-life" situations, and it is arguable whether he survives by his wits or not, as is seen in the incident with Sunny and Maurice.

Language, Symbols, and Imagery

Some of *The Catcher in the Rye*'s symbols have become so well known that they are alluded to by people who have never read the novel. Holden's red hunting hat, for example, is one of the most recognized literary objects. An essay based on the symbolic meanings of the color red throughout the novel is possible. Symbolism is one of Salinger's dominant stylistic techniques in this novel, and analysis of symbolism can open up a wealth of possible essay topics. Similarly, Salinger works with many motifs. A motif can be any image, situation, idea, or incident that is repeated in different ways to elaborate a theme. For example, Holden often seizes opportunities to dance with various characters and then judges them on how well they dance. He is always pleased when someone proves to be a good dancer. What does dancing signify to Holden?

The catcher in the rye is another widely recognized symbol, but its analysis can be broadened to consider other situations where images and descriptions of falling and catching are brought in. Another element of the story that is repeated and so becomes worthy of critical attention is the lagoon in Central Park. Holden is preoccupied with what happens to the lagoon's ducks during winter. Similarly, Holden constantly attempts to make, or thinks about making, numerous telephone calls. These calls often fail to achieve what Holden hopes they will achieve. Why is he so inept at making phone calls? In contrast, although the museum and the carrousel are only discussed in depth once each, the amount of detail that Holden provides about each place also flags them as being noteworthy.

Sample Topics:

1. **The motif of catching and falling:** Why does Holden dream of being the catcher in the rye? What other incidents in the novel evoke ideas of catching and falling?

An important symbol in the novel is the catcher in the rye. The verb *to fall* has connotations that date back to biblical times. Humankind is often described as having fallen from grace because Adam and Eve ate from the tree of knowledge. How does this idea connect to Holden's situation and his fantasy of catching the children who might fall? Other important incidents in the novel that describe scenes of falling or catching include the anecdote he tells about James Castle, the references to Allie's baseball mitt, the children's possible fall off the carrousel, and Holden's near fall into the Central Park lagoon. Essays on this topic can take any combination of the incidents for analysis.

2. **The symbolism of the ducks:** Why is Holden obsessed with the ducks in the park? What does the ducks' absence from the Central Park lagoon in chapter 20 signify?

The first time Holden lets slip his fascination with the ducks is during a conversation with Mr. Spencer. His preoccupation with the ducks recurs throughout the novel. Toward the end of the novel, Holden visits Central Park to verify the whereabouts of the ducks. During this visit, he finds out that the water is only partly frozen and that the ducks have disappeared. How does this relate to Holden? Essays on this topic could analyze the importance of the ducks to Holden and determine how the duck episode in chapter 20 highlights the precarious position Holden finds himself in as he hovers between thoughts of life and death.

3. **The motif of telephone calls:** Why does Holden spend so much time thinking about whom he can call? Why does he rarely follow through on his impulse to make a call? What prompts him to actually pick up a phone?

When Holden arrives at Penn Station from Pencey, he enters a phone booth and wastes 20 minutes thinking about whom he could call but then finding reasons not to call each person. At another point in the novel, he claims that he always forgets to write down people's phone numbers in his book—which is why he cannot call anyone. When he does finally make a call, it is often so late at night that the person being called is alarmed or distant. He calls Faith Cavendish too late, he disturbs Mr. Antolini and his wife late at night, and he telephones Sally not only very late but also while he is drunk. The calls usually have a negative outcome for Holden, as he is unable to communicate what he wants from the other person. Essays on the significance of telephone calls could also consider other forms of abortive communication, such as undelivered messages or Holden's failure to play by the rules in the oral expression class that he flunks at Pencey.

4. **The symbolism of the Museum of Natural History and the carrousel:** What does the Museum of Natural History represent? What does the carrousel represent?

Holden explains that he loves the museum because it is unchanging. However, he acknowledges that the people visiting the museum change, which contributes to making a museum visit different each time. Thus, the museum connotes ideas of both dynamism and stasis. However, to begin with, Holden clings to its associations with stasis. What other characters, places, or objects are unchanging? Why does Holden want things to remain static? When Holden eventually goes inside the museum, he acts as a guide to two young boys. How does he respond to his new role in the museum? The carrousel is a comparable symbol to the museum. A carrousel never changes and never progresses. The horses take the riders back to where they started. Reaching for the gold ring, however, the children may fall and would learn a life lesson. At the end of the novel, Holden is happy watching Phoebe on the carrousel and significantly elects not to have a ride himself. Does this suggest that Holden has grown up? The significance of the museum and the carrousel could be explored in a paper.

Compare and Contrast Essays

The Catcher in the Rye presents many workable topics for comparisons both within the novel and with other rebel or coming-of-age texts or films. There are a number of possible other texts with which it could be compared, such as Mark Twain's *Adventures of Huckleberry Finn* or F. Scott Fitzgerald's *The Great Gatsby*. Holden's character could also be compared to other infamous teenage rebels of the 1950s, such as Jim Stark, from the movie *Rebel without a Cause*. This essay topic could interact with an analysis of the historical context.

Within the novel itself, Holden can be compared to both Ward Stradlater and Robert Ackley, his fellow pupils at Pencey. His relationships with both young men are crucial in setting up the character of Holden at the start of the novel and exposing some of his insecurities, as well as some of his strong points. It is also possible to compare other characters who seem to have a certain synchronicity with one another. For example, Holden often deliberates on whether to call Sally or whether to call Jane. Each girl represents something different to Holden. Comparing and contrasting the two young women in terms of their behavior and the way Holden approaches each of them could connect with many of the central themes of the novel.

Sample Topics:

1. **Holden versus Stradlater:** How would you describe Holden's attitude toward athletic types? Why does Holden punch Stradlater? How is their fight a turning point for Holden?

   Holden shares a room with Stradlater at Pencey, but the two boys do not have much in common beyond the financial status of their respective families. Holden writes a composition for Stradlater that Stradlater rejects. Why is Holden so hurt by this rejection of his work? Another discussion that the two boys have involves Jane Gallagher and whether Stradlater has had sex with her. Why is this information so important to Holden? A comparative essay on this topic would look at the two characters' attitudes to women, their roles in the world, and their behavior during their fight. This approach could also address some of the themes of the novel, such as sexuality and coming-of-age, and the motif of catching and falling.

2. **Holden and Ackley:** What is the nature of the relationship between Holden and Ackley? Why does Ackley visit Holden in his room? What similarities are there between the two boys?

Holden portrays Robert Ackley as an unhygienic outcast. He states that he wishes Ackley would not bother him in his room, yet he invites Ackley to join him on a trip to the movies. Beaten up and bleeding from his fight with Stradlater, Holden retreats into Ackley's room. Why is Holden so cruel about Ackley? Conversely, why is he so tolerant of him? What does Holden's contradictory behavior reveal about his insecurities? An essay on this topic could analyze the two boys' behavior and their respective attitudes toward Stradlater and Pencey. An essay on this topic should look at similarities between the two boys that Holden himself may not accept or admit.

3. **Holden's girlfriends—Sally and Jane:** Why does Holden call Sally when he wants to call Jane? What are the differences between Jane and Sally? What makes Sally more approachable than Jane to Holden?

The two girls are both similar in age to Holden. Although he seems more intent on communicating with Jane, nonetheless it is Sally to whom he speaks on the phone and with whom he has a date. The girls seem to have aspects in common. For example, both girls share a history with Holden, although Holden has been more affected by his past with Jane. However, both girls disappoint Holden in similar ways, since they have joined the superficial world of adulthood and are more confident with their sexuality than Holden. An essay comparing and contrasting the two girls would likely interconnect with an analysis of the themes of communication, relationships, sexuality, and coming-of-age.

4. **Teenage rebels—Holden Caulfield and Jim Stark:** Why are both young men alienated from their society? How do they resolve their situations?

Jim Stark from the movie *Rebel without a Cause* (1955) has become the archetypal teenage rebel, along with Holden Caulfield. The two boys follow similar life trajectories. In both works, the troubled young man repudiates his society and condemns it as being full of phoniness and unnecessary conformity. They both put themselves in dangerous situations that test their mettle and cause each boy to flirt with death. At the end, both return to the family unit because their experiences have forced them to accept the reality of the world and their role in it. Essays comparing these two rebel stories could focus on characterization, plot, context, theme, or philosophical issues.

Bibliography and Online Resources

Alsen, Eberhard. The Catcher in the Rye. *A Reader's Guide to J. D. Salinger.* Westport, CT: Greenwood Press, 2002. 53–77.

Bloom, Harold, ed. *Modern Critical Interpretations: J. D. Salinger's The Catcher in the Rye.* Philadelphia: Chelsea House, 2000.

French, Warren. "The Holden Caulfield Story." *J. D. Salinger, Revisited.* Boston: Twayne, 1988. 33–62.

Lundquist, James. "Against Obscenity: *The Catcher in the Rye.*" *J. D. Salinger.* New York: Ungar, 1979. 37–68.

Pinsker, Sanford. *The Catcher in the Rye: Innocence under Pressure.* New York: Twayne, 1993.

Rosen, G. "A Retrospective Look at *The Catcher in the Rye.*" *J. D. Salinger: Modern Critical Views.* Ed. Harold Bloom. New York: Chelsea House, 1987. 95–109.

Salzberg, Joel. *Critical Essays on Salinger's* The Catcher in the Rye. Boston: G. K. Hall, 1990.

Salzman, Jack, ed. *New Essays on* The Catcher in the Rye. Cambridge: Cambridge University Press, 1991.

Steed, J. P., ed. *The Catcher in the Rye: New Essays*. New York: Peter Lang, 2002.

Stevenson, Juliana. "J. D. Salinger: The Influence of an Author and His Writings on 1950s America." 2 March 2007. <http://honors.umd.edu/HONR269J/ projects/stevenson.html>.

"A PERFECT DAY
FOR BANANAFISH"

READING TO WRITE

WRITING A paper on "A Perfect Day for Bananafish" is complicated by the fact that aspects of the short story are open to conjecture. For example, we do not know exactly what happened to Seymour Glass during World War II, we do not know precisely the nature or cause of his current psychosis, and we do not know definitively why he commits suicide. As a consequence of this uncertainty, the key to understanding this short story is inference. Inference is a process that allows the reader to reach a conclusion or make a logical judgment on the basis of suggested or implied evidence rather than on the basis of direct or explicit observation. In other words, when trying to make sense of "A Perfect Day for Bananafish," readers must read between the lines to figure out what is not being said explicitly, in addition to paying attention to what is actually being said. Communication between the characters in the story and, as a corollary, between Salinger and his readers is not always straightforward. In fact, the story showcases some of the impediments to candid communication between human beings. Thinking about the theme of communication and the problems that prevent characters from attaining authentic interpersonal relationships could generate many worthwhile essay topics.

The limitations of communication are illustrated by the telephone conversation between Seymour's wife, Muriel, and her mother that constitutes the first part of "A Perfect Day for Bananafish." The following excerpt from this long dialogue exemplifies many of Salinger's trademark techniques that allow extra information to be inferred beyond what is directly stated by the characters:

> "Muriel. My word of honor. Dr. Sivetski said Seymour may com-*plete*ly lose contr—"
>
> "I just *got* here, Mother. This is the first vacation I've had in years, and I'm not going to just *pack* everything and come home," said the girl. "I couldn't travel now anyway. I'm so sunburned I can hardly move."
>
> "You're badly sunburned? Didn't you use that jar of Bronze I put in your bag? I put it right—"
>
> "I used it. I'm burned anyway."
>
> "That's terrible. Where are you burned?"
>
> "All over, dear, all over."
>
> "That's terrible."
>
> "I'll live."
>
> "Tell me, did you talk to this psychiatrist?"
>
> "Well, sort of," said the girl.
>
> "What'd he say? Where was Seymour when you talked to him?"
>
> "In the Ocean Room, playing the piano. He's played the piano both nights we've been here."
>
> "Well, what'd he say?"
>
> "Oh, nothing much. He spoke to me first. I was sitting next to him at Bingo last night, and he asked me if that wasn't my husband playing the piano in the other room. I said yes, it was, and he asked me if Seymour's been sick or something. So I said—"

The first feature to notice about this passage is the extensive use of dialogue. The dialogue mimics real conversation in the way that the characters cut each other off, jump from one topic to another, and use slang and other colloquial language. The majority of "A Perfect Day for Bananafish" relies on dialogue, as opposed to narration, to drive the plot forward and develop characterization. Examining Salinger's use of dialogue and the different effects of dialogue usage could be a productive way to start thinking about essays that focus on elements of Salinger's unique writing style. One effect of using so much dialogue is that the narrator does not intervene often to comment on the characters, provide description, or set the scene. As a result, little judgment is made on the characters or their actions by the narrative voice. This contributes to the overall mood of ambiguity and uncertainty.

Despite the shortage of narration, the observant reader can start to decode Salinger's perspective on the characters and their behavior by reading more closely. Salinger's perspective is conveyed through his tone, which is achieved through a buildup of deceptively small details. A technique that Salinger exploits repeatedly in his dialogues is the use of italics to stress words or syllables. In the passage above, the first three lines contain three examples of italicization. These exaggerated stresses highlight the ordinary words being spoken, resulting in a sense that Salinger is mocking his characters' lack of intelligence and lack of understanding. Muriel's two italicized words show that she gives more importance to vacations and the inconvenience of packing than the more urgent concern of Seymour's possible total breakdown. The device of repetition is used to similar effect as that of italicization. The mother's lack of intelligence is brought out when she comments twice, "That's terrible," in response to the fact that Muriel is sunburned. The repetition suggests that the mother does not have much worthwhile to say and that she relies on clichéd phrases, even if she is essentially well intentioned.

Salinger also uses specific allusions and references in "A Perfect Day for Bananafish" that add to this effect of sardonic mockery of his characters and their priorities. In the excerpt, Muriel's mother asks her daughter whether she had used the jar of Bronze that had been packed for her. This leads to a discussion about how sunburned Muriel is even though she used the product. Later, Muriel mentions that the psychiatrist she has met in Florida has not provided much advice on Seymour's condition because he was too busy playing Bingo. It seems as if everyone is more concerned with trivial pastimes than with seriously addressing Seymour's problems. An analysis of Salinger's use of allusion throughout the story could consider how allusion expands the story's meaning.

A close examination of all these small details and techniques in the passage inevitably raises more general questions about the text. For example, why are these characters mostly concerned with superficial aspects of life? Why is Salinger's tone so critical of his characters and their interests? What is the problem with Seymour? Why is Muriel so unconcerned about him? What is Seymour's relationship like with his wife? Searching for textual evidence to help answer these questions will provoke ideas that could lead to the genesis of many valid papers based on thematic analysis, characterization, or historical and social context.

TOPICS AND STRATEGIES

This section will discuss various topics for essays on "A Perfect Day for Bananafish" and will suggest different approaches to those topics. The topic suggestions are meant as a starting place for you to stimulate your own ideas and ultimately to generate your own topic for your essay. The material should be used as a resource to help prompt your own ideas related to the topic, not as a blueprint for a perfect essay.

Themes

Despite being a short story, "A Perfect Day for Bananafish" engages with many themes. It also raises many questions—questions that Salinger does not necessarily answer. A good starting place for searching for themes in a short story is the title. In this case, the title alludes to a comment Seymour makes to Sybil when they go swimming. He tells her that she should keep her eyes open while swimming because it is "a *perfect* day for bananafish." Immediate questions come to mind when reading this. Why does Seymour tell Sybil this (especially given the fact that bananafish do not exist)? Why does he say this at precisely the moment that he does? The bananafish are associated with sickness and death. Is Seymour hinting at anything? Since Salinger chose this phrase as the title of the story, we know that it must be significant to understanding Seymour and the story somehow.

Generally speaking, the character traits and behavior of the protagonist reinforce or amplify important themes of a short story. In "A Perfect Day for Bananafish," Seymour has problems with his wife and his wife's mother, but he also is out of step with his society, which is causing him serious inner conflict. What is the nature of his conflict with his wife and his mother-in-law? Why does he find it so difficult to fit into his society? Why is he able to relate to children but not to adults? What causes him to go over the edge and kill himself? Answering these questions might cause you to consider themes such as marriage and other personal relationships, communication, and the different perceptions that people have of the same person or the same event. All of these themes could provide the basis for a good essay.

Sample Topics:

1. **Personal relationships:** How does Salinger portray marriage in the story? How does he present family relationships?

To write an essay based on an examination of personal relationships, determine what Salinger's attitude is toward them by looking at the different marriages and the different family relationships depicted in the story. The marriage between Seymour and Muriel is shown as one that is unhappy, empty, and distant. What does Salinger suggest is responsible for making an unhappy marriage? Why are Muriel and Seymour so uncaring toward each other? Although Salinger's perspective on this marriage could be the basis for a thesis on its own, the topic can be broadened to consider personal relationships in general. Look at other family relationships in the story. How does Salinger represent them? Are there any similarities between his representation of the married relationship and, for example, the mother/daughter relationship? A paper could examine the way that difficult personal relationships affect a particular character. Another productive line of enquiry would be to examine what Salinger insinuates are the causes of difficult personal relationships.

2. **Communication:** Which characters are able to communicate successfully, and which fail to make themselves understood? What causes communication to fail or succeed in the story? What is Salinger's judgment on communication in society in general?

To write an essay on this topic, begin by identifying the different instances of attempted communication between characters in the story and decide whether they are successful or whether they fail in some way. Compare and contrast hostile conversations where there is mutual misunderstanding and avoidance of real issues with direct and honest conversations where genuine emotions are expressed. By paying close attention to details and reading between the lines, Salinger's attitude toward the state of interpersonal communication in postwar America can be inferred.

3. **Sickness and death:** What does Salinger suggest are the causes of Seymour's psychological problems? What are the links between Seymour's sickness and "banana fever"?

To get started on a paper connected to ideas of sickness and death, pinpoint all the parts of the text where Salinger alludes to or refers directly to these themes. During the conversation between Muriel and her mother, there are several mentions of symptoms of Seymour's illness. Why has he become so aggressive and hostile? The bananafish story also involves disease and death. Is the death of the bananafish related to Seymour's suicide? Closely examine the final paragraph of the story and consider some of the small details. Why was Seymour carrying a gun? What does it mean that he uses a German gun to kill himself? Why does he look at his sleeping wife twice before shooting himself? Salinger's perspective on these themes can be found by his hints and suggestions rather than by direct statements.

4. **Perception:** Why does Salinger show that the characters have contrasting feelings and attitudes toward each other? What is the significance of the various assessments the characters have of the same events?

From the beginning of the short story, it is clear that Muriel and her mother view Seymour's condition very differently. Her mother sees him as dangerous whereas Muriel does not seem particularly worried by his behavior. In contrast, the child characters seek Seymour out and see him as fun and interesting. A topic could address how perception affects judgment. In what ways do our knowledge and experience of people and situations affect the way we respond to them? There are several instances in the short story where characters make quick judgments of each other with consequences for either themselves or the other person.

Character

There are different ways that character studies can be approached, but the literary element of characterization opens up many possibilities for essay topics. Looking closely at the secondary characters, for example, can be constructive. Sybil's mother in "A Perfect Day for Bananafish" appears only briefly in the story, so we never see her change or develop in any way. She is a flat and static background character. Nevertheless, several observations can be made about her characterization. Although the story furnishes less than a page on which to base an analysis of her, it can still be noted that Mrs. Carpenter is more interested in the conversation with Mrs. Hubbel about fashion than with her daughter's conversation about "see more glass." Overall, she is irritated by her daughter and cannot wait to get rid of her so that she can have a martini and gossip with Mrs. Hubbel. Salinger mocks Mrs. Carpenter through her affected speech patterns: She calls her daughter "pussy," refers to herself in the third person as "Mommy," and comments that a fashion item is "darling." This all leaves the reader with the impression that she is self-absorbed and shallow. In this way, she is used to embody the idea that adult women in postwar America are only interested in superficial matters, especially the products of a consumer society.

Sample Topics:

1. **Adult secondary characters:** What are some of the traits that the adult secondary characters have in common? What techniques does Salinger use to convey the traits of the adult secondary characters? What ideas do these secondary characters embody?

   A paper on this topic could consider the different devices and techniques Salinger uses to present adult secondary characters even though they are all flat and static. How does he manage to convey information about them although they may appear only briefly in the story? Similarities as well as differences would need to be taken into consideration to determine if the characters all serve the same purpose or if there are distinctions among them. What seems to be Salinger's tone and attitude toward his adult characters? An essay on this topic would probably interact with thematic and historical/contextual analysis as well.

2. **Seymour's breaking point:** Why does Seymour commit suicide? In what ways does Seymour's character change in the short story?

One interesting aspect of this short story is that the reader is given a great deal of insight into Seymour from the other characters, although their judgments vary considerably. How does Seymour's behavior agree or contrast with the other characters' judgments? A paper on this subject would need to weigh the different viewpoints given about Seymour in order to reach a conclusion on why Seymour shoots himself. Another source of information is the narrator's descriptions of Seymour's actions when he is on the beach, in the elevator, and in the hotel room. Small details that Salinger adds in these sections provide many hints as to Seymour's personality and frame of mind.

3. **The presentation and function of child characters:** How does the story portray children and childhood? What techniques does Salinger use to distinguish his child characters from his adult characters?

This essay would have to look very closely at the child Sybil Carpenter and examine the methods of characterization that Salinger uses to make her a convincing girl in the story. Although the other child, Sharon Lipschutz, is not presented directly, we hear about her from Sybil. Do the two girls seem to have any traits in common? How does Seymour respond to the two children? The essay might consider why the children respond differently to Seymour than all the adults do. In Greek mythology, a sibyl was a woman who could foresee the future. How might Seymour (and Salinger) see Sybil's role in the future?

History and Context

Approaching a short story through consideration of its time and place is always a valid means of analysis. "A Perfect Day for Bananafish" was first published in 1948. The early and middle decades of the 20th century were filled with major events that shaped the people who lived through them. Salinger, born in 1919, grew up through the Depression years of the 1930s, witnessed the political upheavals of the first half of the 20th century such as the emergence of communist and fascist states, and eventually joined the American military to fight the Nazis in Europe in the early 1940s. He returned to the United States at the end of World War II; "A Perfect Day for Bananafish" was written shortly after his wartime experiences. In light of this, Seymour's psychological problems could be understood as what we would now call post-traumatic stress disorder, which would have probably been called "shell shock," combat stress, or even war neurosis in 1948. Using awareness of how war affects soldiers, we can view Seymour's behavior from an alternative standpoint.

At the end of World War II, the United States emerged as the country with the strongest economy. The United States soon became seen as the land of opportunity and, capitalizing on the economic foundations established during the war, American society became increasingly prosperous in the postwar years. Not all Americans shared in this newfound affluence, but middle-class white America was able to enjoy such luxuries as purchasing the latest consumer products and taking vacations in Florida. However, this changing America, with its focus on materialism, was not greeted enthusiastically by writers such as Salinger. Salinger questioned whether the values that were driving Americans in their daily lives—the pursuit of wealth and the pursuit of comfort—were values that were desirable or admirable in a world that could have been dealing with far more important concerns of the period, such as racial prejudice. Were Americans more concerned with trivia than with substance? Were Americans becoming self-absorbed because they were obsessed with consumer products and image? Was reading magazines rather than poetry symptomatic of the fact that Americans were becoming intellectually dull? These are all areas of discussion that Salinger raises in many of his short stories and that would make interesting topics for an essay mixing sociological analysis with literary analysis.

Sample Topics:

1. **World War II and postwar America:** In what way has the war affected Seymour? How does Seymour, as a war veteran, differ from the characters who did not leave America during the war? What aspects of America does Salinger show to be changing in the postwar years? How do the characters respond to these changes?

Over 16 million Americans served in World War II, approximately 13 percent of the total population of that time. About 400,000 were killed during the war. Although these men and women have been celebrated as protectors of liberty, the treatment of veterans has not always been as commendable as it could have been. The story mentions that a doctor is horrified that the army released Seymour from hospital since he clearly was in no fit state to be discharged. How easy was it for war veterans to integrate back into society after combat experience? What has the war and the lack of medical support done to Seymour? Seymour's tattoo (which may or may not exist) is mentioned by Muriel. If it exists, what might it suggest may have happened to Seymour in Europe? How sympathetic are the other characters shown to be to his condition? How does he contrast with all the other guests in the hotel? Many of the background characters who are mentioned have family names that are of European and, in some cases, German or Jewish origin. How has the war changed the face of America? The story portrays a United States where everybody seems to have money. Notice Muriel's comment when she says, in a very condescending tone, that people who may have driven down "in a truck" were sitting next to her in the hotel restaurant. How do people behave with their newfound wealth and leisure time? What is the role of women in this changing world? Does Salinger portray women negatively or with sympathy? A paper could show how Salinger uses the Florida setting to exemplify how America was changing.

2. **The emptiness of American society:** Why does Seymour call his wife "Miss Spiritual Tramp 1948"? How does Salinger critique the world of Muriel, her mother, and the Florida hotel guests?

We learn from the story that Seymour had sent his wife a copy of German poems, but she lost the book and never read the poems because they were in German. She prefers to read women's magazines or shop. She was outraged that he had expected her to buy a translation or learn German. It is widely assumed that the poet Seymour is alluding to is Rainer Maria Rilke, whose poems often focus on problems of isolation and anxiety. Why does Seymour feel alone? Why is he so anxious about the world? What aspects of his society does Salinger show him to be hostile to? What elements of modern life absorb the other characters? Why does Seymour accuse his wife of being spiritually empty? Is there any textual evidence that supports a view of Muriel as self-absorbed and vapid? Papers could address any combination of these questions to explore Salinger's critique of America's spiritual emptiness.

3. **A culture of consumption:** How does the Florida setting depict a world based on consumption and materialism? What allusions and symbols does Salinger incorporate to show his attitude to consumption?

To write an essay on this topic, you might analyze the activities and topics of conversation in which the adult characters engage. The opening line of the story introduces a world that is controlled by people—"advertising men"—who are trying to sell society some product. There are also two important allusions to consumption. The first one is Sybil's question to Seymour whether he has read *Little Black Sambo*. In this story, a boy has to sacrifice his red coat, blue trousers, and purple shoes to some tigers but eventually outsmarts the beasts to return home and eat 169 pancakes for dinner. The second important allusion to consumption is the bananafish tale. What are the similarities and differences between the two stories? How do the two tales help us understand Sybil and Seymour? What do they reveal about Salinger's perspective on America in the late 1940s?

Philosophy and Ideas

Salinger is a writer who explores many ideas of a philosophical nature in his work. These universal ideas offer another way to approach his stories. Some of these philosophical concerns may have been debated for hundreds of years, while others may have only gained attention in modern times because they arise out of situations created by modern society.

We can go back to the Bible to see that questions about the relationship between innocence and experience have been important for a very long time. What causes the movement from a state of innocence to a state of experience? Why is a state of innocence usually described as being preferable to a state of experience? Similarly, the debate over image and substance has also been discussed for hundreds of years. In contrast to these philosophical concerns, the concept of alienation is one that has only been pondered most extensively since the end of the 19th century. Alienation can be defined as a feeling of dissociation or isolation. Thinking about philosophical issues, whether they originate from ancient or relatively modern times, could yield many meaningful essay topics.

Sample Topics:

1. **Alienation:** In what ways is Seymour alienated from his society? What are the causes of his alienation? Do any other characters feel the effects of alienation?

   An essay centered on a discussion of alienation would need to focus primarily on the character of Seymour and consider the reasons why he is so disconnected from his society. What are the elements of this society that cause him to feel like an outsider? What are the values of the individuals and society in Florida? This essay would be closely linked to the historical context, since the causes of alienation vary according to historical period.

2. **Innocence versus experience:** How does Salinger contrast the states of innocence and experience? In our society, we tend to think of children as being pure and innocent. Does Salinger depict Sybil as being in a state of innocence, or are there some aspects of her characterization that show she has been contaminated by the world?

Since the time of the ancient Greeks, Western thought has often been dualistic, seeing everything as composed of a pair of warring opposites. Furthermore, there has been a tendency in Western thinking to make absolute judgments between the two parts of the pair, praising one while rejecting the other. Since the story of Adam and Eve, the state of innocence has been valued while the state of experience has been condemned, because interaction with the world is thought to corrupt our better, purer natures. An essay based on the duality of innocence versus experience would logically look at children as embodying innocence and at adults as representing experience. But is this division clear-cut in Salinger's story? Why does Seymour put an end to swimming with Sybil even though she says she has not had enough?

3. **Image over substance:** Why is Muriel so concerned with her appearance? Beyond her appearance, what other things interest her? There is a saying that we should not judge based on appearance. If that is true, why are superficial appearances so important for some characters?

Philosophers might argue that society today is under the spell of seductive, glamorous brand names. However, many people feel that a world based on materialism is a spiritual wasteland. In other words, a world of materialism has no substance; it relies on image to sell itself, but there is nothing worthwhile behind the image. What does Salinger show to be the consequences for someone who cares only about image? For those who want substance in their lives, where will they find it in a materialistic society? To write an essay on this question, start by looking at Seymour and his responses to the world and the people around him.

Form and Genre

Salinger's work has mostly been in the form of fictional prose, and he has written many short stories. Short stories, because of their brevity, have a limited number of characters and a limited number of events that propel the plot forward. One aspect that differentiates one short story from another is structure, the way an author organizes and orders the different parts of the short story to make a whole.

Structure may be influenced, to a certain extent, by the genre of a short story. A mystery story usually centers on a crime, and the plot is built around solving that crime. Suicide is considered by some people to be a crime, and Seymour's decision to kill himself is certainly baffling. The reader must attempt to solve the mystery in order to make sense of the story. How has "A Perfect Day for Bananafish" been structured, and what is the effect of the author's choice of organizing the elements the way he did?

Sample Topics:

1. **"A Perfect Day for Bananafish" as a three-act play:** The story has many similarities to a three-act play. Why did Salinger structure his story in this way? What is the effect of his telling the story this way?

   If the story is analyzed in this way, the first act of the play is Muriel's phone conversation in the hotel room, the second act takes place on the beach, and the third act is the brief scene back in the hotel room. The parts where the narrator provides limited information about a character's behavior, such as when Seymour folds up his clothes on the beach, could be understood as "stage directions." An essay could examine Salinger's use of dramatic techniques in the construction of "A Perfect Day for Bananafish," taking into consideration the effects the techniques have on the telling of the story.

2. **"A Perfect Day for Bananafish" as a mystery short story:** Why does Seymour kill himself?

An essay based on an examination of this story as a mystery would need to consider the different elements of a mystery and see whether the story fulfills these criteria. Does the story have a problem that needs to be solved? Does it have suspense? Does it have clues to help solve the problem? Are there any "red herrings" thrown in by the author to mislead the reader? An essay based on analyzing the story as a mystery would link to the character study of Seymour's breaking point discussed in the character section of this chapter.

Language, Symbols, and Imagery

Salinger's distinctive style and use of language offer other ways to analyze the story. The style of a particular writer is produced by choice of words (diction), grammatical structures, use of literary devices, and all the possible parts of language use. Owing to the brief form of the short story, Salinger relies on devices such as allusion, dialogue, and symbolism to add layers of depth. For an understanding of an author's purpose, analysis of short stories often involves analysis of the literary elements and devices that the author has used.

As mentioned in the "Reading to Write" section, Salinger's use of allusion provides shades of additional meaning that could easily be missed in a cursory reading of the text. Salinger's allusions are not always obvious and assume a shared inventory of knowledge between writer and reader. However, understanding the full implications of the allusions may require further research. Reading T. S. Eliot's *The Waste Land*, for example, would unearth many areas of revealing overlap between the poem and the short story. Dialogue is Salinger's main method in "A Perfect Day for Bananafish" for advancing the plot and revealing characterization. Having characters talk about a person can divulge what each person is like. The things that are left unsaid can be equally illuminating.

The way a character is made to talk can have multiple purposes, such as conveying a sense of time and place or unmasking conflict. What are the effects of Salinger's extensive use of dialogue? Symbolism poses a special problem with Salinger, as his symbols often allow multiple interpretations. Overall, Salinger's style could be described as cryptic, but it certainly creates the potential for a range of essay papers.

1. **The symbolism of the bananafish:** What are the possible meanings of the bananafish? What is the effect of conveying important ideas through this symbol?

   The use of symbolism is a notable part of Salinger's style that contributes to the meaning of his work; an analysis of this symbolism could form the basis of an essay. In "A Perfect Day for Bananafish," the bananafish are the most obvious symbol. What does the tale Seymour tells Sybil about bananafish mean? Are the different references to color in the short story linked to the bananafish tale in any way? For example, Sybil is wearing a yellow bathing suit when they go swimming, whereas Seymour's trunks are blue. What else in the story is blue or yellow? There are also several references to feet throughout the story. Why does Seymour kiss Sybil's foot and then get so angry at the woman in the elevator for possibly looking at his feet? Does this link back to the bananafish tale somehow? The bananafish swimming into a hole has obvious sexual connotations. Does the phallic appearance of the bananafish convey other possible symbolic interpretations? Does the story contain any other phallic or sexual references?

2. **Allusion to *The Waste Land*:** Why does Salinger allude to T. S. Eliot's poem? How does this allusion increase our understanding of the story?

   During his conversation with Sybil, Seymour observes that Sharon Lipschutz's name keeps being mentioned: "How that name comes up. Mixing memory and desire." This final phrase is an allusion to T. S. Eliot's poem *The Waste Land*. Eliot's poem is prefaced by a quotation in Greek and Latin that is sometimes translated as "I saw with my own eyes the Sibyl at Cumae hanging in a cage, and when the boys said to her 'Sibyl, what do you want?' she replied, 'I want to die.'" Eliot's poem then starts the first section which is entitled "The Burial of the Dead" with the lines:

> April is the cruellest month, breeding
> Lilacs out of the dead land, mixing
> Memory and desire . . .

Memory, death, and the relationship between the past and the present are thematically significant in *The Waste Land*. Similarly, in "A Perfect Day for Bananafish," this complex allusion to Eliot's poem elucidates Seymour's psychology. How has the contrast between past and present affected Seymour to the point that he wants to die? What might be the role of memory in Seymour's psychological problems? Why does Salinger include a suggestion that Sybil might "want to die"? An essay could analyze the connections between the two texts.

3. **The use of language to develop Muriel's character:** How does the way Muriel speak shed light on her character? What devices in Muriel's speech does Salinger deploy to critique Muriel's character?

Diction, sentence structure, and formality or informality of language can not only communicate information about a character but can also be used by an author to critique the character. How does Salinger use Muriel's speech to mock her? Dialogue often discloses conflicts among characters. What conflicts does Muriel's dialogue make known? How does Salinger deploy small details, such as tone or the stance and gestures that accompany her speech, to furnish additional information about her? What is not said can be as significant as things that are said. How do the things that Muriel avoids talking about clarify her motivations and intentions? An essay on this topic would need to combine analysis of language, character, and historical and social context.

Compare and Contrast Essays

A good place to start when thinking of a topic for a comparison/contrast essay is to select two characters to compare. However, be sure not to choose two totally distinct characters. In order to have a valid topic for discussion, pick two characters who provide some purpose for the comparison. For example, the characters may bring out certain aspects of a theme. "A Perfect Day for Bananafish" has several female characters who have similar traits and could be used as the basis of a comparison, bearing in mind that Salinger was using them in his story for a purpose and to embody specific ideas. Some of Salinger's characters reappear in a slightly different form in other short stories in the *Nine Stories* collection. There are many possible character combinations from the different stories that would make interesting comparisons and that connect to key Salinger themes and concerns.

Sample Topics:

1. **Older women compared to little girls:** How do the adult female characters differ from the child female characters? Are there any similarities between the two groups of female characters?

   For this topic, a straightforward comparison between Muriel and Sybil would be possible since there is a great deal of information on both of these female characters. Salinger focuses on and ridicules many of Muriel's character traits in the opening section as she waits for and makes her phone call to her mother. How do these traits compare to those of the child Sybil? Do the two females have anything in common? This topic could be expanded if more of the adult female characters are taken into consideration and pitted against the other girl child (Sharon Lipschutz) we hear about. Muriel's mother or Sybil's mother might add to the overall impression that Salinger presents of adult women. Keep in mind, though, that it is advisable to keep a balance between the number of characters being compared on each side. To this end, if you discuss only two child characters, you should balance this with a focus on two adult characters (not three or four).

2. **Comparison of husband and wife:** How do Seymour and Muriel talk about each other? How do they react and behave with each other? How do they react and behave with other people?

Most people expect a husband and wife to have something tangible that keeps them together. Although divorce was not as common in 1948 as it is now, it is difficult to imagine that Seymour and Muriel were ever in love since they are so unsympathetic toward each other. However, there must have been some reason why they got married. What traits might Seymour have appreciated in Muriel that we can still see? What traits might Muriel have appreciated in Seymour that we can still see? What do we learn about these two characters through their interaction with others? An essay might appraise what Salinger wanted to show through Mr. and Mrs. Glass's contrasting portrayals, their relationship, and its brutal end.

3. **Comparison of veterans:** Seymour is not the only war veteran in Salinger's *Nine Stories*. Sergeant X in "For Esmé—with Love and Squalor" shares comparable trauma in the war and suffers psychologically as a result. However, this soldier does not commit suicide. What allows Sergeant X to be saved whereas Seymour cannot be saved?

The veteran character who has disengaged from his society features in both "For Esmé—With Love and Squalor" and "A Perfect Day for Bananafish." These veterans offer the potential for a comparison. There are many similarities between the two characters and many significant differences. What point was

Salinger trying to make through his portrayal of these damaged soldier characters? According to Salinger, what can help a soldier reintegrate into society?

Bibliography

French, Warren. "A Nine Story Cycle." *J. D. Salinger, Revisited.* Boston: Twayne, 1988. 65–69.

Goldstein, Bernice, and Sanford Goldstein. "Zen and *Nine Stories.*" *J. D. Salinger: Modern Critical Views.* Ed. Harold Bloom. New York: Chelsea House, 1987. 81–93.

Wenke, John. *"Nine Stories." J. D. Salinger: A Study of the Short Fiction.* Boston: Twayne, 1991. 31–38.

"UNCLE WIGGILY IN CONNECTICUT"

READING TO WRITE

"**U**NCLE WIGGILY in Connecticut" is the only Salinger short story that was made into a movie with his consent. Hollywood managed to turn the acerbic short story into a tear-jerker titled *My Foolish Heart* (1949). The experience so soured Salinger, who was given no creative input, that he never again sold film rights to his work. Ironically, Salinger's characters in the short story are clearly avid moviegoers. In the passage below, Eloise jokingly mentions that her daughter resembles Akim Tamiroff. Born in Tbilisi, Georgia, Tamiroff perhaps embodies foreign mystique to Eloise, who claims, earlier in the story, that she "love[s] him." Similarly, a visit to the movies offers a few hours of escapism from the humdrum banality of life in suburban Connecticut. Another form of escapism that Eloise utilizes is excessive alcohol consumption. Drinking cocktails in the afternoon releases her to talk about her dissatisfaction with her marriage and life. By the time the events in the following excerpt take place, the two women have drunk to the point that Mary Jane has splashed some of her highball on the floor:

> "Leave it. *Leave* it," said Eloise. "I hate this damn rug anyway. I'll get you another."
> "No, look, I have more than half left!" Mary Jane held up her glass.
> "Sure?" said Eloise. "Gimme a cigarette."

Mary Jane extended her pack of cigarettes, saying "Oh, I'm dying to see her. Who does she look like now?"

Eloise struck a light. "Akim Tamiroff."

"No, seriously."

"Lew. She looks like Lew. When his mother comes over, the three of them look like triplets." Without sitting up, Eloise reached for a stack of ashtrays on the far side of the cigarette table. She successfully lifted off the top one and set it down on her stomach. "What I need is a cocker spaniel or something," she said. "Somebody that looks like me."

"How're her eyes now?" Mary Jane asked. "I mean they're not any worse or anything, are they?"

"God! Not that I know of."

"Can she see at all without her glasses? I mean if she gets up in the night to go to the john or something?"

"She won't tell anybody. She's lousy with secrets."

This brief passage provides a wealth of information about the characterization of Eloise, which could become the foundation of a character analysis. The first sentence displays her dislike of her environment. She is not concerned about the rug that Mary Jane has stained. She is more bothered about keeping Mary Jane drinking; she craves sympathetic companionship and an excuse to drink. Next, her lack of interest in her daughter is laid bare. At first, Mary Jane's question about Ramona's appearance is evaded with humor, as Eloise endeavors to derail the conversation by mentioning Tamiroff. An explanation for her lack of interest becomes apparent when she finally concedes that her daughter takes after her husband and her mother-in-law. This image of a room filled with people with a similar physical appearance accentuates Eloise's sense of isolation and her status as outsider in this suburban milieu. While she may be joking about getting a cocker spaniel so she would have someone on her side, this quip reveals both her need for a loyal companion and her critical appraisal of her own lack of beauty. However, her response to her dreary situation is largely entropic. Her entropy is epitomized by her lackadaisical movements throughout the story; in this excerpt, she barely extends her arm to get an ashtray.

Essay topics related to symbolism, theme, and philosophical ideas are all suggested by this extract. Ramona's glasses play a critical role at the end of the story, and their importance is set up here. Why is Eloise so disparaging of her own daughter? How does the child's chronic myopia symbolically elucidate fundamental aspects of both Ramona's and Eloise's characters? The themes of antagonistic husband/wife relationships, regret, honesty, and bitterness are touched on in this passage and could be used to generate papers. Eloise can open up to her old friend Mary Jane about the regrets she has for the way her life has turned out. Her dishonest relationship with her husband, Lew, has extended into an essentially dishonest relationship with her neglected child, who has become one of the targets of her bitterness. Ramona has retreated into the secretive world of her imagination. A discussion about forms of escapism also presents a possible topic for an analysis.

As is usual with Salinger, this story is subtle. Eloise's characteristics are never baldly stated; rather, they are hinted at through lines of dialogue or slight movements. Themes and philosophical ideas are developed through symbolism, allusions, tone, and choice of diction. However subtle the conveyance of ideas is, the dominant mood of bitter defeat and disillusionment does not cede space for the sentimental interpretation that Hollywood produced.

TOPICS AND STRATEGIES

The remainder of this chapter will present possible topics for essays on "Uncle Wiggily in Connecticut." The suggested approaches should inspire novel ways to tackle a topic.

Themes

Eloise's regret and bitterness are the result of the legacy of her past combined with the frustrations of her present. Under the influence of alcohol, Eloise reveals that before she got married, she had been in love with another man with whom she was able to laugh and have fun. This man, the reader presumes, was Walt Glass. In *Franny and Zooey*, Walt is described as Bessie Glass's "only truly lighthearted son." In "Uncle

Wiggily in Connecticut," his tragic death is explained as having been caused by an exploding stove in Japan during World War II. This pointless and unheroic death has turned Eloise from a fun-loving young woman into a bitter and angry mother and wife. Her pain is still so omnipresent that she chooses not to tell her husband the truth about her former love because she fears that his jealousy of her past might tarnish her memories. Eloise cautions Mary Jane never to be honest with a man about her romantic past. Sadly, Eloise's relationship with Lew is built on a foundation of lies and dishonesty. At the start of their relationship, Lew lied to Eloise to impress her, by pretending that Jane Austen was one of his favorite authors. Now, the dishonesty is being passed on to their daughter, who is suffering the consequences of Eloise's inability to make peace with Walt's death. Eloise has degenerated from an authentic, good person when she was with Walt into an inauthentic termagant trapped in the suburbs, where she unleashes her acrimony on other family members.

Sample Topics:

1. **Bitterness and regret:** What does Eloise feel she has lost as a consequence of Walt's death? How has Eloise's disappointment with her life caused her to behave toward her family? How has her bitterness altered her personality?

The presence of bitterness serves as notice of rage and regret. Bitterness can stem from an inability to move on with life when a loved one's life is taken unexpectedly. This sense of loss can be all-consuming. For Eloise, the memory of Walt acts as a constant symbol of what has been lost. Eloise's bitterness is indicated by negativity and harshly critical attitudes toward others. An essay on this topic could discuss Eloise's bullying demeanor with friends, family, and her maid; her critical gossip about acquaintances; and other manifestations of her bitter attitude.

2. **Living in truth:** In what ways is Eloise dishonest with her husband? How is Eloise dishonest with herself?

As a young woman, Eloise enjoyed a time where the person she loved would say what was on his mind to the people he met. Walt was honest and direct with her, but he could be equally plain-spoken to a train conductor whom he happened to encounter. This forthright and emotionally candid attitude allowed Eloise to live in truth with herself. An essay on this topic could analyze what aspects of Eloise's current life are inauthentic and how this has affected her. The title of this short story expresses the joining together of the two sides of Eloise. The Uncle Wiggily allusion is linked to her happier times, while her life in Connecticut is equated with her current inauthenticity.

Character

The three main characters in this short story are all sufficiently well-developed that an analysis of them could become the basis of an essay. Eloise is the most dynamic character since she undergoes an epiphany about her own behavior at the end of the story. As she picks up her weeping daughter's glasses, Eloise is able to empathize with her child's pain and starts to cry too. She is also crying out of misery at the way her own life has turned out. She realizes that a random series of events has changed her into a person who is spiteful and vicious to others. However, one question that the story does not answer is whether this momentary flash of empathy and understanding will alter Eloise's future life. Doubt arises about the lasting nature of her epiphany because Eloise is extremely drunk. The popular expression *in vino veritas* (in wine, truth) proposes that when someone drinks, they lose emotional inhibitions and confess truths that they would normally keep concealed. The expression also suggests that when he or she is sober again, the person might feel regret and embarrassment for having let the mask slip. Thus, there is a possibility that Eloise will return to her usual bitter self the morning after this drinking binge.

Mary Jane's primary function in the story is to act as a foil to Eloise. A foil is a character whose traits are placed in juxtaposition to those of the principal character with the purpose of accentuating key characteristics of the protagonist. Mary Jane is not a dynamic character; she does not change through the course of the story. However, the narrator does provide important details about her. For example, she is weak and easily persuaded to stay and drink. She is not intelligent or particularly curious about anything except gossip. She is able, though, to ask probing questions that lead to revelations about Eloise's character. Mary Jane is also used by Salinger to set off the other secondary character, the neglected and unappealing Ramona. Ramona is a unique creation for Salinger in that she is a child character who is not precocious or particularly endearing. Her nose-picking and detachment are off-putting. Her self-contained ways hint at a history of having to be self-sufficient and expecting little from adults. As an unprepossessing child, she becomes an unusual Salinger character to analyze.

Sample Topics:

1. **Eloise:** How does Eloise develop throughout the course of the story? How has Eloise changed since she was a young woman?

An essay dealing with the character of Eloise would likely interact with an analysis of the themes already discussed, namely regret, bitterness, and living in truth. In such an essay, different aspects of her characterization could be dissected for an understanding of how Eloise's pain surrounding her past has led her to exteriorize her anger by being cruel to other people.

2. **The character foil—Mary Jane:** How does Salinger use Mary Jane to develop Eloise? What traits do we learn about Mary Jane as a character in her own right?

Even though Mary Jane is primarily used as a foil, she still needs to have integrity as a character in order for the story to be credible. She could be analyzed simply through her function as a foil, whose characteristics are used to highlight Eloise's crucial traits. Another approach would be to analyze Mary Jane as a secondary character, independent of her impact on Eloise's development.

3. **Ramona—like mother, like daughter:** Which of Ramona's traits suggest that she has not been given much attention by adults? How does Ramona's pain mirror her mother's suffering?

Children are often the unwitting victims of their parents' problems. Ramona is being raised in a neighborhood with no other children, yet her mother does not seem interested in spending time with her. On the contrary, her child is an embarrassment as she stands in the living room picking her nose and talking to her imaginary friend. Eloise keeps sending her to the maid for care and attention. An essay on this subject could examine how Ramona's behavior is a consequence of her home environment. For example, Eloise's mourning for her dead (and, therefore, invisible) lover has a direct bearing on Ramona's imaginary friends' characteristics.

History and Context

"Uncle Wiggily in Connecticut" was first published in 1948 in the *New Yorker* magazine. The story is steeped in World War II and post–World War II situations and references. Both Eloise and Mary Jane were in college during the early years of the war, and both left college prematurely because of liaisons with men in the armed forces. The approximately half a million deaths in the United States' armed forces during World War II meant that many women suffered the loss of a husband, fiancé, or other loved one. Some women never married (or remarried) as a consequence of their losses in the war. As is the case with Eloise, those who did try to move on with their lives may have been haunted by the belief that they had lost their one true love. Other features of the postwar situation often hindered women from finding alternative fulfillment in their lives. Job opportunities were limited for women. Many ended up in the type of work that Mary Jane appears to do: secretarial services. Social pressure urged middle-class women to become wives and mothers, satisfied with domesticity. Eloise's drinking proves the folly of thinking that the bourgeois domestic realm could satisfy all women. To acquire a symbol of status in this period, people might engage a maid. Given the race relations and economic realities of the late 1940s, the maid was often an African-American woman who was forced to live apart from her own family. Having a maid creates even more unnecessary leisure time for Eloise. Eloise's situation, which has largely been forged by the time in which she lives, has shaped her into a frustrated and discontented woman.

Sample Topics:

1. **World War II and its aftermath:** How has the war contributed to Eloise's depressed and angry condition? How have the mores and social conventions of the postwar era contributed to the formation of Eloise's unfulfilled life?

A paper on this topic could assess to what degree Eloise embodies an amalgamation of circumstances and attitudes created by her time and place. For example, women are no longer pressured to stay in loveless marriages because divorce is more socially acceptable today. Also, there is a greater range of opportunities for women outside the conformist world of domesticity today than in 1948.

Philosophy and Ideas

The master-slave relationship is a conflictual dynamic that has been theorized by many philosophers, notably Georg Hegel (1770–1831). In the master-slave relationship, one person commands the other. However, the master is dependent on the slave for recognition, because a person can only be a master if there is a servant/slave who acknowledges his or her dominance. The master may try to conceal this irony from the slave by assertion of power to make the slave feel totally impotent. The master-slave relationship is usually characterized by mutual rancor and disdain. In "Uncle Wiggily in Connecticut," the maid Grace is a servant, not a slave, but the dynamics are comparable because Grace is denied autonomy and self-determination as a result of her live-in position in the household. Eloise is struggling to impose her authority on Grace, who does not demonstrate a suitable degree of deference to Eloise. Eloise pays her back with arbitrary cruelty to assert her power. Grace seems "annoyed" when Eloise goes into the kitchen to get ice because her reading is disturbed. Tellingly, Grace is reading *The Robe* by Lloyd C. Douglas (1942), an adventure story that tells the tale of the Roman soldier who won Christ's robe as a gambling prize. It is a book that promotes the authority of Christ as the ultimate master. Furthermore, the text addresses the nature of the master-slave relationship, ultimately showing that the relationship breaks down very quickly if the master recognizes the full humanity of the slave and friendship develops. Eloise denies Grace her full humanity by referring to her as "whosis" and insulting her behind her back. Grace's choice of reading material and her attitude toward Eloise indicate that the maid resents her position and treatment in the household.

While Eloise could not conceive of friendship with her servant, she relies heavily on her relationship with Mary Jane to shore her up. With this old college friend, she can speak the truth and allow her emotions to show. As a support system to help people cope with their lives, friendships are an essential part of growing up. The fact that Ramona has no friends, apart from imaginary boyfriends, is a disturbing feature of her life. Since her mother has a rather strained relationship with her, Ramona has no one with whom to share her thoughts, leaving her isolated and uncommunicative. If imaginary friends are Ramona's way of dealing with her loneliness, Eloise's methods of escapism from her miserable life—alcohol and cruelty—are equally pathetic.

Sample Topics:

1. **The master-servant relationship:** How does Grace confound Eloise's expectations of a master-servant relationship? How does Eloise make herself feel superior to Grace?

People are constantly engaged in power struggles. An essay on this topic could analyze the dynamics of Eloise and Grace's interaction within the framework of the master-slave relationship. An essay on this topic could also take into consideration the social context of race relations in the late 1940s to see how Grace is reaching for self-assertion within her limited realm. Grace's reading material adds another dimension to the dynamic, since it reveals her interest in the notion that her ultimate master is God, not the drunken, vicious woman for whom she works.

2. **Friendship:** How does Mary Jane provide support for Eloise? What role do Ramona's imaginary friends play in the child's life?

Women turn to conversation with their female friends when they want to work through problems. Eloise chooses not to be a friend to her husband, believing that sexual tensions intervene in possible honesty between men and women. An essay on this topic could analyze the role of friendships in the short story. Another approach would be a comparison between Eloise's relationships with men and Ramona's relationships with her make-believe friends, highlighting similarities and differences.

3. **Escapism:** Why does Eloise drink? Why is Eloise so cruel to other people?

Escapism is the tendency to retreat from unpleasant situations by whatever means that allow reality to be kept at bay. Eloise uses alcohol in an attempt to numb her pain, although ironically it causes her true feelings to surface. In a way, her critical comments about other people are a means to make herself feel better about her own life. An essay on this topic could consider how Eloise has created a modus operandi that enables her to avoid dealing with the reality of her miserable and unfulfilled life. This essay would probably overlap with an analysis of the themes of regret and bitterness. The topic could be extended to include Ramona. How does Ramona use her imagination to create a better world for herself?

Language, Symbols, and Imagery

The title of this short story identifies its two main symbols. Howard Garis (1873–1962) was a prolific writer in the first half of the 20th century who was particularly noted for his Uncle Wiggily series of children's books. Uncle Wiggily Longears, the main character of this series, was a "nice old gentleman rabbit." Uncle Wiggily is characterized by a positive attitude toward life, always assuming the best of everyone. Another quality that Uncle Wiggily is renowned for is his love of children. Uncle Wiggily is adored by his numerous nieces and nephews, and he is equally generous and caring toward them. The overall goal of the Uncle Wiggily books was to instruct children in fundamental Christian values, such as treating people with love, compassion, and generosity. So even though Walt's joking comment to Eloise when he called her ankle "Uncle Wiggily" can be understood on a literal level—her ankle must have wiggled to cause it to twist—the allusion carries with it both positive and profoundly ironic overtones. This darker side of the allusion is conveyed through Eloise's final epiphany as she picks up her child's glasses and repeatedly mutters, "Poor Uncle Wiggily." She acknowledges that the "Uncle Wiggily" component of her personality has been whittled away, in the same way that she is contributing to the erosion of her child's niceness.

The second half of the title, "in Connecticut," establishes a jarring contrast with the first half. Connecticut is the place where Eloise has lost her associations with Uncle Wiggily. She has mislaid her joie de vivre and love of people; her spirit is closed to life and even to her own child. As the story shows, Mary Jane has problems reaching and departing from the house. The house in Connecticut is so forgettable that Mary Jane gets lost trying to find it, even though she has been to the house on two previous occasions. The house is equally difficult to leave; even the weather conspires with the house to prevent easy escape. The descriptions that are provided of the house and its surroundings resonate with Salinger's distaste for this bourgeois class and its values. Each room in the house has a particular function and code of behavior attached to it. The household of women brought together on an icy winter's day is a household of tensions and divisions.

Sample Topics:

1. **Uncle Wiggily:** What does Uncle Wiggily symbolize in connection with Eloise? What does Uncle Wiggily symbolize in connection with Ramona?

   When Eloise mutters "Uncle Wiggily" repeatedly at the end of the short story, it is because she has had an insight into her own personality and behavior. She becomes aware of how much she has changed since she was a young woman in love with Walt Glass. Why does she say "Uncle Wiggily" over and over again? What does Uncle Wiggily mean to her? An essay on this topic could examine the connection between Eloise and her daughter, which is evinced through the symbol of Uncle Wiggily. Ramona's crying and her thick eyeglasses trigger memories for Eloise of when she was still a "nice" girl who was capable of loving and being loved by Walt. An essay could even compare mother and daughter since the daughter's behavior often parallels features of her mother's past and present life.

2. **The suburban Connecticut house:** What imagery used throughout the story contributes to the impression of the house being like a dark, unwelcoming jail? How does the description of each room in the house convey the tensions and divisions of the female "inmates"?

Although the suburban house is a short distance away from the local train station and New York, it nevertheless seems to be a place that is difficult to reach. Its sense of isolation is compounded by the wintry weather that acts as a backdrop to the story. The house is an unapproachable, dark, and somewhat dirty structure, cut off from the rest of the world by "filthy slush" and full of angry, unfulfilled women. An essay on the suburban house could analyze how the descriptions of the house and the activities that take place inside it reflect Salinger's loathing of upper-middle-class suburban life and the values associated with it. Another approach would be to analyze the symbolic meanings attached to the imagery linked to the house. For example, there are many references that describe which rooms are left in the dark and which have lights switched on. The absence or presence of light communicates the state of mind of the person in that room. Each room in the house acts as a mini-domain for each woman. Trespassing into another woman's realm is fraught with tension. For example, Eloise frequently sends Mary Jane and Ramona to the kitchen, which is a place dominated by the presence of the hostile Grace.

Compare and Contrast Essays

Walt Glass is a character who is mentioned in both "Uncle Wiggily in Connecticut" and the "Zooey" section of *Franny and Zooey*. Both "Uncle Wiggily in Connecticut" and "Zooey" address the psychological problems of struggling with an inauthentic life. The action in "Uncle Wiggily in Connecticut" unfolds in a suburban Connecticut house, whereas the plot of "Zooey" plays out in the Glasses' Manhattan apartment. However, in each story, the house or apartment is deployed by Salinger to add to the story's meaning through its imagery and through the occupancy of each room by a specific character. In both cases, entering another person's room leads to conflict or resolution of conflict. Notably, both stories depict an epiphany for the main female character in another character's bedroom. Arguably, both Franny and Eloise are able to move forward and improve the quality of their lives after their moment of clarity in these bedrooms. Salinger uses his settings symbolically to reinforce characterization and plot. However, a significant difference between the two locations is that while Salinger deplores suburban life, he concedes the possibility that New York City life has the potential to withstand the phony, conformist values of suburbia.

Another interpretation of Eloise would describe her as a personification of defeat. Given that she is drunk, her realization about her child's unhappiness and her role in that misery may simply dissipate in the morning. With this interpretation, Eloise could be compared to Seymour Glass in "A Perfect Day for Bananafish," another character who is trapped by the trite superficiality of middle-class values in the postwar era. Both stories were originally published in 1948, and they are the first two stories in the *Nine Stories* collection. Seymour and Eloise are two characters who abhor the world they find themselves in and have given over to despair. Interaction with children in each case stimulates awareness of their condition, although they respond to their moment of understanding differently.

Sample Topics:

1. **A suburban house versus a Manhattan apartment:** How does Salinger use each building to convey the values of the community in which it is located? How does each dwelling amplify the conflict among its various occupants?

An essay analyzing the two buildings could compare the different rooms in each home and determine the function of each room. This topic could be extended to encompass the imagery that is used to describe each room and how that imagery elucidates aspects of characterization. (For an analysis of aspects of the Glasses' Manhattan apartment, refer to the "Language, Symbols, and Imagery" section of the chapter on *Franny and Zooey.*) Another approach would be to make parallels between features of each home and the social values that Salinger is either critiquing or promoting through those features.

2. **Eloise and Seymour Glass—embodiments of defeat:** Why are Eloise and Seymour at odds with their family and the society in which they live? How has each character responded to his or her feelings of alienation, frustration, and cynicism?

Seymour Glass and Eloise are both caught up in the WASP (white Anglo-Saxon Protestant) society that Salinger repeatedly pillories throughout his work. The phoniness, superficiality, and banality of middle-class white America in the postwar years causes people who are sensitive, intellectual, or passionate to wither up and retreat into a protective shell. In the case of Seymour, that protective shell is the armor of insanity: a sane response to an insane world. Eloise, on the other hand, has retreated into a persona that is hard and uncaring, and her authentic self is shriveling up inside her. An essay examining these two characters could compare the way they treat their spouses (who embody some of the worst qualities of the society they hate) and how their interaction with a child causes an awakening. The essay could also contrast the ways they have responded to their situations, and the final outcome of their struggles with a phony world.

Bibliography

French, Warren. "A Nine Story Cycle." *J. D. Salinger, Revisited.* Boston: Twayne, 1988. 69–70.

Wenke, John. "Nine Stories." *J. D. Salinger: A Study of the Short Fiction.* Boston: Twayne, 1991. 38–41.

"JUST BEFORE THE WAR WITH THE ESKIMOS"

READING TO WRITE

IT IS usually impossible to predict whether a boy and a girl will find each other interesting. Franklin Graff is not obviously physically appealing when Ginnie Mannox meets him for the first time:

She looked around the room, mentally rearranging furniture, throwing out table lamps, removing artificial flowers. In her opinion, it was an altogether hideous room—expensive but cheesy.

Suddenly, a male voice shouted from another part of the apartment, *"Eric? That you?"*

Ginnie guessed it was Selena's brother, whom she had never seen. She crossed her long legs, arranged the hem of her polo coat over her knees, and waited.

A young man wearing glasses and pajamas and no slippers lunged into the room with his mouth open. "Oh. I thought it was Eric, for Chrissake," he said. Without stopping, and with extremely poor posture, he continued across the room, cradling something close to his narrow chest. He sat down on the vacant end of the sofa. "I just cut my goddam finger," he said rather wildly. He looked at Ginnie as if he had expected her to be sitting there. "Ever cut your finger? Right down to the bone and all?" he asked. There was a real appeal in his noisy voice, as if Ginnie, by her answer, could save him from some particularly isolating form of pioneering.

In this excerpt, Franklin is depicted as slovenly and, in Ginnie's words, "goofy." A character study of this 24-year-old should evaluate his physical, mental, and behavioral characteristics carefully to determine what it is that captivates Ginnie.

Ginnie enters the Graff household in a hostile and spiteful frame of mind. She believes that Selena Graff has been exploiting her by not paying her share of their taxi fare home from tennis every week. Her condescending and peremptory attitude to the Graffs is based on the fact that she considers herself better than Selena. Ginnie has dismissed Selena as "the biggest drip" at their school. Nonetheless, Ginnie has been playing tennis with her on a weekly basis, partly because Selena's father furnishes the girls with free tennis balls. Failing to recognize that she could be perceived as exploitative, Ginnie insists that Selena contribute to the taxi fare as well. As she sits waiting for Selena to bring the money, Ginnie evaluates the Graff living room in a snobbish and arrogant way. Her thought processes of rearranging the furniture and redecorating aspects of the room reinforce how Ginnie has elevated herself and her opinions to a plane superior to everything and everyone in the Graff household. However, the presence of a young man has the power to modify her entire demeanor and attitude toward the Graffs. Ginnie's shift in attitude could be analyzed from different angles to create a selection of essay topics. Firstly, Ginnie could become the focus of a character study. Alternatively, her transformation could be approached through an analysis of the themes of pity and adolescent friendships. Her altered outlook also serves to comment on a bizarre interplay between the value of money and the value of a person.

Why does Ginnie respond to Franklin? He has poor posture, he swears incessantly, and he has no valid occupation. He walks in on Ginnie with a bleeding finger, which he proceeds to discuss rather than attend to it medically. Before his entrance into the living room, Salinger indicates that Ginnie is at the age where she is apprehensive yet open to meeting young men. This is shown through the detail of her arranging her coat and crossing her legs to prepare herself for an encounter with a strange young man. Her gesture is unknowingly reciprocated by Franklin during the course of their conversation, since he addresses her with "real appeal" in his voice. The desperation of his reaching out to her so instantaneously and directly is highlighted by the final sentence of the extract. Franklin's appeal to Ginnie is described as if her response "could save him from some particularly isolating form of pioneering."

Franklin, too, would make an interesting character for analysis. What exactly is he "pioneering"? A pioneer is someone who leads the way or who is a trailblazer. If Salinger's tone is ironic in this passage, then Franklin's pioneering can be understood simply that he could be the first human being ever to cut his finger down to the bone, but he wants Ginnie to save him from this isolating episode by having her confess that she has had the same experience as him. This would put them on the same level. However, "pioneering" is used more ambiguously by Salinger. The lack of specificity of this line and the fact that he is reaching out so quickly to the girl imply that he wants to be saved from something more profound than a cut finger. The answer to this conundrum may lie in the character Eric, whom Franklin is expecting. Intuitively, Franklin may be looking for someone to rescue him from Eric's controlling friendship. Drifting into Eric's world of effeminacy and homosexuality would be "particularly isolating" in the upper-middle-class milieu from which Franklin is coming adrift. A relationship with a girl would facilitate his return back to social (and sexual) normativity. A possible essay topic that arises from these observations would be an analysis of the 1948 social context and the period's attitude towards homosexuality and nontraditional definitions of masculinity.

The reasons for Ginnie's and Franklin's attraction to each other are never clarified in the story. Salinger uses an open-ended resolution where the characters' actions are subject to multiple interpretations. The ambiguity of the ending would make a possible topic for discussion, and the hints that Salinger provides at these two young people's initial meeting can be used to elucidate whichever conclusion each reader determines the story yields.

TOPICS AND STRATEGIES

Possible topics for essays on "Just Before the War with the Eskimos" will be proposed in the remainder of this chapter. Suggestions on how to tackle those topics should inspire your own ideas.

Themes

Money may buy friendship, but money cannot buy love. At the end of "Just Before the War with the Eskimos," Ginnie Mannox does seem to try to buy Selena's friendship in hope that she can gain access to Franklin. Access to Franklin, Ginnie surmises, could lead to more friendship or even love. What kind of friendship, though, can be bought? In the case of Selena and Ginnie, the two families apparently hail from comparable economic backgrounds, since the children of both families move in the same circles. However, Ginnie labels Selena the "biggest drip" at the school they both attend. A young teenage girl who is excluded from the ranks of the popular may accept friendship on different terms than other people will. Selena, it should be noted, is not prepared at first to "buy" Ginnie as her tennis companion. The issue of who owes whom what threatens to end their fragile friendship. As Ginnie prepares to leave the Graff apartment and magnanimously lets Selena off the debt she believes she is owed, Selena is nonplussed by Ginnie's sudden change of heart. However, she is prepared to take Ginnie's words at face value and agrees that Ginnie can return later that evening to visit her under the guise of friendship. The issue of money and friendship, particularly when male-female attraction is implicated, is convoluted. However, since the ending of the story is indeterminate, some readers interpret Ginnie's about-face at the end of the story as sincere rather than manipulative. An argument could be presented that Ginnie's interaction with Franklin has stirred a degree of pity in her. She has moved away from her petty, capitalist egoism to a place where she can empathize with the Graffs.

Sample Topics:

1. **Money:** How does money threaten to destroy the relationship between Selena and Ginnie? How does money have the power to redeem their friendship?

   How is it possible that a girl who plays tennis every weekend and can afford a taxi home can become irate over $1.90? Why does Ginnie insist on having the money immediately instead of letting Selena bring it to school on Monday? Why would a girl who lives in an expensively furnished apartment with a maid resist paying a small debt? Money has the power to divide and conquer. In elite WASP circles, arguing about money is considered poor taste. An essay on this topic could look at the contradictory attitudes toward money that the two girls demonstrate. Another approach would be to consider how money has specific purchasing power in the world of people like the Graffs and Mannoxs. Can money buy love and friendship?

2. **Friendship:** What is the basis of the friendship between Selena and Ginnie? What is the basis of the friendship between Ginnie and Franklin? What is the basis of the friendship between Franklin and Eric?

What is the basis of friendship? There must be some common ground between two people in order for a relationship to be established. An idealistic view would argue that friendship is founded on unselfish love for another person. In the real world, however, many relationships fulfill a specific function. An essay analyzing this topic would need to scrutinize the different key friendships in the story. What has brought these people together, and what keeps them together? Overall, does Salinger portray friendship as a pure or a self-seeking relationship?

3. **Pity:** How does Ginnie show her pitiless side in the story? What situations cause her to soften and demonstrate some gentleness and compunction?

A society that is ruthlessly acquisitive and competitive can induce its members to become hardened and insensitive to other people. Other people become impediments to the fulfillment of one's personal desires. Several Salinger stories portray teenagers on the brink of transitioning into adulthood. These characters often balk at this transformation because of its accompanying loss of goodness and niceness. There is no easy turning back once a person has crossed over into the domain of hypocrisy and egotism. Teenagers can only struggle against their contamination at the threshold of this transformation. An essay analyzing the theme of pity could look for moments in "Just Before the War with the Eskimos" where the characters reach out to each other with a genuine and compassionate spirit. These moments can be compared with other instances where the characters are the perpetrators or the victims of pitiless behavior.

Character

Franklin Graff, from his sister's perspective, is a "character." Selena notes the apparent individual quality of her brother, but she does not mean her comment in a flattering way. Her lack of interest in her failure of a sibling is counterpointed by Ginnie's enthusiasm for this young man, who neither works nor goes to school. Ginnie's interest cannot be the consequence of his dashing good looks. Franklin slouches, picks at himself, is unshaven, and has a weak heart. On the other hand, he is direct, provokes atypical topics of conversation, and reaches out to the young girl he finds sitting in the Graff living room. Eric does not appeal to Ginnie in the slightest. Salinger presents this effeminate character as melodramatic. He does not engage Ginnie in conversation, so much as regale her with his life story. Ginnie only has opportunity to interject a few words before Eric launches into a fresh tirade. When Ginnie leaves, the narrator points out that she does not bother to say goodbye to this flamboyant character. Why would Ginnie find Eric annoying or repellent? Ginnie is a tall girl of 15 who seems open to meeting new people, especially young men. Salinger presents her as a bit gauche and awkward, but she has no trouble asserting her will over Selena. She has other contradictory traits, and her behavior is unpredictable. Overall, she embodies the conflicts that Salinger believes abound in a wealthy young girl who is approaching adulthood.

Sample Topics:

1. **Franklin Graff:** Which of this young man's characteristics does Salinger use to point out his alienation from society? Why does Ginnie respond positively to Franklin?

An essay on this character could examine the attributes that make Franklin both appealing and off-putting. He clearly does not make his parents proud since he lounges around at home and refuses to work or study. However, there is something authentic about him that Ginnie reacts to with interest and concern. What does he say and do that stimulate Ginnie to want to return to the Graff household in the hope that she might see him again?

2. **Eric:** What techniques does Salinger deploy to insinuate that this character is effeminate and possibly homosexual? What is the nature of the relationship between Eric and Franklin?

Eric and Franklin became acquainted when they were working together in an airplane factory in Ohio during the war. Although Franklin was exempted from combat because of a heart weakened by rheumatic fever as a child, Eric's 4F status is not due to poor health because he claims to have the "constitution of. . . ." The sentence is left unfinished, but the reader can infer that he would have added, ". . . an ox." Openly homosexual men, even if healthy, were not allowed to serve in the American military during World War II. An essay could analyze the traits that Salinger gives Eric to imply that his 4F status is due to homosexuality. Eric and Franklin have been friends for a while by the time the events of the story take place. Why has their friendship flourished?

3. **Ginnie:** How does Ginnie develop throughout the course of the story? How does the indeterminate ending of the short story leave Ginnie's change of attitude toward Selena subject to different interpretations?

Ginnie is an adolescent character who at the start of the story already seems to have mislaid any generosity of spirit or compassion. She browbeats Selena into bringing her money immediately. However, following Selena into her apartment to wait for the money results in a fortuitous meeting for Ginnie. She comes across Franklin, who shows interest in her and is able to connect with her. This connection is confirmed by his strange offering of half a chicken sandwich. An essay could determine whether Franklin's warmth to Ginnie causes her to reevaluate her earlier behavior to Selena. If this is the case, then her holding on to the chicken sandwich links her back to her compassionate, warmer young self. However, another approach could consider whether Ginnie is merely manipulating Selena to gain access to Franklin and whether her holding onto the chicken sandwich has more negative connotations. For further commentary on the sandwich, see the "Language, Symbols, and Imagery" section of this chapter.

History and Context

Modern society has long resisted giving its homosexual citizens the same rights as its heterosexuals. Although attitudes and mores change over time, it was only in the 1960s that gays began to assert their rights and demand full inclusion into society. With biblical prohibitions as support, society has ostracized homosexuals, deeming them inimical to the interests of the community. Openly gay men were exempted from military service during World War II, regardless of how healthy and fit they were. Popular opinion has accused gay men of preying on the vulnerable and attempting to pervert them away from heterosexual lives. In 1948, when "Just Before the War with the Eskimos" was published, homosexuality was commonly classified as a mental illness. Eric's sexual orientation does not seem covert according to the textual clues that Salinger inserts. Eric's outspoken admiration of camel hair and his admission that he has seen Jean Cocteau's "Beauty and the Beast" (1946) are two of the more blatant pointers of Eric's effeminacy, if not his sexual orientation. (Cocteau was openly homosexual and cast his lover Jean Marais as the lead in this film.) What were the possible repercussions of being openly homosexual in a time when it was demonized? How does the period and Eric's presumed homosexuality shape Ginnie's and Franklin's response to him?

Sample Topics:

1. **Homosexuality:** How does Salinger hint at Eric's effeminate behavior and interests? What is the importance of the characters' sexual orientation to the overall story?

Arguments proposing that the main focus of this short story is sexuality are viable. Ginnie is obviously heterosexual and Eric is probably homosexual. Franklin can be seen as essentially heterosexual, but he is perhaps gravitating toward a homosexual lifestyle through his lack of success as a heterosexual. Franklin does not conform to the demands of normative masculinity, and his rebuff by Joan Mannox typifies the likely female response to him. An essay could argue that the story enacts a struggle for Franklin's allegiance by Eric and Ginnie, and this idea garners greater import because of the time in which the story is set. How does the 1948 time frame control how a story about homosexuality can be articulated by Salinger? Is Eric portrayed sympathetically by Salinger? What appears to be Salinger's perspective on openly homosexual men? Salinger's representation of Eric as a homosexual could also be the focus of an essay.

Philosophy and Ideas

When Franklin looks out of his apartment window, he expresses his sense of distance from the people on the streets who are going about their daily business. He condemns them as "fools." He tells Ginnie that, in his opinion, all the people he can see are rushing to the draft board to sign up for a war against the Eskimos. (In 1948, there would have been no awareness among white Americans that the term "Eskimo" is considered offensive by some of the groups of people who have been called this name.) When Franklin makes this statement, he is commenting on the futility of war, since fighting in the Arctic would be self-destructive and essentially pointless. This comment and other facets of his behavior are symptomatic of his feelings of alienation, made known through his expressions of exclusion, unbelonging, and loneliness. Alienation is a common condition for Salinger characters and, like Holden in *The Catcher in the Rye* or Franny in *Franny and Zooey*, Franklin shows that one of the reasons he cannot fit in with the rest of the world is that he does not share the competitive and aggressive mindset that predominates among most 20th-century adults.

Sample Topics:

1. **Alienation:** What physical and mental attributes have caused or contributed to Franklin's disengagement with society? What aspects of his world make Franklin hesitant about joining the ranks of the gainfully occupied?

Franklin Graff is a man of 24 who is still living the life of a boy. He neither works nor studies. Physically, he still resembles a younger male. He is ungainly and slovenly. His comments indicate that he scorns the society of which he is supposed to be a member. His choice of friend shows that he is gravitating toward people who live their life on the margins. An essay on this topic could determine why Franklin has become an outsider from his wealthy and privileged world. Furthermore, the essay could explore the aspects of society that Salinger is critiquing through Franklin. What traits does Franklin reveal that indicate why he is in conflict with society? When he reaches out to Ginnie, will she rescue him from his alienated status, or will she simply provide him with more company in the ranks of the sensitive outsiders?

Form and Genre

Many of Salinger's short stories have a degree of ambiguity that makes it hard for the reader to ascribe a definitive interpretation to the text. This lack of closure to the text is pronounced in "Just Before the War with the Eskimos." Its indeterminate ending raises more questions than it answers. Does Ginnie realize that Eric is homosexual? Does Ginnie recognize a mutual attraction between Franklin and herself? Is Franklin simply being polite to Ginnie? Does he reach out to her as a friendly human being and not on the basis of romantic interest? What is the nature of the friendship between Eric and Franklin? Why does Ginnie not say goodbye to Eric? Why does she quite aggressively create an opportunity for herself to see Franklin again? Why did Salinger choose to end his story in this indeterminate way?

Another technique that this short story deploys, and that Salinger uses in other stories such as "A Perfect Day for Bananafish," is a form that simulates a three-act play. In this case, the first act is the drama that erupts between Ginnie and Selena in the taxi and outside Selena's apartment. The second act takes place in the living room, where Ginnie meets Franklin. The final act is the conversation between Ginnie and Eric. At the end of their exchange, Selena enters and escorts Ginnie off stage.

Sample Topics:

1. **"Just Before the War with the Eskimos" as a three-act play:** Structurally, the story has many similarities to a three-act drama. Why did Salinger structure his story in this way, and what is the effect of telling the story this way?

   In an analysis of the story as a three-act play, one approach would be to consider the roles and movements of the four main characters/actors. Ginnie is the only "actor" who stays on stage throughout the play. The other characters come and go to allow the tension and mystery to build. When Ginnie is alone on stage, the narrator provides information about her behavior and actions, such as when she scans the room looking for a place to secrete the unwanted chicken sandwich. These descriptions of her activities could be understood as stage directions. An essay could appraise Salinger's use of dramatic techniques in the construction of "Just Before the War with the Eskimos," analyzing the effects the techniques have on the plot, characterization, conflicts, and setting.

2. **The open ending of "Just Before the War with the Eskimos":** How does the ambiguous ending of the story connect to the theme of friendship, to the idea of alienation, and to the 1948 context in terms of attitudes toward sexuality, sexual orientation, and gender roles?

   An author makes a conscious choice whether to tie up the loose ends of a story or leave the reader with questions. An essay on this topic could attempt to determine why Salinger left this particular short story so indeterminate. Possible arguments could be created to show how the open-endedness enhances various themes and questions that the story poses. After all, some issues and some relationships can never be understood definitively and concluded neatly.

Language, Symbols, and Imagery

What is the connection between a dead Easter chick and a half-eaten chicken sandwich? The question sounds absurd, but it is the question that Salinger leaves the reader with at the end of "Just Before the War with the Eskimos." In crude terms, the chick would have to grow into a chicken and then be killed in order to turn up in a sandwich. An Easter chick is a symbol associated with Christ's resurrection. Christ rose again at Easter after three days of death. Similarly, the Easter chick would have to be reborn if it is to reappear as a chicken sandwich. The dead Easter chick is found at the bottom of Ginnie's wastebasket. Franklin cuts his finger while rummaging in his wastebasket. His wound has the power to help him bond with Ginnie, and their connection is cemented by his gift to her of the chicken sandwich. However, Ginnie does not want to eat the sandwich, although she holds on to it in the same way that she did to the Easter chick. These symbols, therefore, engage with the conflicting notions of life and death. They also incorporate ideas of regeneration, resurrection, divinity, and the power of gifts. On the other hand, they are tainted by the stain of uselessness. As a consequence of this mélange of associations, these objects present a variety of angles for analysis.

Sample Topics:

1. **The Easter chick and the chicken sandwich:** What point does Salinger make by establishing a connection between the Easter chick and the chicken sandwich at the end of the story? Is it a positive or negative quality in Ginnie when she holds onto objects that should be thrown away?

A piece of junk or a gift with regenerative powers? Salinger does not provide easy answers to the complex symbol of the chicken sandwich. Is Ginnie irresolute or compassionate when she fails to throw out the dead chick? An essay on these symbols could weigh their different possible interpretations and evaluate what they add to the story's overall meaning. One way that this topic could be extended is to determine whether Franny's uneaten chicken sandwich in *Franny and Zooey* has any connection to this unwanted sandwich. Why are chicken sandwiches in Salinger texts associated with rejection, alienation, niceness, and difference?

Compare and Contrast Essays

Several Salinger characters teeter on the threshold that separates adolescent sensitivity and adult cruelty. Salinger shows that the transition from one state to the other is inevitable but that many people are apprehensive about entering the adult world. The apprehension stems from the fear that adulthood entails relinquishing qualities that define them as human, such as empathy, kindness, and sincerity. Worse, the traits and behavior they must assume in order to participate in mainstream society are likely to make them live a meaningless and inauthentic life. Ginnie is poised on the brink of becoming an adult. She already demonstrates characteristics that are emblematic of Salinger's critical perspective on mainstream American life. She is egocentric, greedy, spiteful, and uncaring. This character is similar to Eloise in "Uncle Wiggily in Connecticut," although Eloise is older and has passed over the threshold that separates authenticity from phoniness. However, Eloise is not so far advanced and lost in adult cruelty and hypocrisy that she cannot still remember a time when she was "nice." Arguably, Ginnie also reconnects to her nicer self as a result of her interaction with Franklin.

Sample Topics:
1. **Ginnie and Eloise:** What character traits does Salinger give these two women that indicate that they have been negatively affected by their upper-middle-class WASP environment? Which incidents in their respective stories allow each woman to manifest aspects of a more authentic self?

The endings of "Just Before the War with the Eskimos" and "Uncle Wiggily in Connecticut" present the possibility for a comparative essay, even though both tales terminate ambiguously. Eloise and Ginnie are portrayed initially as banal female Salinger characters. However, throughout the course of each story, each woman provides a glimpse of a nicer persona that existed before she was corrupted by her society. Each female character is reminded of a better way of behaving by another character. Significantly, the end of each story is indeterminate. Does each woman change, or is her final behavior transitory and/or insincere?

Bibliography

French, Warren. "A Nine Story Cycle." *J. D. Salinger, Revisited*. Boston: Twayne, 1988. 70–72.

Goldstein, Bernice, and Sanford Goldstein. "Zen and *Nine Stories*." *J. D. Salinger: Modern Critical Views*. Ed. Harold Bloom. New York: Chelsea House, 1987. 81–93.

Wenke, John. "Nine Stories." *J. D. Salinger: A Study of the Short Fiction*. Boston: Twayne, 1991. 41–43.

"THE LAUGHING MAN"

READING TO WRITE

MALTREATED AND misunderstood or monstrous and macabre? The fictional Laughing Man, created by John Gedsudski to entertain 25 young boys in an after-school club, is both compassionate Robin Hood and ruthless criminal mastermind. He is hideously ugly but inspires love and devotion from a select few. The facial feature that makes the Laughing Man so grotesque is his nose. In the passage below, Gedsudski's superhero is described:

> The nose itself consisted of two flesh-sealed nostrils. In conse-
> quence, when the Laughing Man breathed, the hideous, mirthless
> gap below his nose dilated and contracted like (as *I* see it) some
> sort of monstrous vacuole. (The Chief demonstrated, rather than
> explained, the Laughing Man's respiration method.) Strangers
> fainted dead away at the sight of the Laughing Man's horrible face.
> Acquaintances shunned him. Curiously enough, though, the ban-
> dits let him hang around their headquarters—as long as he kept
> his face covered with a pale-red gossamer mask made out of poppy
> petals. The mask not only spared the bandits the sight of their fos-
> ter son's face, it also kept them sensible of his whereabouts; under
> the circumstances, he reeked of opium.

What is the nature of the relationship between a storyteller and his story and his audience? Telling stories to children has many possible functions. Stories may be used to entertain, to convey moral messages, or to teach a child about culture or religion. The primary tool of a story-

143

teller is words. Through words and the process of creative narration, the storyteller can insert himself in the plot, the characters, and the context of the story. The construction of the story becomes linked to the construction of identity for both the storyteller and the audience. If Gedsudski acts out his own life struggles through his story, his young audience participates in those struggles through their mental association with the superhero character. This nexus among storyteller, story, and audience presents several potential essay topics. The most obvious avenue of exploration is to determine the degree to which the Laughing Man's antics are used to act out Gedsudski's life situation. Another important issue to consider is the role of fantasy in the Laughing Man story. How does the serialized narrative inform the reader about the Chief's insecurities, fears, dreams, and self-image?

The excerpt implies that Gedsudski's principal insecurity is his physical appearance. Earlier in the story, the narrator spends an entire paragraph outlining the Chief's physical appearance. Too short for a man and simian, the Chief's worst feature is his nose. It is described as "large and fleshy." Seemingly, Gedsudski transfers his paranoia about his ugly nose into the Laughing Man narrative, where its unsightliness is concealed behind a poppy-petal mask. The idea of masking offers another possible essay topic. At several instances throughout both the Laughing Man tale and the external frame story related by the former Comanche Club member, there are moments where characters are masking their true feelings or when certain truths are unmasked. The young Comanche Club boys are oblivious to the limitations of their Chief's physical beauty. They all admire, love, and respect him. In the all-male world that they inhabit for a brief time every day after school, Gedsudski is invincible. To them, he is the superhero of his fantasies. Only with time and experience can the narrator look back on his youthful time with the Comanche Club and begin to intuit why the Chief killed off the Laughing Man character.

A frame narrative is a literary technique where one story is embedded within another story. The first story usually starts and finishes the story, while the second story is completed within this outer "frame." The internal, framed story usually reveals some important truth about the outer story. "The Laughing Man" can be analyzed as a story within a story since the Laughing Man narrative provides psychological insight into some of the characters in the external story. Structurally, the short story has three layers of narrative: the story of the Comanche Club boys and their time spent with the Chief, the Laughing Man stories, and the retrospective comments of the older narrator looking back on his young self. These three narrative strata are stacked together in the excerpt.

Salinger uses parentheses to contrast the ignorance of the nine-year-old boy with the understanding of his older self, as is shown in the excerpt above. The parentheses incorporate information that is mostly derived from more mature reflection. This device allows the primary narration to retain the innocence of the young boy who did not understand the nature of the relationship between the Chief and Mary Hudson or between the Chief and the Laughing Man. This immature perception of the unfolding events establishes a perspective for the story that obliges the reader to infer what happened between the adult characters. Even the mature narrator claims to be unsure of what happened. As the passage shows, Salinger's choice of narrative voice advances thematic concerns that could be the basis of an essay. Since the narrator is an older man looking back on his youth, the theme of the loss of innocence is paramount. Additionally, the Comanche Club and the Laughing Man both acquire symbolic significance now that the narrator has more experience of the world. The passage also raises questions about relationship problems and the definition of masculinity.

TOPICS AND STRATEGIES

Further topics for essays on "The Laughing Man" will be discussed in the remainder of this chapter. Some general approaches that could be used to write about those topics will also be outlined. These topics and approaches should be used as a resource to help generate your own essay subjects and theses.

Themes

"The Laughing Man" is a short story narrated by a man who is relating events from his childhood. A child of nine years has limited experience of the problems and pain that can accompany romantic relationships. While a child may divine that something is wrong between two adults, he might not be able to grasp the complexities of that problem. Thus, although that child may be able to recount the details surrounding a crisis in a relationship, the nature of that crisis could be unknown. This is what happens to the narrator as a young boy. Only as an older man reflecting on his past can he piece together the fragments of information to infer what may have happened between the Chief and Mary Hudson. This mature reflection also allows him to discern the Chief's motives for ending the Laughing Man serial story. As a boy, he was only aware of his own misery when Gedsudski killed off the Comanche Club's super-hero. As a man, he is able to suspect that the Chief's pain may have been conveyed through the story's ending. As a child, he was more aware of the Comanche Club boys' bodily and physical responses to the Chief's termination of their boyish fantasy world. As a man, he can understand that a part of the innocence of his childhood died on that day. The all-male world that the narrator had been enjoying in the Comanche Club was ruptured by the intrusion of a woman. The narrator as a young boy believes firmly that there is behavior suitable for a boy and behavior suit-able for a girl. His identity as a male is forged through his activities with the Chief and the other Comanche Club members. The presence of a woman seems to threaten the integrity and stability of this masculine space. Ironically, the Chief's unhappy relationship with Mary Hudson teaches the narrator a fundamental lesson about being a man.

Sample Topics:

1. **The loss of innocence:** What events cause the narrator to mature? How does the narrator view his youthful Comanche Club experience?

   Specific events in each person's life may stand out in his or her memory as having been critically formative. Often, the scat-tered memories that a person recalls from childhood revolve around some tragic or painful occurrence. With hindsight, those painful memories are understood as having altered fun-damental attitudes toward life. Experience leads to knowledge; knowledge contributes to maturity. What was the narrator's life like as a Comanche Club member? How did his perspec-tive change as a result of the Chief's decision to kill off the Laughing Man? An essay on this topic could examine how the narrator's innocence was gradually corroded throughout the duration of the summer of 1928.

2. **Relationships:** How do the characters respond to their relationship problems? How do the child characters differ from the adults in the way they handle relationships?

Children tend to be more straightforward in their interactions with other people than adults are. They can be sensitive to an adult's mood but will lack the vocabulary and the emotional experience to deal with the problem with subtlety. An essay on this topic could discuss the various types of relationships in the story or just select one of the more important relationships and appraise how each character manages his or her emotional stress caused through interaction with other people.

3. **Masculinity:** What qualities does the young narrator associate with masculinity? Why is the presence of Mary Hudson seen as a threat to the ethos of the Comanche Club?

In 1928, there were strict expectations about the way a man should behave and the way a woman should behave. Transgressing the roles assigned to one's gender could result in verbal belittlement. For example, in the Laughing Man tale, Mademoiselle Dufarge is probably referred to as a "transvestite" because she wears pants. The boys have a code of masculinity in their Comanche Club that Mary's presence threatens to undermine. How does Mary defy gendered codes of behavior? How does she ultimately gain acceptance from the boys? An essay could analyze the challenges both to the norms of masculinity and to the expectations associated with femininity that are depicted in the story. The "History and Context" section provides more information on New York City's social norms in the 1920s.

Character
This short story offers detailed psychological insight into John Gedsudski. The reader also learns about his physical appearance and his inter-

personal strengths and weaknesses. Access to his fantasies is provided through his transference of his own life situation into his serial story of the Laughing Man. The stories provide valuable information about his character since they are paraphrased with little interference from the narrator. However, the information in the Laughing Man narrative must be deciphered with care, and appropriately speculative language should be used when writing about ideas derived from the tale. The knowledge about the Chief that can be culled from events involving the Comanche Club's activities can be considered a more reliable source of information. Nonetheless, an essay dealing with the Chief cannot ignore that this information is sometimes subject to the young narrator's deficient perspicaciousness so far as the adult world is concerned. In contrast, the narrator presents himself in a more direct way since he has knowledge of his own emotions and feelings at the time the events occurred.

Sample Topics:

1. **John Gedsudski (the Chief):** What qualities does the Chief demonstrate through his role as mentor and tutor to the boys of the Comanche Club? What character traits are revealed when the Chief starts dating Mary Hudson?

   Different approaches are possible for an essay on this topic. One option would be to consider the development of the character. To create a valid thesis for this kind of character study, you would need to assess how this character changes throughout the course of the story. How does Gedsudski change toward the boys after he meets Mary Hudson? Another approach would be to analyze the Chief through the allegorical rendering of his life in the Laughing Man serial. For further details on this approach, see the sections "Language, Symbols, and Imagery" and "Compare and Contrast Essays."

2. **The narrator:** What traits define the narrator as a young boy? What insights on his life has the narrator achieved through retrospection?

   An essay on this topic would probably be linked to the theme of the loss of innocence. Although distance from the main events of the story has been created by the narrator's matura-tion, the plot is still largely articulated from the perspective of the innocent young boy with interjections from the older man. One approach to this character would be to analyze his progression from a state of innocence to a state of experience. Another approach would be to consider the young boy's role in understanding the relationship between John and Mary.

History and Context

In 1928, New York was the largest city in the world and was growing steadily as a result of African-Americans fleeing oppression in the South and a vast influx of European immigrants. The latest dance craze for young people was the Charleston. Charlie Chaplin was a popular Hollywood movie star. Children did not sit in front of the television for their entertainment; it had only just been invented. The novel *Lady Chatterley's Lover* by D. H. Law-rence was banned because of its sexual content. Although it was widely believed that women did not have the intellectual capacity to vote, women were enfranchised in 1920 in the United States. Women's newfound sense of liberation was typified by the flapper, a woman who enjoyed a hedonis-tic lifestyle of dancing, drinking, and smoking. She cut her hair short and wore shorter dresses than had been seen in previous centuries. In other words, middle- and upper-class women were challenging the status quo that had pressured them to stay in the background as mothers and wives. As Mary Hudson proves to Gedsudski and the Comanche Club boys, women could excel at activities such as baseball, which had been deemed unladylike and beyond women's capacities. Women were also experiment-ing with their sexuality in a new way. However, despite Margaret Sanger's birth control movement in the 1920s, contraceptive techniques were still haphazard and unreliable. In the lingering Victorian climate of the 1920s, discussions about sex and contraception were considered disgraceful. Abortion was a taboo subject, but an illegal and often dangerous abortion could be procured with money and contacts.

Sample Topics:

1. **New York City, 1928:** How does the 1928 time period affect the events and outcome of the short story? How does the con-text of the 1920s help the reader understand Mary Hudson's behavior?

Mary Hudson has to fight to be considered capable of playing baseball. How else does Mary challenge the norms of womanhood in 1928? There are suggestions (although nothing is confirmed) that, by the end of the story, Mary has become pregnant and that this is the cause of the problems between her and Gedsudski. Using the Laughing Man serial narrative and the final appearance of Mary in the park as evidence, an essay could examine what might be going on behind the scenes with Mary and her father and Gedsudski. Another essay on this topic could use the 1920s backdrop to explain the secretive nature of some aspects of the story and to analyze why Mary and the male characters behave the way they do toward one another.

Philosophy and Ideas

Why do children around the world study literature? A story can transport a child into the past or the future, or to a different place in the present. Human society has been shaped by stories, from early creation myths to modern legends of people achieving massive financial success after having started life in poverty and hardship. Beyond being a form of entertainment, stories can offer knowledge of our world. In "The Laughing Man," there are two main stories that provoke awareness and understanding of the world. The first tale is, patently, the Laughing Man adventure narrative. The Comanche Club boys are described as imagining themselves to be descendants of this superhero. During their ordinary school day, the Laughing Man stories resonate in the boys' day-to-day life, making the mundane appear potentially exciting. The story allows the boys to reconceptualize themselves; it stimulates their imagination to see the possibilities around them. The second important story is the narrator's relation of the events of 1928, when John Gedsudski was the Comanche Club Chief. Through the process of narration, the narrator is trying to make sense of the events that proved critical to his development. A simple story taught him multiple lessons. With the death of the Laughing Man, the narrator as a young boy learned about mortality, finality, the harshness of the world, and the inevitability of transformation. The power of stories in "The Laughing Man" is paralleled by the importance of role models in a young person's life. The Comanche Club boys embrace both Gedsudski and the Laughing Man as formidable male role models in their young lives. The danger of role models is that they can exercise excessive sway over their younger followers, and their position of power could be misused.

Sample Topics:

1. **The power of stories:** How do stories and storytelling affect the narrator in "The Laughing Man"? Why do the Comanche Club boys give such importance to the Laughing Man narrative?

   Stories and storytelling have always played a significant role in the education and acculturation of young (and old) people. How important are stories and storytelling in "The Laughing Man"? How does the process of interpreting stories help the narrator understand his own life? An essay on this topic could consider the impact of stories on the narrator or Gedsudski. Stories have a powerful effect on an audience, but Gedsudski also wields great power in the way he chooses to tell his story.

2. **Role models:** Why do the Comanche Club boys look up to John Gedsudski and the Laughing Man? What effect do the Chief and the Laughing Man have on the young boys?

   The reasons different role models inspire people vary, but, in general, the role model has qualities, attitudes, or attributes that seem admirable and desirable. An essay on this topic could examine how the Chief and his alter ego, the Laughing Man, inspire the boys in his care. This essay could also assess whether Gedsudski abuses his position of power over the boys or whether he teaches them an invaluable life lesson.

Form and Genre

The literary technique of relating a story within a story is a fairly common narrative form that writers use. This technique is known as a frame story. Authors usually deploy the story within the story because of its function in providing insights on the external story. Often, the significance of the internal story will not be made explicit by the author, but the internal story can serve as a kind of allegory for events that happen in the external story. When discussing the use of the frame form in connection with "The Laughing Man," two key questions to consider are why Salinger chose to tell his story using this technique and how this form aids in achieving the goal of the story. The story within the story can also be interpreted through analysis of its allegorical function. An allegory is a story where all the characters and events can be understood as referring, indirectly, to another story or situation. An allegory comments on certain people and events without expressly naming them. It can also be used to satirize or lambaste people in a fictional arena without the repercussions that could occur if the same hostility and fears were expressed about those people directly.

Sample Topics:

1. **"The Laughing Man" as a frame story:** What insights on the events and characters in the external story are revealed though the drama of the internal story? How does the device of a frame story aid in accomplishing the goal of the short story?

The narrator undertakes a journey of growth and awareness through his reevaluation of Gedsudski's Laughing Man narrative. Through hearing the Laughing Man story installment by installment, the reader is able to follow and experience the narrator's journey along with him. An essay analyzing the short story's frame technique could discuss how this form enhances and bolsters some of the main themes and ideas of the story, such as the loss of innocence and the power of stories. The essay could also show how the story within a story is used by Salinger to contribute to the overall framework of conflict between the fantasy world of children and the painful realities of the adult world. As children negotiate the transition between the two worlds, they undergo stages of increasing understanding. How does the frame story reflect this?

2. **The Laughing Man serial narrative as an allegory:** In the Laughing Man saga, who does each character represent in the

main story? What do the Chief's embellishments (in terms of his presentation of the characters in his serial) reveal about his psychological frame of mind and his attitude to the characters in the main story?

If the Laughing Man is understood as the alter ego of John Gedsudski, the other characters in the adventure tale can be identified as corresponding to people in the life of Gedsudski. Are there any characters in the Laughing Man story who do not feature in the main story? Can the reader infer who the additional characters represent in Gedsudski's life? An essay on this topic could analyze who each character symbolizes in the superhero tale and assess how the way that Gedsudski presents them in his story reveals Gedsudski's attitude toward them in his own life. Additionally, the events in the narrative could be an allegorical representation of what is transpiring in the Chief's relationship with Mary Hudson. Since ideas can only be inferred in analyzing the Laughing Man story, an essay on this topic must provide strong textual evidence for any inference that is proposed.

Language, Symbols, and Imagery

As the older, unnamed narrator looks back on his childhood, chunks of his past acquire symbolic weight. It is a common process for humans to reflect on their past and to create links of cause and effect that help explain their current attitudes and behavior. As humans, we have a tendency to make our past into a coherent narrative in which each event logically follows the preceding event. As a consequence of this process, certain people and occurrences stand out in our memory as having contributed significantly to our psychological growth in either a positive or a negative way. Furthermore, adults are inclined to romanticize the period of childhood. With time and distance, it appears to be a carefree, innocent era in stark contrast to the burden of adult responsibilities. The narrator presents his time in the Comanche Club from this idealistic slant. He conjures up memories of baseball games and visits to museums as part of a tight-knit group of boys led fearlessly by the Chief, their icon of successful manhood. The Laughing Man serial adventure story stimulated the narrator's boyish imagination and allowed him to transport himself to a more exciting fantasy life. With hindsight, the narrator suspects that the Chief acted out the drama of his own life through the fictional events, albeit with an added coating of machismo and bravado. The gap that existed between Gedsudski's actual life and his fictional counterpart is symbolized by the poppy-petal mask. The Chief was masking his real feelings from the boys and probably from Mary Hudson. His physical limitations and emotional pain, however, were actualized through his story. The story permitted a glimpse behind his everyday mask.

Sample Topics:

1. **The poppy-petal mask:** What is the function of the poppy-petal mask in the Laughing Man serial narrative? What is the function of the poppy-petal mask in the main story of the Chief and the Comanche Club boys?

   The poppy-petal mask is mentioned at various moments throughout both the Laughing Man adventure story and in the main story of the nameless narrator's experience in the Comanche Club. Masks generally symbolize the concealment of one's true self. Without being able to see a person's face, it becomes difficult to read their reactions or have knowledge of their emotions. A mask is associated with performance, the acting out of simulated emotions and responses to situations. An essay on this topic might address the following questions: Why does the Laughing Man wear a mask? How could this mask be transposed to Gedsudski's own state of being? When and why does Gedsudski wear a mask in his actual life? Why does Omba attempt to replace the mask over the Laughing Man's face, and why is this described as an "act of mercy"? When the narrator sees something resembling a poppy-petal mask at the end of the story, why does this upset the boy so much? What has been revealed to the narrator by the Laughing Man's unmasking?

2. **The Comanche Club:** What is the narrator's attitude toward his time in the Comanche Club? How did the Comanche Club help form the man that the narrator became?

When the narrator gets lost in the Palisades one afternoon, he has faith that the Chief will find him if he sits down and waits. For the narrator, the Chief is a person whom he trusts implicitly. Why does the narrator have so much confidence in the Chief? How does the Chief command respect from his "tribe"? The club itself symbolizes many things to the narrator since it is attached to memories of his carefree and innocent childhood. An essay on the symbolic function of the Comanche Club could take into consideration the effect of the club on the boys, the role of the Chief in creating a protective "tribal" ambiance in the club, and the importance of fantasy and imagination in establishing the loyalty of the tribe to their Chief.

Compare and Contrast Essays

Although the Laughing Man was discussed briefly as the alter ego of John Gedsudski in the "Form and Genre" section as a part of the allegorical analysis, a comparison can also be made focusing on John Gedsudski and the Laughing Man in isolation from the rest of the characters. In an essay on this topic, the purpose of the paper could be to decide how the similarities and differences between the two characters provide psychological insight into the Chief. The other main character in this short story—the narrator—also supplies possibilities for comparison. The protagonist of Salinger's "De Daumier-Smith's Blue Period" is a comparable young man to the narrator in the sense that he gets involved in an episode with an older woman that culminates in a growth of understanding and maturity. With both male characters, this step forward into the adult world is presented by Salinger as essential. The stories show that however compelling the innocence of boyhood may seem, men must leave this safe haven behind in order to function effectively. Furthermore, both stories share a focus on the role of the artist and art in society. This is a theme that runs throughout several of Salinger's works, such as *Seymour: An Introduction,* and the artist is portrayed comparably in each text.

Sample Topics:

1. **The Laughing Man compared to John Gedsudski:** What are the similarities between John Gedsudski and his fictional creation, the Laughing Man? How do the differences between the two characters inform the reader about Gedsudski's fears and fantasies?

Many people wish that their physical appearance was different. Many people fantasize and daydream, giving themselves more admirable traits and qualities than they have in their real life. In some cases, people express such fears and dreams through artistic representation. Which physical and mental attributes (which he manifests through his depiction of the Laughing Man) does the Chief dislike in himself? An essay comparing these two characters would need to take into consideration the gap between fantasy and reality. Gedsudski's unintentional revelations of his own strengths and weaknesses help the reader understand why his relationship with Mary Hudson is beset by problems.

2. **The unnamed narrator in "The Laughing Man" versus Jean de Daumier-Smith:** How does a woman inadvertently teach both young men some fundamental truths about life? In retrospect, how does each male character look back on his youthful innocence?

Defining moments in a person's life may come to symbolize the transition from innocence and ignorance to knowledge and understanding. In both "The Laughing Man" and "De Daumier-Smith's Blue Period," the male protagonists relate their story from a position of greater wisdom as they mull over a critical period in their past. This retrospection shows each character as having successfully moved beyond the ignorance of his earlier condition to a state of greater understanding of himself and his world. An essay on these two men could be approached through an analysis that compares the development of each male character that has culminated in his ability to assess his past more objectively. In both cases, artistic representations, women, and a significant male father figure play a role in each boy's development.

3. **The role of art and the artist in "The Laughing Man" and "De Daumier-Smith's Blue Period":** How is the artist portrayed in each short story? What is the function of art in each short story?

The role of the artist and art in society is a common theme in Salinger's work. Although the artistic medium differs in the two stories, artists in each story suffer comparable angst. Perhaps more important, some of the creative products in each case (the serial story in "The Laughing Man" and Sister Irma's painting in "De Daumier-Smith's Blue Period") are received comparably by their audience. Another similarity between the two stories is the connection between the artist and his or her artistic creation. An essay on this topic could analyze the bond between artists and their art, the way their art is received by audiences, and the long-term effect of their art on their audience.

Bibliography

French, Warren. "A Nine Story Cycle." *J. D. Salinger, Revisited.* Boston: Twayne, 1988. 72–74.

Goldstein, Bernice, and Sanford Goldstein. "Zen and *Nine Stories.*" *J. D. Salinger: Modern Critical Views.* Ed. Harold Bloom. New York: Chelsea House, 1987. 81–93.

Wenke, John. "Nine Stories." *J. D. Salinger: A Study of the Short Fiction.* Boston: Twayne, 1991. 43–46.

"DOWN AT THE DINGHY"

READING TO WRITE

THE JEWISH presence in the United States has been consolidated by waves of immigration from Europe throughout the centuries. In the late 19th century, Jews fleeing persecution in the Russian empire and other parts of Eastern Europe accounted for a notable increase in the United States' Jewish population. As a consequence, in the early decades of the 20th century, anti-Semitic sentiments started to escalate. Immigration restrictions were put in place. Tapping into the anti-Semitic zeitgeist of the 1930s and 1940s, some American politicians and prominent figures felt comfortable making hostile comments about the hypothetical threat that Jewish people posed to the United States' national security.

In this story, the maid Sandra has referred to her employer as a "sloppy kike." Considering the anti-Semitic climate in the United States in the mid to late 1940s, Sandra's confident and flippant slurs are par for the course. She is not troubled by guilt or shame for the derogatory name she has called Mr. Tannenbaum. Her only concern is whether the child who overheard her will repeat what he knows to his mother. If he does, she runs the risk of losing her job:

"I'm not worryin' about it," Sandra responded. "The last thing I'm gonna do is worry about it. Only, it drives ya loony, the way that kid goes pussyfootin' all around the house. Ya can't hear him, ya know. I mean nobody can hear him, ya know. Just the other day I was shellin' beans—right at this here table—and I almost stepped on his hand. He was sittin' right under the table."

"Well. I wouldn't worry about it."

"I mean ya gotta weigh every word ya say around him," Sandra said. "It drives ya loony."

"I still can't drink this," Mrs. Snell said. ". . . That's terrible. When ya gotta weigh every word ya say and all."

"It drives ya loony! I mean it. Half the time I'm half loony." Sandra brushed some imaginary crumbs off her lap, and snorted. "A four-year-old kid!"

"He's kind of a good-lookin' kid," said Mrs. Snell. "Them big brown eyes and all."

Sandra snorted again. "He's gonna have a nose just like the father." She raised her cup and drank from it without any difficulty.

Rather than accept any kind of responsibility for the consequences of her prejudice, Sandra blames the child for her predicament. Even though Lionel is only four years old, Sandra cannot see beyond what she perceives as his Jewish genetic inheritance. The child creeps around his parents' house. This comment insinuates that there is something underhanded about the boy, tapping into a common stereotype that Jews cannot be trusted because they are likely to use dishonest means to get what they want. Furthermore, Lionel cannot be considered handsome by Sandra because his nose is going to become quintessentially Jewish. Anti-Semitism is still a major issue in the world today, and an essay on this critical topic could consider it within the context of the attitudes of the postwar period in the United States. In the story, Sandra does not doubt for one moment that Mrs. Snell shares her sense of superiority toward the Jewish Tannenbaums.

Salinger's loathing of anti-Semitic sentiment is brought out through his characterization of Sandra and Mrs. Snell. He clearly attributes racial hatred and stereotyping to ignorance. The two women are shown in this extract as extremely limited in their cognitive skills. Their vocabulary is repetitive and unsophisticated. Mrs. Snell is preoccupied with her cup of tea and fails to see why Sandra would waste time worrying about her quandary. The two women never consider the pain Sandra may have caused to a young child and his family. They place the blame squarely on Lionel because he inhibits Sandra from freely speaking her mind. Analysis of the two women can be approached from different angles. For example, they could be the subjects of character studies, they could be discussed from the viewpoint of class since they are the domestic servants of the wealthier Tannenbaums, or they could provide textual evidence for an analysis of the theme of communication.

The most significant sentence in the excerpt that showcases Sandra's unquestioning anti-Semitism is the final sentence, which explains how she drinks from her cup of hot tea "without any difficulty." On the one hand, this sentence can be read literally. Mrs. Snell is struggling to drink her tea because it is so hot, whereas Sandra is able to ingest hers easily. On the other hand, this sentence immediately follows her extremely offensive observation about Lionel's nose resembling his father's. Thus, the descriptive sentence seems to refer back to her prejudiced comment because of its textual contiguity. In other words, her racism surfaces without any difficulty. Salinger's stories are permeated by ambiguities and uncertainties in terms of plot, characterization, and, in this case, language. The plot of "Down at the Dinghy" hinges on language confusion when Lionel mistakes "kike" for "kite." The problems that are inherent in communication and language could become the subject of an essay. As this short story demonstrates, a single word can cause chaos.

TOPICS AND STRATEGIES

The balance of this chapter will suggest topics related to "Down at the Dinghy" and a variety of approaches that could be used to write essays on those topics. The suggested ideas should be used to help develop your own slant on these topics.

Themes

Can a Jewish child grow up in the United States without ever being singled out as a target for anti-Semitic prejudice? Should a young child be taught about the evils of racism? Boo Boo Tannenbaum, in "Down at the

Dinghy," is faced with the critical choice of instructing her young son in the realities of the adult world or leaving him in his innocence for a while longer. She decides to leave him in his current state of knowledge, which she deems suitable for a four year-old. In Lionel's world, the venomous domestic help has called his father a "sloppy kite." This phrase would have various negative connotations for the boy since Sandra's tone would no doubt have conveyed her racist hatred. The boy has had a brief history of being pained by other people's unkind words and, on each occasion, has run away from home to escape his hurt. Since his mother must fear for his safety whenever the boy disappears, she may feel that it is better for him to learn the full truth about other people's cruelty when he is better able to manage that knowledge.

Having a conversation with someone where certain things are left unsaid, where the full truth is not disclosed, or where the two conversers are talking at cross-purposes is, sadly, very common. In this story, there are several conversations where the communication is not completely successful for various reasons. One of the reasons communication can fail is that one or both of the participants in the conversation are playing a role. The motive for playing the role can be positive. This is the case when Boo Boo pretends to her son that she is an admiral, in the hope that he will respond to her "man to man." The motives for role-playing can also be negative. This is the case when Sandra pretends to be interested in the history of Lionel's running away from home. She probably hopes to demonstrate concern for her employer's child and put herself in a good light, thereby minimizing the chance of being dismissed from her job.

Sample Topics:

1. **A child's innocence:** How does Lionel respond to assaults against his innocent outlook on life? How do Sandra and Boo Boo relate to Lionel's innocent condition?

Many human beings, be they child or adult, do not enjoy having their illusions of a perfect world shattered. An essay on this topic could discuss Lionel's behavior when incidents in his short life have forced him to face evil and negativity. Why does he run away? Why does he never get very far? Adults who have lost their innocence take up different stances toward a child's innocence, often depending on their relationship with a particular child. A mother will usually try to protect her child, whereas a prejudiced stranger might doubt a child's presumed innocence. Sandra, for example, talks as if Lionel was born with the negative characteristics and values that she attributes to Jews. Thus, another approach to this topic would be to analyze how adults react to a child's presumed innocent condition and why they do so.

2. **The failure of communication:** How do the different conversations in the story fail to convey truth and understanding between the conversers? What features of the different conversations cause communication to break down?

The story is structured around three conversations. The first one involves Sandra and Mrs. Snell, who interrupt each other constantly, talk at cross-purposes, and ultimately do not complete the most critical part of their dialogue. The second conversation occurs when Boo Boo joins the two older women in the kitchen and they discuss Lionel's habit of running away. The tenor of this conversation is in marked contrast to the one the women shared prior to Boo Boo's entrance. The third conversation involves Boo Boo and her son. It, too, stumbles against misunderstandings and deception, even though Boo Boo's motives are to help her son. An essay on the subject of communication could analyze how these three conversations are marred. What happens during conversations that prevent people from properly listening or understanding each other?

3. **Role-playing:** Why do the adult characters assume different roles for themselves and pretend to be people they are not? How does Lionel react to his mother's role-playing?

When someone plays a role, he or she adopts a different personality in order to achieve a specific goal. This short story depicts all its featured adult characters as playing roles in different ways. Mrs. Snell uses fashion accessories to prove to the world that she is worth more than being "just a cleaner" might imply. Sandra switches personality the minute her employer enters a room. Her vitriolic, angry demeanor metamorphoses into that of a concerned and loving member of the household. Boo Boo acts out the role of admiral in an attempt to catch her son's imagination and interest. An essay on this topic might evaluate the success of each adult's role-playing. What are the motivations for role-playing in adults? Does role-playing achieve its goals?

Character

Sandra is a character whom Salinger has rendered with few redeeming traits. She is racist, vicious, unintelligent, and hypocritical. Her representation conveys Salinger's antipathy for anti-Semitism. Sandra cannot stoop much lower than accusing a four-year-old child of being the problem because he overheard her derogatory comments. Salinger signals his distaste for this character through her dialogue and mannerisms. Mrs. Snell is not spared the taint of mockery and disdain either. Although she is not actively anti-Semitic in the way that Sandra is, she passively accepts everything she hears at the kitchen table. She does not remonstrate with Sandra. Her proposal is simply that Sandra should start looking for a new job. Boo Boo's entrance into the kitchen establishes a marked contrast between the two working women and their employer. Boo Boo is young and physically childlike, whereas the two domestic helpers are old and womanly. In other Salinger works (*Franny and Zooey* and *Raise High the Roof Beam, Carpenters and Seymour: An Introduction*), Boo Boo is referred to as if she is the most psychologically stable of all the Glass brothers and sisters. She certainly leads the most conventional lifestyle of all the Glass siblings: married with children. "Down at the Dinghy" is the only Salinger text where Boo Boo claims the primary role.

Sample Topics:

1. **Working women:** How do Sandra's syntax and diction indicate her lack of education and intelligence? How is Sandra's physical appearance used to demean her character?

Salinger usually depicts characters who are obliged to do domestic work for a living sympathetically. Sandra, however, is so lacking in intelligence and empathy for others that she is one of Salinger's least likable secondary characters. Sandra is used by Salinger to represent specific human qualities and traits. An essay could analyze the qualities that Sandra personifies. This topic could be extended to include an appraisal of Mrs. Snell. Her pretentiousness and self-absorption fortify Salinger's contemptuous portrayal of these working women. How does Salinger use class stereotypes to characterize them? An essay could consider the irony of activating class stereotypes in a story that aims to expose the insidious nature of Jewish racial profiling.

2. **Boo Boo Tannenbaum:** What techniques does Salinger deploy to make Boo Boo appealing to readers? How does Boo Boo differ from Sandra and Mrs. Snell in terms of physical appearance, attitudes, and behavior?

In most of Salinger's fiction, women who are wealthy wives and mothers are portrayed as superficial and narcissistic. Boo Boo, however, is shown to be a supportive, loving mother and wife. Even though she is part of a visibly Jewish family, her assimilation into upper-middle-class American society is evinced by the lake house and the engagement of domestic staff. What allows Boo Boo to transcend the banality of WASP values? The narrator describes her as "a stunning and final girl." Why does Salinger present her sympathetically? An essay on Boo Boo could analyze her qualities and traits that prevent her from being sucked into suburban vacuity.

History and Context

Jews have never been readily embraced by Christian America since their early arrival from Europe in the late 1700s. Salinger's father was Jewish, and his grandfather was a rabbi at one time in his life. However, Salinger's father married a Christian, and business success made moves into better houses in desirable WASP neighborhoods possible. Even if the Salinger family did not affirm their Jewish faith and identity, Salinger could not fail to be aware of the anti-Semitic climate of the United States as he was growing up. Nevertheless, "Down at the Dinghy" is the only one of Salinger's published short stories that addresses the issue of racism. "Down at the Dinghy" was originally published in 1949 in *Harper's* magazine. The period before and after World War II was an age when anti-Semitism was rampant in the United States, even though more than half a million Jewish men fought for the United States in the war. Despite official restrictions that were put in place to limit Jewish immigration and despite the reluctance of the United States government to rescue Jews from the Holocaust, the Jewish population in America continued to grow as people sought sanctuary from persecution from around the world. A common mind-set in this period was that Jews were not only different from Christians but also inferior. This assertion of fundamental difference justified exclusionary and racist treatment against the Jewish population. Salinger sought to show in his story how children as young as four years old can be the targets of racism.

Sample Topics:

1. **Anti-Semitism in the United States in the mid-20th century:** Anti-Semitism in the United States was widespread in the period after World War II. How does Salinger show racism to be a normalized American attitude among the non-Jewish population in his story? How does anti-Semitism in the story affect its victims?

Salinger depicts the corruption of a child's innocence through anti-Semitism. For an essay on this topic, you would probably need to do some historical research in order to obtain information concerning the treatment of Jews in the United States during this period. One place to look for articles and references on American anti-Semitism is the Jewish Virtual Library (http://www.jewishvirtuallibrary.org). A possible approach to this topic would be to examine the connection between racism and ignorance, jealousy, and resentment, since this is a link that Salinger stresses in this story. Another approach could assess the different responses to anti-Semitism that are shown through the different characters. For example, how does Boo Boo react when learning of her maid's anti-Semitism?

Philosophy and Ideas

Boo Boo tells Sandra and Mrs. Snell that her son has a history of running away from home. He reacted strongly when another child told him that he stank, causing him to flee into Central Park. He also ran off after hearing a friend's comment that there was a worm in her thermos flask. After overhearing Sandra's derogatory comment about his father, young Lionel runs down to a dinghy and acts out another escape. All of these escapades have happened within the four years of the child's short life. Thus, the boy seems to have a heightened sensibility and sensitivity, making him a typical Glass child. Lionel drops his Uncle Seymour's goggles into the water when he is sitting in the dinghy. This establishes a bond between the two characters, especially since Seymour committed suicide shortly after having gone swimming. However, since the boy is still so young, his mother is able to steer him out of his emotional retreat from the horrors of the adult world by bribing him with keys, pickles, and an outing to the station. Her mothering abilities are presented in the story as superior. She deploys several strategies to try to communicate with her son, gain his trust, and make him tell her the nature of his problem. The trust is created by an exchange where she gives her son a bunch of keys and he looks at her with "pure perception." Lionel throws the keys into the lake—as presumably Boo Boo had known he would—and, at this moment, mother and son understand each other perfectly.

Sample Topics:

1. **Sensitivity and sensibility:** How does Lionel demonstrate a heightened response to matters of feeling? How does he show that he is emotionally sensitive? What qualities make Lionel a typical Glass child?

The accounts of Lionel's behavior portray him as special: He is not a typical four-year-old boy. His penchant for marbles, his silence, and his precocious refusal to be manipulated by Boo

Boo's role-playing categorize him as a classic Glass child. How else is Lionel set up by Salinger to be a prototypal Glass child? When his mother eventually gives him the bunch of keys, what might be the basis of the child's "pure perception"? What is he is able to intuit at that moment? How does Salinger portray this child's unusual behavior? An essay on Lionel's sensibility and sensitivity could analyze the child from the angle that he is one of Salinger's quintessential gifted children.

2. **Motherhood:** What qualities does Salinger propose make Boo Boo an effective mother? How does she win the battle of wills with her son?

Boo Boo is described as physically childlike, yet she is adult enough to be able to connect with her child and salve his mental wounds when he is suffering emotionally. What techniques does Boo Boo use to make her son return to the real world and abandon his fantasy of escape? How successful are these techniques? An essay on the concept of motherhood could determine whether she has indeed "lost" the race at the end of the story or whether she wins. Parents often let their child win a running race or a game in order to bolster that child's self-esteem. Another approach to this topic would be to consider the possibility that Salinger is ironic in the final sentence of the story. In what ways could Lionel be understood as having "won" the confrontation with his mother and his conflict with the adult world? If this child is put in the context of other Glass children and special child characters, remaining an innocent child and eating pickles is infinitely more desirable than being taught the realities of anti-Semitism.

Language, Symbols, and Imagery

When Lionel throws a pair of underwater goggles into the lake, his mother informs him that they once belonged to his Uncle Seymour. This information changes the reader's understanding of the significance of the goggles. From being a commonplace object that could readily be found in a boat, the goggles acquire associations with death and the rejection of middle-class values. "A Perfect Day for Bananafish" describes how going swimming with a child was Seymour's final activity before committing suicide. As a result of Lionel's action, the goggles sink to the bottom of the lake. His decision to flip them into the water is a spontaneous response to his mother's request for an explanation as to why he is running away from home. Thus, he becomes tied to Seymour through the object, but he also could be interpreted as intuitively repudiating everything that the goggles signify. Keys are objects that are connected to adult responsibility. Young children rarely have keys and therefore are often fascinated by them, seeing them as toys. When Boo Boo throws her son the set of keys, his eyes are described as registering "pure perception." The bunch of keys is seemingly an object of barter that both mother and son understand and agree on. Boo Boo's decision to give Lionel the keys is the event that leads her son to allow her to board the dinghy and comfort him. Before this moment, the dinghy has been his sacred domain, a symbolic place of isolation and escape. The goggles, the keys, and the dinghy are three elements of this short story whose symbolic meaning could be the focal point of an essay.

Sample Topics:

1. **The goggles, the keys, and the dinghy:** How do the three objects link to Lionel's desire to evade the horrors of the adult world? Why does Lionel not want his mother to join him in the boat?

Why does Lionel respond to emotional pain with flight? An essay on these symbolic objects could approach them through an analysis of the interplay between a child's world and an adult world. In "A Perfect Day for Bananafish," Seymour prefers the innocence of children to adult hypocrisy and banality. In Sybil Carpenter, Seymour possibly perceives the inevitable corruption of a child's innocence caused by interaction with the world. What are the differences between Sybil and Lionel in terms of the way they interact with the adults around them? How is Lionel's attitude toward the adult world acted out through his handling of the goggles, keys, and dinghy? When his mother hands her son the keys, she appears fully aware that he is going to throw them in the lake. Why does she give them to him? Symbolically, what is she giving him the key to? What does he perceive at the moment she tosses them to him? After he throws the keys in the water, he sobs and turns to his mother for consolation. What is the connection between throwing the keys away and his subsequent behavior?

Compare and Contrast Essays

Salinger's child characters are often shown to be mentally assaulted by the adult world's hypocrisies and evils. To protect their innocent goodness, these children retreat into a fantasy world where they can shut out the threat the adult world poses. Through insularity and isolation, they can retain their integrity, although Salinger shows that they cannot elude the pull of the adult world forever. Lionel and Ramona in "Uncle Wiggily in Connecticut" are two very young child characters who, for comparable reasons, have devised strategies to help them cope with adult attacks on their innocent goodness. A significant difference between them, though, is that Lionel has a supportive and caring mother, whereas Ramona's mother is the main cause of the child's suffering. Nonetheless, adults are the ones who threaten the rectitude of the children's world, and their shared response to adult brutality is a retreat into the imagination with the creation of an alternative world.

Sample Topics:

1. **Lionel and Ramona:** Why do these two young children feel under attack from the adult world? How do they each try to create a safe place where they can be in control of what happens to them?

An essay comparing these two children could analyze them from the perspective of children's innocence versus adult corruption. How does each child attempt to retain the purity of his or her mind and existence? How does each child try to avoid being implicated in the duplicity of the adult world? How do adults both help and damage the children? What is Salinger's perspective on children's innocence?

Bibliography

French, Warren. "A Nine Story Cycle." *J. D. Salinger, Revisited*. Boston: Twayne, 1988. 74–76.

Goldstein, Bernice, and Sanford Goldstein. "Zen and *Nine Stories*." *J. D. Salinger: Modern Critical Views*. Ed. Harold Bloom. New York: Chelsea House, 1987. 81–93.

Wenke, John. "Nine Stories." *J. D. Salinger: A Study of the Short Fiction*. Boston: Twayne, 1991. 46–49.

"FOR ESMÉ—WITH LOVE AND SQUALOR"

READING TO WRITE

The title of the short story "For Esmé—with Love and Squalor" identifies the critical contrast between love and squalor that structures
the story, determines the characterization, and governs the thematic
focus. In the first half of the story, when Sergeant X meets Esmé in an
English tearoom, the seeds of love and compassion between two lonely
people are sown. When the protagonist is deployed in Germany and
suffers the ravages of war, he narrates the squalid part of the story.
Salinger uses a shifting narrative point of view to register the deteriorating mental state of his protagonist. In Germany, as the following excerpt illustrates, Sergeant X writes about himself in the third
person:

Written in ink, in German, in a small, hopelessly sincere handwriting, were the words "Dear God, life is hell." Nothing led up to
or away from it. Alone on the page, and in the sickly stillness of the
room, the words appeared to have the stature of an uncontestable,
even classic indictment. X stared at the page for several minutes,
trying, against heavy odds, not to be taken in. Then, with far more
zeal than he had done anything in weeks, he picked up a pencil
stub and wrote down under the inscription, in English, "Fathers
and teachers, I ponder 'What is hell?' I maintain that it is the suffering of being unable to love." He started to write Dostoyevski's
name under the inscription, but saw—with fright that ran through

his whole body—that what he had written was almost entirely illegible. He shut the book.

An essay might map the evolution of the narrative point of view and link it to the development of X's character. The effect of using a third-person limited narrative point of view to write about himself emphasizes X's sense of dislocation. A loss of identity is one legacy that the brutality of combat has bequeathed to him. Suffering from shell shock, his sensitive nature is subject to numerous assaults from the carelessness and thoughtlessness of those in contact with him. His isolation and alienation from other soldiers and from those back home in the United States is underscored by his decision to refer to himself as Sergeant X. A man without a name and without the resolve to call himself "I" is nobody.

The force that can compel X to evolve from nobody to somebody is the force of love. An analysis of the theme of love could consider the relationship between X and Esmé and discuss how love and compassion heal the damaged solider and allow him to return to the land of the living. At the time when X is reading the Nazi woman's inscription, he is lost in squalor. Nonetheless, as the excerpt shows, he still affirms the redemptive power of love. The assertion that "life is hell" resonates with X, since he is being pummeled by his own private demons. The imagery used in the excerpt reinforces notions of stagnation, isolation, and decay. The words are "[a]lone on the page." The alliteration used in the phrase "sickly stillness" helps convey the idea of life as an endless experience of suffering. Reading the Nazi woman's words is a turning point for X. He musters all his resources to resist their destructive pull into the void. He attempts to fight back with more words, the words of Father Zossima, a Russian priest who exhorts other characters to love and forgive, from Fyodor Dostoyevsky's *The Brothers Karamazov* (1879–1880). Father Zossima's message is one of universal love. Directly following the statement that X quotes, Father Zossima adds that the purpose of life is to recognize the moment of love when it is offered. With the recognition of love, the priest argues, a human being then has the capacity to say, "I am and I love." Love allows forgiveness of other's sins, kindles an appreciation of the divine, and awakens a sense of self in unity with others.

The tragedy for Sergeant X is that his words of love are "illegible." The German words of the Nazi woman are fixed in time and place. Nothing is attached to them; they are not part of a dialogue. They stand as a final judgment. X wants to enter into a dialogue through his application of Dostoyevsky's words, but he does not have the power to invalidate the words of the Nazis. This implies that, at this moment in the story, affirmation of love cannot conquer squalor. An essay could analyze how the two forces of evil and good battle in X's mind. Following Father Zossima's reasoning, the story appears to show the triumph of love, and this is made clear by Salinger through X's ability to refer to himself as "I" at the beginning of the story. The transcendent experience of love can be fleeting, but this should not negate its lasting effect throughout a person's life. However, the tone and diction used by X to refer to his wife and his mother-in-law seemingly relocate X firmly back in squalor.

An overall message of universal love is one that Salinger has returned to in several of his works. Zooey and Buddy Glass promulgated comparable ideas in *Franny and Zooey* and *Raise High the Roof Beam, Carpenters and Seymour: An Introduction.* Comparative essays become possible as a result of the thematic similarities between these texts. Seymour is a World War II veteran who also does not survive the war with all his "faculties intact." In "A Perfect Day for Bananafish," Seymour loses himself in an insipid marriage, living in a banal society. At the beginning of "For Esmé—with Love and Squalor," we find X in a comparable situation, living with a wife who inhibits him from doing what he wants to do, enforcing the socially correct course of action on him. An essay could compare these two characters in terms of their response to their war experiences. Is it knowledge of love that saves Sergeant X and lack of love that pushes Seymour to commit suicide?

TOPICS AND STRATEGIES

Possible essay topics will be discussed in the remainder of this chapter. Various approaches to those topics will also be proposed. These suggestions should help you generate your own ideas and approaches to writing a paper on "For Esmé—with Love and Squalor."

Themes

Love is usually pitted against hate. However, in this short story, the apparent opposite of love is squalor, the state of being filthy or wretched.

Squalor encompasses suggestions of foulness and dirtiness, brought on by poverty or, sometimes, moral degradation. This unusual yoking together of love and squalor is occasioned by Esmé. She requests that Sergeant X write a short story for her about squalor. In an English setting, her precocious choice of this word reeks of class privilege. The slums of London were regularly labeled squalid by the upper classes, and the pejorative use of the word implies a state of moral ruin for the people who live in squalid conditions. When Sergeant X finds himself immersed in the squalor of Nazi Germany, the connotation of moral degradation is applicable. There is no morality in a society that can carry out the annihilation of people based on nothing more than ethnicity or religious belief. Sergeant X ponders the possibility that life is hell. If squalor is the maltreatment of humans by humans, love is instated as its opposite in this story. Love is not defined as romantic love between two people but rather is a universal love, founded on forgiveness and charity. Love is an approach to life wherein a person recognizes the connection between self and other. When one stranger reaches out in compassion to another stranger, an act of love occurs. For this transmission of love to take place, there must be human contact. Relationships in this short story, however, do not all have the purity of Esmé's friendship with Sergeant X. Sergeant X's comrade-in-arms, Clay, shows how relationships can fail to attain a moment of understanding. In this story, there are more relationships that are marked by battles for supremacy and control than there are relationships that are giving and unselfish.

Communication is the key to forging effective relationships. A variety of forms of communication are illustrated in "For Esmé—with Love and Squalor." Predictably, there is dialogue. The conversation with Esmé, however, contrasts significantly with X's exchange with Clay in terms of tenor and content. Another form of communication is writing. Again, Esmé's letter is distinguished from the letter that X receives from his brother. Finally, communication can occur nonverbally. Esmé offers Sergeant X a kiss, using her brother Charles as their go-between. She also sends X her watch as a symbol of her love. In general, communication can create a bond between two people or it can prompt someone to doubt the value of life.

Sample Topics:

1. **Love:** How does "For Esmé—with Love and Squalor" reveal itself to be a love story? How is the love between the characters

shown? What social and personal factors obstruct the transmission of love between characters?

Essays on the theme of love can be approached from different angles. One possible approach is to analyze the occurrences of love that the story describes and show the power they have to overwrite the incidences of squalor. Another essay could focus on the different manifestations of love to demonstrate how love takes different forms. Esmé demonstrates a kind of maternal love toward Charles, who seems to want to keep Esmé's attention focused on himself. The love between Esmé and Sergeant X could be described as filial, symbolized by Esmé's gift of her father's watch to X. The act of "writing" the short story for Esmé can be analyzed as an act of love. The notion of universal love is also introduced by means of the quotation from Dostoyevsky. See the "Reading to Write" section for a discussion of this quotation.

2. **Squalor:** In this story, what aspects of the war-era society are presented as squalid? Why is Esmé drawn to squalor? How does X manage to elude succumbing to squalor?

"Squalor" is an unusual word choice from an unusual child character. In this story, squalor functions as the iniquitous underbelly of humankind that, during the time of World War II, seemed to have the capacity to overturn all that was affirmative in human interactions. The Nazi mentality, epitomized by Joseph Goebbels, and the seeming ease with which so many people accepted Nazi tenets showed how the evil side of humans could prevail. An essay on the theme of squalor could examine the irony of Esmé's being drawn to squalor. For her, squalor is equated with the realities of adult life. What has happened to this young girl that makes her reject everything "childish and silly"? Other approaches would be to discuss the prevalence and meaning of squalor throughout the story or to analyze which characters are linked to squalor and why. Which characters attempt to rise above their squalid condition, and which characters are at home in squalor?

3. **Communication:** In the story, which conversation epitomizes successful communication and which conversation illustrates unsuccessful communication? Similarly, which letter exemplifies how communication can be beneficial and which letter depicts how communication can be damaging?

An essay based on this theme could analyze both the positive and the negative that can result from an act of communication. This essay could discuss the different forms of communication that are described in the story in order to determine what leads to effective or ineffective communication. Letters and dialogue are the main forms of communication in the story, but there are also other types of communication. Orders from one human to another, messages, books, gestures, humor, and physical appearance are other ways that humans communicate critical information to each other in this story.

4. **Relationships:** Identify the different types of relationships that are presented in this story. What point is Salinger making about human interaction through his presentation of these various relationships? How does Salinger portray marriage in the story? How does he present family relationships?

To write an essay based on an examination of relationships, a first step would be to determine what Salinger's attitude is toward them by looking at the different types of relationships depicted in the story. For example, X's marriage is portrayed as restrictive. Take a look at other family relationships in the story. How does Salinger represent them? For example, what is the nature of the sibling relationship between Esmé and Charles? A paper could examine the way that difficult personal relationships affect a particular character. Such an essay could examine the relationship between X and his jeep partner Clay. This relationship is critical in that each man depends on the other for his safety, yet at the same time, there is a gulf of misunderstanding between them. An alternative line of enquiry would be to examine what Salinger imputes as the causes of difficult personal relationships.

Character

Esmé's upper-class English upbringing has left its mark on her. However, the truth behind the stiff upper lip is made manifest by certain physical signs and certain topics of conversation that she touches on with Sergeant X. For example, when talking about her parents, Esmé bites her fingernails. When she bids X goodbye, her hand is damp with nervousness. She admits that her own father accused her of being humorless. Esmé is a 13-year-old orphan who appears to be emotionally responsible for her younger brother, Charles. Later, she writes that she has been "justifiably saddled" with responsibilities when her aunt becomes ill with streptococcus. This is a child who has been raised to accept her responsibilities and duties. The fact that there is so little indication of her trauma is more surprising than the fact that there are slight signs of a lack of composure. The most surprising aspect of Esmé's character is her capacity to reach out to strangers with compassion. The character she extends her compassion to is Sergeant X, a multifaceted soldier character who is shown in three different time frames. In each setting, his personality has altered. Essays on this character could trace his development throughout the story. Although his conversation with Esmé is sometimes awkward and sometimes antagonistic, both realize that a moment of affinity has transpired as a result of their meeting. Their encounter is definitely not a meeting of the body, not exactly a meeting of the mind, but more a meeting of the soul.

Similarly, Charles's presence in the English tearoom creates a moment of joy for X. The young boy acts on impulse and, like many small children, wants to be the center of attention even in an adult conversation. The boy's riddle provides one key to his function as a character in the short story. The riddle's answer speaks of two walls coming together. The endless repetition of it achieves the goal of bringing two strangers together.

Sample Topics:

1. **Esmé:** In what ways does Esmé stand out to X when he sees her for the first time in the children's choir? Why does Esmé talk to

Sergeant X in the tearoom? What makes Esmé's conversation with X an important part of both their lives?

A character study on Esmé would have to acknowledge that she is presented by Salinger with both positive and negative qualities. X's first sighting of Esmé shows her to be bored and slightly arrogant, even as she sings angelically. Her arrogance is brought out later in her conversation with X. Notably, she thinks X, as an American, will be impressed by her title. Her precociousness is mocked by her tendency to misuse and mispronounce certain words. On the other hand, her negative qualities are overridden by her positive traits. Her kindheartedness and her recognition of X's loneliness resonate in his otherwise empty life. A paper on Esmé could also analyze how she embodies the essence of universal love, the force that has the power to conquer squalor.

2. **Sergeant X:** How does Sergeant X develop throughout the story? Why does he not survive the war with all his "faculties intact"? How does Esmé help him?

A sensitive soul will have a difficult time in a war environment. X's isolation is described by Salinger right from the start, as all the soldiers keep to themselves in his military unit. X's cavalier attitude toward his fate is signaled by his feelings toward his gas mask and toward lightning. However, a 13-year-old girl is able to connect with him and make him grasp that life is about love. An essay on X could either chart his development throughout the story or show how he embodies a conflict between love and squalor, or argue that X illustrates that being open to relationships can help overcome alienation.

3. **Charles:** How does Charles personify innocence and spontaneity? What is Charles's function in the short story?

The innocence of young children holds redemptive power for adults in many Salinger stories. Charles is not presented as an angelic child. Esmé struggles to make him behave in public, and he sulks when X destroys his riddling fun by giving the answer. He is spoiled and indulged. Conversely, there is nothing phony about him. His behavior confirms that he has not yet been molded by his society to repress his emotions or act according to social mores. An essay on Charles could examine his presentation as a quintessential Salinger child character.

History and Context

In 1942, every G.I. preparing to go to England was given a manual titled *Instructions for American Servicemen in Britain*. This guide attempted to clarify some of the common misunderstandings that occur between Americans and the English. American good intentions notwithstanding, the predominant English attitude toward American G.I.s when they went to England was "They are overpaid, oversexed and they are over here!" From the English perspective at that time, Americans were loud, uncultured, and boorish. Esmé's labeling of Americans as "animals" who go around punching and insulting everyone reflects a common English attitude toward the visiting horde of American soldiers. Since she lives in Devon, a quiet and rather isolated region of England, an American presence would have been the talk of the town. Stereotyped perceptions of each side of the Atlantic still abound, but the British mix of fascination and antipathy toward Americans was solidified during World War II. X's conversation with Clay is juxtaposed with his dialogue with Esmé to bring out the contrasting features of each exchange. Regurgitating an English stereotype of Americans, Esmé cruelly observes to Sergeant X that he seemed "quite intelligent for an American." X rightly reprimands her for this brash generalization. However, Salinger then gives us X's dialogue with Clay, an insensitive American character who fits the British stereotype aptly.

Many soldiers suffer psychological trauma as a result of combat. Definitive statistics on soldiers who may have been affected as a consequence of World War II are hard to find. Many may not have had their symptoms properly diagnosed, and some may have tried to deal with their combat stress without official treatment. Sergeant X is described as a "young man who had not come through the war with all his faculties intact." The story mentions that X has been in hospital for two weeks.

The details of his hospitalization are not provided, but X still has symptoms such as a lack of concentration, tics, shaking hands, and sensitivity to bright light. The implication is that he has been discharged and put back into service prematurely. In what ways does X differ from Clay—as a soldier and as a human being? Why has Clay passed through the war unscathed?

Sample Topics:

1. **The American G.I. in England:** How does Salinger both challenge and bolster English stereotypes of the American G.I.? How does Esmé both dismantle and confirm American stereotypes of the British?

The small town Devon setting is a perfect locale for the conflict between American soldiers and English civilians to be enacted. The traditional 1940s English lifestyle of tea and church exists in stark contrast to the tense existence of a group of American soldiers waiting to be shipped overseas for D-Day. Esmé's interest in the American presence, however, would have been typical. An essay on the topic of English and American stereotypes could compare the representations of Esmé and Clay to determine how Salinger plays into but also questions the common stereotypes of that time. The essay could also take into consideration the English choir coach and Miss Megley. Where does Sergeant X fit into the English/American divide? Why is Clay associated with a German setting rather than an English or an American one?

2. **World War II and combat stress:** Why would Sergeant X be the kind of character who might suffer psychological stress as a result of a war environment? As suggested by the story, what is Salinger's attitude toward war and the type of man who is able to succeed as a soldier?

Clay is used as X's foil. An essay on combat stress and men's reactions to the experience of war could compare the two main soldier characters. Salinger's portrayal of Clay is not sympathetic. What qualities allow Clay to breeze through war without struggling psychologically? In contrast, how does Salinger set up Sergeant X as a character who would likely be damaged by war? The two men's superior, Bulling, is characterized as someone who fits in the world of war. What is the unpleasant trait that Salinger reveals about this background character? This essay could also draw on some of the background characters Salinger uses to critique the general population's understanding of shell shock. For example, how does Salinger use Clay's girlfriend as a background character whose attitudes are detrimental to the well-being of a soldier with combat stress?

Philosophy and Ideas

Writing is a process that facilitates an exchange of ideas between people. Depending on the purpose of the writing, the process of writing can be therapeutic for someone who is trying to make sense of a particular incident in life. For the reader of the written word, the letter or the book can provide access, intentionally or unintentionally, into the inner workings of another person's mind. When X writes the short story for Esmé, with its required quantity of squalor, he is allowing the young woman to understand how she affected his life and helped him heal. Alternatively, the letter that X receives from his brother requesting swastikas and bayonets as souvenirs gives X insight into his brother's selfishness and lack of empathy. At its negative extreme, the process of writing becomes a chore and a battle site. Filling out Bulling's forms, for example, deteriorates into an irritating obligation that complicates the soldiers' lives simply because Bulling has the power to make it complicate their lives. Thus, writing (and reading) engages with the idea of power on many levels.

Sample Topics:

1. **The written word:** How does writing or reading have the power to heal? How does writing or reading have the power to hurt?

"For Esmé—with Love and Squalor" is a short story that addresses the power of the written word and the writing process. One approach to this topic could examine the different instances where writing has the power to heal a character and contrast it with the occasions where the written word has the ability to wound. How does the nature of the relationship between writer and reader affect the writing process? This topic could also interact with an analysis of the theme of communication.

Form and Genre

One of the first choices a writer must make when contemplating the telling of a story is to decide whose voice will operate as narrator. Most stories adopt one narrative point of view and use it consistently throughout the course of the story or novel, but many writers have experimented with the use of narrative points of view to add complexity and variety to their telling of a story. Multiple narrative points of view permit multiple perspectives on the same events. A shifting narrative point of view usually casts a new light on the plot and the characters of the narrative. In the case of "For Esmé—with Love and Squalor," the narrative point of view changes three times. However, the distinctive aspect of the shift is that the narrative voice does not change. What would cause a single character to narrate his story using three different personal pronouns?

Sample Topics:

1. **The use of different narrative points of view:** What different narrative points of view does the story use? How does each narrative point of view mirror the psychological status of Sergeant X at different moments throughout the plot?

A person without a clear sense of identity may find it difficult to refer to himself using the personal pronoun "I." Referring to oneself in the third person may be seen as symptomatic of a certain pathology. An essay on the shifting narrative points of view used in this short story could trace the moments at which they alter and relate them to X's sense of self at each moment. This essay could also include an analysis of the symbol of Goebbels's book and the quote from Dostoyevsky that X writes in the margins. How does Father Zossima's message also tie into ideas of whether a person has the capacity to talk of himself or herself as "I"? For more information on this topic, refer to the "Reading to Write" section of this chapter.

Language, Symbols, and Imagery

The primary purpose of a wristwatch is to tell the time. Wearing a watch can thus act as a reminder of the passage of time. Some people choose to wear a watch because it was given to them as a gift, and being in constant contact with the gift might make the wearer feel closer to the person who gave it to him or her. Esmé's watch is far too big for her, but she wears it nonetheless. The watch was given to her by her father just before she and her brother Charles were evacuated. Her father was subsequently killed in the war. When Sergeant X tries to initiate a conversation about the watch, Esmé changes the topic. Her love for her father and her pain at his death are still very evident. Since her father has died, his watch is one of the mementos that she has left of him. Her decision to send the watch to a virtual stranger can be seen as a very altruistic gesture. The watch does not survive its journey across Europe intact, but it achieves its purpose of bringing hope to a soldier contemplating the jaws of hell. The symbol of the watch contrasts with the book by Joseph Goebbels (1897–1945), the Nazi Party's propaganda minister, that Sergeant X comes across in Germany. Goebbels helped orchestrate the waves of misinformation that created a climate of hatred toward the Jews. Sergeant X picks up Goebbels's *Die Zeit Ohne Beispiel* and reads a note in the margin that states, "Dear God, life is hell." This piece of marginalia has been written by a member of the Nazi Party whom X has recently arrested. All the symbolic associations of this book and the comment X reads in it build up to a serious crisis for X as he mulls over the possibility that, indeed, life is hell. The power of love articulated by Dostoevsky's character, Father Zossima, is X's response to the void. However, the fact that X is unable to read his own inscription suggests that darkness is claiming him. Still, it cannot be ignored that his soul tries to counter the supremacy of hatred.

Sample Topics:

1. **Esmé's watch:** Why does Esmé send her father's watch to Sergeant X? How does the gift help X start the process of healing from his war trauma?

When Esmé wears the watch, it is too big for her child's wrist. What does this symbolize? Like Sergeant X, Esmé's watch does not survive the war intact. Why does the arrival of the watch make X feel sleepy? An essay analyzing the significance of the watch to the story could consider its importance to Esmé, its relation to the theme of time, and its power to help X emerge from the darkness of his own internal hell.

2. **Goebbels's book:** The author of *Die Zeit Ohne Beispiel* is Joseph Goebbels. What does this book represent to Sergeant X? How do the two notes written in the margins of the book symbolize a battle between evil and good (or hatred and love)?

An essay on the symbolic meanings of Goebbels's book could also interact with an analysis of the power of the written word. The book becomes a site for a struggle between words of anguish and words of love. For further insight on the meanings of the two messages, refer to the "Reading to Write" section of this chapter. Why is it significant that the book is authored by Goebbels? What does Goebbels represent to the tormented X?

Compare and Contrast Essays

The soldier damaged by his encounter with war is a figure that Salinger presents twice in the *Nine Stories* collection. However, Seymour Glass in "A Perfect Day for Bananafish" is unable to emerge from his private hell, unlike Sergeant X. Ostensibly, the two characters have much in common. They are married to women who do not seem to understand them well, and they are at odds with the people around them. Their sensitivity sets them apart from other people. Both seem doomed to follow the same path to self-destruction, yet Sergeant X is pulled back from the brink by the gesture of love he receives from two small children. Seymour Glass, in contrast, chooses suicide after his interaction with a small child. How do the children in the two stories differ? Why do they affect the two soldiers in contrasting ways? The tenor of the soldiers' conversations with other characters is important for an understanding of why the protagonists react the way they do. In "For Esmé—with Love and Squalor," Sergeant X has two lengthy conversations. The first conversation occurs with the child Esmé; the second conversation involves X's comrade-in-arms, Clay. The two conversations take place in distinct settings, and the circumstances that provide the backdrop to the conversations contrast significantly.

1. **Comparison of soldiers with combat stress:** Seymour in "A Perfect Day for Bananafish" and Sergeant X in "For Esmé—with Love and Squalor" share comparable trauma in the war and suffer psychologically. However, X starts the process of recovery, whereas Seymour commits suicide. What allows Sergeant X to be saved?

The soldier character who has disconnected from his society features in both "For Esmé—with Love and Squalor" and "A Perfect Day for Bananafish." These soldiers could be compared in an essay, as there are many similarities and many significant differences between the two characters. What point was Salinger trying to make through his portrayal of these damaged soldier characters?

2. **X's conversation with Esmé compared to X's conversation with Clay:** Where does each conversation take place? What are the topics of conversation between X and each character? How does each conversation affect Sergeant X?

When X sees Esmé for the first time, she is in a church singing in a more or less harmonious choir. Later, she accosts him in a tearoom where people are enjoying an afternoon English tea. In contrast, X and Clay converse in Germany in X's room. This room is described as if it were a cell, with a naked lightbulb and rudimentary furniture. A comparison could examine the two settings to show how they amplify the contrasts in the two conversations. Furthermore, the topics of conversation could be compared to determine why Esmé is able to connect with the lonely soldier whereas Clay only succeeds in alienating him further.

Bibliography

French, Warren. "A Nine Story Cycle." *J. D. Salinger, Revisited.* Boston: Twayne, 1988. 76–78.

Goldstein, Bernice, and Sanford Goldstein. "Zen and *Nine Stories.*" *J. D. Salinger: Modern Critical Views.* Ed. Harold Bloom. New York: Chelsea House, 1987. 81–93.

Wenke, John. "Nine Stories." *J. D. Salinger: A Study of the Short Fiction.* Boston: Twayne, 1991. 49–53.

———. "Sergeant X, Esmé, and the Meaning of Words." *J. D. Salinger: Modern Critical Views.* Ed. Harold Bloom. New York: Chelsea House, 1987. 111–18.

"PRETTY MOUTH AND GREEN MY EYES"

READING TO WRITE

THE ENGLISH essayist Joseph Addison (1672–1719) is credited with coining the axiom, "Arguments out of a pretty mouth are unanswerable." In "Pretty Mouth and Green My Eyes," Arthur is suffering an internal conflict that is caused by the contrast between his wife's attractiveness and the ugly lies she feeds him. While he is aware that his wife, Joanie, is betraying him with various other men, he is paralyzed by inaction because of his positive memories of how she once made him feel. In the excerpt below, however, the reader does not witness Joanie arguing her way out of an awkward situation. In a bizarre twist, the speaker of the "pretty" words is Lee the lawyer—Arthur's supposed best friend. In a lengthy telephone conversation, Lee uses verbal and psychological guile, imbuing his empty words with sincerity and concern, all with the intention of deceiving Arthur:

"*Wait* a second—I'll *tell* ya, God damn it. I practically have to keep myself from opening every goddam closet door in the apartment—I swear to God. Every night I come home, I half expect to find a bunch of bastards hiding all over the place. *El*evator boys. De*liv*ery boys. *Cops*—"

"All right. All right. Let's try to take it a little easy, Arthur," the gray-haired man said. He glanced abruptly to his right, where a cigarette, lighted some time earlier in the evening, was balanced on an ashtray. It obviously had gone out, though, and he didn't pick it up. "In the first place," he said into the phone, "I've told you many, many times, Arthur, that's *exactly* where you make your biggest mistake. You know what you do? Would you like me to tell you what you do? You go out of your way—I mean this, now—you actually go out of your way to torture yourself. As a matter of fact, you actually in*spire* Joanie—" He broke off. "You're bloody lucky she's a wonderful kid. I mean it. You give that kid absolutely no credit for having any good taste—or *brains,* for Chrissake, for that matter—"

"Brains! Are you kidding? She hasn't got any goddam brains! She's an animal!"

The gray-haired man, his nostrils dilating, appeared to take a fairly deep breath. "We're all animals," he said. "Basically, we're all animals."

"Like hell we are. I'm no goddam animal. I may be a stupid, fouled-up twentieth-century son of a bitch, but I'm no animal. Don't gimme that. I'm no animal."

Throughout this dialogue, Lee battles with his own ego, which nearly causes him to slip up and reveal to Arthur that he is more cognizant of Joanie's state of mind than he should be. For example, in the passage, he is on the verge of suggesting that Arthur's paranoia has incited Joanie to be unfaithful. With this near indiscretion, the reader can sense that Joanie's motivations for her infidelities may have been a prior topic of conversation between Lee and her. Lee then compounds his arrogant, manipulative treatment of Arthur by informing the tormented man that he fails to recognize that his wife has "good taste" and "brains." Lee's addendum at this point reeks of self-importance. After all, he is lying next to Joanie and so can be seen as an example of her "good taste."

This excerpt touches on many themes for an essay. The foremost themes are honesty, deception, and relationships. Lee is supposedly a friend of Arthur, yet he is sufficiently hypocritical to spend time reassuring Arthur of Joanie's honor while she is lying next to him listening to his insincere dialogue with her husband. Thus, the deception functions on several levels. The romantic triangle prompts different emotions in each participant, depending on that person's awareness of the truth of the situation. Lee alternates between smugness and pique in the passage above. He is offended by the suggestion that his lover is no more than a brainless animal. Perhaps he feels that Arthur's comment is an indictment of his own taste and sexual behavior. Joanie's silence in the excerpt is representative of her behavior throughout the story. She appears largely indifferent to Arthur's distress. Arthur, in his state of ignorance, is in emotional turmoil. Arthur, Lee, and Joanie could each become the focus of a character study.

Arthur's final comment in the excerpt critiques the modern urban condition. The 20th century is condemned for its capacity to disturb the human psyche. In Salinger's New York City, the pressures to survive and the inauthenticity of society's values lead people to be ego-driven and selfish. Loneliness, alienation, neurosis, and obsession have become commonplace. Relationships are based on self-seeking individualism. Everyone is out for what he or she can get, even if it is at someone else's expense. However, Arthur asserts that he is still able to rise above his animal instincts and behave in a civilized manner with others. He associates his wife, on the other hand, with raw animalism. An analysis of the meaning of animal references and imagery becomes possible with this story, as does a consideration of the relationship between a debased society and the behavior of its human members. How has the urban landscape provoked regression in humans? Can some people transcend the negative influences of their society? These are just some of the critical questions that the story poses.

TOPICS AND STRATEGIES

Suggested topics for essays on "Pretty Mouth and Green My Eyes" will be the focus of the remainder of this chapter. Additionally, the chapter will propose general approaches that could be used to develop those topics. These proposals should help you generate your own creative approaches to the topics.

Themes

In Salinger's vision of the 20th century, human relationships often boil down to a form of mutual mistreatment. Emotions are controlled. Trust is a luxury. In the case of the two main male characters in "Pretty Mouth and Green My Eyes," an enemy could not betray Arthur more convincingly than his purported friend, Lee, does. Arthur is surrounded by deception, but he is aware of only one face of that dishonesty. He knows his wife is betraying him, yet he puts his misguided faith in his work colleague. In this sense, Lee's deception is crueler than Joanie's, because Lee compounds the deception by offering Arthur advice and encouraging him to think well of Joanie. His hypocrisy is excessive. On the other hand, Arthur breaks one of the cardinal rules of 20th-century friendship: He discloses genuine emotion turmoil. Possibly the consequence of too much alcohol or possibly the result of overwhelming feelings, Arthur lets his public mask slip in front of Lee and shows him his vulnerabilities. This is a mistake, and Arthur quickly realizes it. Even though he is ignorant of Lee's connivance in his wife's infidelity, he knows the mores of his society sufficiently well to understand that openly confessing weaknesses brings rejection and pity rather than sympathy and compassion. In this society, there is no place for love. However, Arthur still retains links to purer human emotions. He can remember a time when his relationship with his wife was a source of joy. He is unable to sever all ties with his humanity, even if everyone around him has degenerated into an animalistic, corrupt state. However, like so many other Salinger characters, Arthur proves that a person who lives in a society founded on phoniness will find it very difficult to resist inauthenticity. Many of the themes raised in this short story touch on the notion that the modern urban condition has displaced people from a genuine and caring way of being. Essays on the themes of deception, betrayal, honesty, relationships, love, or emotions could illuminate Salinger's hostility to society's hypocritical values and standards in the story.

Sample Topics:

1. **Honesty and dishonesty:** What acts of deception and betrayal does Salinger depict in the short story? Do any of the characters expose an honest side of their personality?

The short story pits honesty and openness against dishonesty and deception. However, the forces of dishonesty strongly outweigh the voices of honesty. Even the characters who display a degree of honesty in one area of their lives are fundamentally dishonest in other areas. For example, even if Arthur is direct with Lee about his personal feelings and fears, he misrepresents the truth in his professional capacity. An essay on this topic either could focus on dishonesty, deception, and betrayal as independent themes or could negotiate the interplay between honesty and dishonesty.

2. **Failure:** How does Arthur respond to his sense of failure in his personal and professional lives? In what ways is Joanie a failure? How is Lee shown to fail at the end of the story?

The story illustrates failure as an integral component of everyone's life. The nature of that failure, though, differs for each character. Some characters are delusional about their successes and failures. Only Arthur demonstrates any awareness of his own weaknesses and limitations, although the text implies that Joanie and even Lee at the end of the story are reacting to professional and relationship disappointments. This topic could be approached through an analysis of the characters' frustrations and disenchantments and a consideration of the different ways that each character handles his or her failures.

3. **Emotional turmoil:** How does each character manifest his or her emotional confusion? How do social norms dictate, to a certain degree, how the characters deal with their emotions?

Twentieth-century humans, in Salinger's fictional world, like to think of themselves as sophisticated and in control. However, situations can arise that undermine an individual's conviction of his or her own emotional strength. Arthur confesses his emotional weakness. In Arthur's telephone conversation with Lee, Lee clearly thinks of himself as having greater emotional control than Arthur. By the end of the story, however, Lee's urbane and patronizing demeanor falters when he is confronted with Arthur's own face-saving duplicity. An essay on this theme could chart the dynamics of the story's emotional chaos, assessing how the characters fluctuate between emotional strength and emotional weakness.

4. **Dissimulation:** How does each character conceal his or her true intentions and feelings? How does Arthur's legal case enact the theme of dissimulation?

Arthur admits that he lost his legal case partly as a result of a chambermaid airing dirty laundry. The sheets stained with bedbugs contradict the lawyers' evasions and misrepresentations of their clients' hotels. How is this unveiling of the truth paralleled in the conversation between Arthur and Lee? All three main characters dissimulate to differing extents. Salinger presents dissimulation as a consequence of the phoniness and insincerity of society. Essays examining dissimulation could approach it through an analysis of the three characters' contributions to the inauthentic world in which they live, with its spurious relationships, occupations, and values.

Character

Arthur, Lee, and Joanie all present possibilities for a well-developed character study. Arthur is emotionally unstable, not only during his conversation with Lee but also in his life in general. He confesses that he feels the urge to search his closets when he comes home, in order to root out his wife's lovers. In his imagination, all sorts of men are hiding in his apartment. His paranoia and instability cause him to suppose that Joanie is capable of sexual conduct with any man she happens to meet. In reaction to his vulnerability regarding his wife's sexuality, he derides the idea that Joanie is intelligent. To him, she is merely physical and animal. Joanie is a more challenging character to write about because most of the information the reader receives about her is channeled through the hostile antipathy of her husband. On the other hand, Arthur's is also the only voice that outlines a more complex side of the woman who spends most of the story passively smoking by the side of her lover while he is in a heated conversation with her husband. At one time, Arthur reveals,

Joanie was capable of spontaneous gestures of generosity and love. Although different sides of Arthur and Joanie are shown throughout the story, Lee is the character who seems the most corrupted and hardened by modern urban life. The reader is never shown a caring or compassionate side of Lee. Throughout the short story, Lee's primary concern is himself. Whether Arthur will find out about the affair and whether their law firm won its case seem to be all that bothers him. Everything he does and everything he says is deliberate and mannered. Flickers of emotion are detectable only when his stability and ego are jeopardized. Aspects of characterization within this romantic triangle are made evident through dialogue, mannerisms, behavior, memories, and patterns of speech.

Sample Topics:

1. **Arthur:** What is the basis of Arthur's internal conflict? Why does Arthur bare his soul to Lee during their first conversation? Why is Arthur reluctant to end his marriage with Joanie?

   Lawyers are popularly imagined to lead comfortable lifestyles, free from the stresses of economic survival that trouble people with less remunerative careers. A character analysis of Arthur could analyze the contradiction between his elevated status in society and his unstable, depressed, and neurotic private self. Why does he fantasize about returning to the Army? Why does he pathetically strive to reclaim his self-respect with Lee in their second conversation?

2. **Lee:** What is Lee's attitude toward Arthur? What is Lee's attitude toward Joanie? How does Lee try to stay in control in his relationships with Joanie and Arthur? How is his equilibrium shaken at the end of the story?

   Lee's hair has been freshly trimmed, yet he allows it to be fashionably longer on top. He politely asks his lover whether she will be troubled if he answers his ringing telephone. Everything about Lee is considered and mannered. An essay on Lee could assess how he tries to maintain control in a delicate situation. However, there are moments when he loses sight of the role of "concerned friend" that he is feigning. What causes Lee to slip out of the role that he is playing? What mannerisms indicate Lee's loss of control? Does Lee care about anything other than himself?

3. **Joanie:** What aspects of Joanie's behavior indicate that she is insecure? What is Joanie's relationship like with her husband? What kind of a liaison does she have with Lee?

An essay on Joanie must not forget that much of the information about her is filtered through the perspective of her disillusioned husband. However, some of his assertions are verified by her behavior during the conversation between Lee and Arthur. Is she concerned about Arthur's feelings? Does she display any signs of nervousness or anxiety as she waits for the conversation to finish? Is her claim that she feels like a "dog" an indication of remorse? According to Arthur's version of events, how has Joanie changed since they were first married?

History and Context

As 20th-century U.S. cities grew to accommodate expanding populations, the sense of belonging to a community dwindled. Neighbors could be strangers. Families could be dispersed over different continents. An increasing reliance on self was necessary in order for people to survive in an advanced capitalist system that promoted competition and acquisition. Those who find themselves dislocated in urban sprawl, using communication forms that negate the need for face-to-face contact, might feel alienation in one of three forms. First, there is alienation from oneself. The modern urban condition makes it difficult for people to be authentically themselves. Second, midcentury urbanites became alienated from their fellow city dwellers. Third, alienation can be experienced from the society in which the individual lives. The three forms of alienation are brought together in the three main characters of "Pretty Mouth and Green My Eyes." Suburbanization was originally advocated as the solution to urban alienation. Arthur has bought into the midcentury fantasy that escape to the Connecticut suburbs could allow a "normal goddam life." New York, he feels, is an artificial place that is full of neurotics. However, Salinger's other stories frequently depict the Connecticut suburbs as a soulless and superficial domain where alienation is even more likely than in New York City.

Sample Topics:

1. **The modern urban condition:** What are the dominant features of interpersonal relationships in New York City as shown in the story? How do the three main characters convey their alienation from one another, from their society, and from their own selves?

In Salinger's urban world, the character who is aware of his or her sense of dislocation from mainstream values and attitudes is the character who struggles most with life. Nervous breakdown or excessive drinking are some of the pitiful responses used by these sensitive characters to ward off their feelings of horror and repulsion. An essay on this topic would probably focus on Arthur. He is neurotic, obsessive, depressed, and lonely. Which of his behavioral patterns indicate his neurosis and his loneliness? Compared with Arthur, Joanie and Lee have a different way of negotiating relationships with other people and with their society. How do the characters' various ways of communicating highlight their different answers to the modern urban condition?

Philosophy and Ideas

The term "romantic triangle" describes a relationship involving three people, wherein each person has a distinct relationship with the other two. The term also connotes that the triangular structure is unsatisfactory to at least one of the three members. In the scenario in "Pretty Mouth and Green My Eyes," Arthur is the only one of the three who is ignorant of the intricacy of the triangle. He labors under the misconception that Lee is a close friend who can advise him on his marital problems. Joanie and Lee, who are in a position of knowledge, can feel superior to Arthur because of his misdirected emotional outpouring.

Participating in a covert romantic triangle necessitates playing roles and wearing masks. In many career positions, but particularly for a lawyer, the job description might require that the successful candidate mask his true feelings, both negative and positive, in the name of professionalism. Arthur is defending a chain of hotels that has substandard hygiene practices. Nevertheless, a lawyer is paid to defend the client, regardless of guilt or innocence. In the private arena, too, masking is often a normal feature of interpersonal relationships. Evidently, this can be the case if someone has something to hide, as do Lee and Joanie. However, there are other motives for masking the truth. Arthur, at the end of the story, lies in order to retain his dignity in front of his colleague. Being perceived as weak or needy can be damaging both personally and professionally.

Sample Topics:

1. **The romantic triangle:** How is power distributed among the three players in the love triangle? What emotions do the three players feel as a result of participating in a romantic triangle? How does the story's triangle reflect the breakdown of values and authenticity that Salinger perceives in 20th-century society?

An essay on the romantic triangle could take one of several approaches. One approach to the topic would be to analyze the dynamics among the three characters, determining who has power in the triangle and how that power manifests itself. Possibly, more than one character has some form of control over another member of the triangle. A different approach would be to assess the social and personal elements that have caused each character to become entangled in a triangle (wittingly or unwittingly) and what impact the triangle has on each of them. Another angle would be to connect the romantic triangle to history and context. With this approach, the triangle could be used to highlight how the three players and their behavior within the triangle typify the alienated modern urban condition.

2. **Masks and masking:** Which characters conceal their true feelings and why? Which plot events indicate that Salinger is portraying a society where appearance is more important than reality?

In the mid-20th century, airing one's dirty laundry in public is perceived as breaking the unspoken rules of society. The seamy side of life, like the personal skeleton in everyone's closet, is not supposed to be made public. Everything is fine; everything is rosy. For the individual and society to perpetuate this happy myth, unhappy and complex realities must be repressed and denied. An essay on the notion of masking could approach the topic on both a personal and societal level, as Salinger addresses both perspectives in this short story.

Form and Genre

A story with a twist catches a reader by surprise. If the ending is indeterminate, it leaves the text subject to various interpretations. The ambiguous ending is a technique favored by Salinger in the *Nine Stories* collection. As a formal technique, it presents the potential for analysis, since an essay could pursue lines of inquiry such as the effects of using this technique on theme, characterization, and philosophical ideas. Salinger uses the surprise ending less frequently than the open-ended story, but notably "A Perfect Day for Bananafish" also terminates counter to the reader's expectations. The surprise, yet indeterminate, ending of "Pretty Mouth and Green My Eyes" leaves the reader uncertain about the characters' true motives and reactions and provokes a reconsideration of everything that has occurred throughout the story. Salinger's refusal to provide the reader with a solid base from which to analyze the plot and the characters is buttressed by the choice of a third-person objective narrative point of view and the use of dialogue as the driving forces of the story. Both of these narrative techniques establish distance between the reader and the inner workings of the characters' thought processes. This results in a situation where the fictional world mimics the actual world: People's motives and emotions are essentially unknowable.

Sample Topics:

1. **The indeterminate and surprise ending of "Pretty Mouth and Green My Eyes":** Why does Salinger not clarify Lee's reaction to Arthur's second telephone call? How does the surprise ending affect the reader's understanding of the story?

   Interpersonal relationships are often fraught with tensions that arise because another person's behavior seems inexplicable or bizarre. Unlike in most novels or films, a person's motivations for behaving in a certain way may never be clarified in our real-life human interactions. Even if an explanation is attempted, the rationale may still seem illogical. These factors could be considered in tandem with an analysis of the surprise ending of "Pretty Mouth and Green My Eyes." An essay analyzing Salinger's indeterminate, surprise resolution and denouement could be discussed on the basis of the uncertainty it imposes on the reader's knowledge of the characters, their motivations, and the ultimate meaning of the story itself. How does this ambiguity create parallels between the fictional and the actual world?

2. **Third-person objective narrative point of view and the use of dialogue:** Why does Salinger choose to establish distance between the reader and the thought processes of his characters? What stylistic and language techniques does Salinger employ to make his dialogue simulate actual dialogue?

   Among other techniques, Salinger makes Arthur lie, repeat himself, use slang, stress specific words, interrupt Lee and cut him off, and swear. These techniques help simulate the authentic speech of a man who has drunk too much and who feels the urge to communicate with someone. An essay analyzing Salinger's use of dialogue could take various approaches. One approach could be to analyze the stylistic devices used to convey and create a credible dialogue. Critics have regularly praised Salinger's effective replication of believable dialogue. Another approach would be to link an analysis of the use of the third-person objective narrative point of view with an analysis of the dialogue to show how they work together to bring out Salinger's perspective on the story's themes of dissimulation, dishonesty, alienation, loneliness, and relationships.

Language, Symbols, and Imagery

Salinger's characters are often prolific smokers, and Lee and Joanie are no exception to this trend. The way characters hold a cigarette, the point at which they choose to inhale or exhale, and their decision to fiddle with an ashtray or a cigarette shed light on their psychological state at any given moment. For example, the decision to light a cigarette often indicates tension or stress. However, smoke, fire, and ash can also be used symbolically to add shades of meaning to a situation. For example, if a scenario is shrouded in smoke, this might imply that someone or something is not being seen clearly. Similarly, in "Pretty Mouth and Green My Eyes," references to body parts and the various colors associated with those body parts expand a character's traits and add complexity to his or her representation. In addition, this story deliberates on the duality between animal (uncivilized) and human (civilized) behaviors, challenging the inevitability of the feral nature of human behavior in the 20th century as Salinger sees it. Animal imagery and animal references place this duality at the forefront of the story.

Sample Topics:

1. **Smoke, cigarettes, ash, and fire:** How does Salinger use these four elements to comment on the state of the relationship between Joanie and Lee at different moments throughout the development of the story? How does Lee's smoking and fiddling with the ash and the ashtray give clues to his frame of mind?

   A fire is alive and vibrant. Ash is dead matter. Cigarettes can have a calming effect, since smoking can steady a person's nerves. In the 1950s, smoking was considered fashionable, the preserve of the stylish. Thus, smoking could be a means of communicating a certain image to the rest of society. Smoke, on the other hand, is noxious and obscures clear vision. An essay considering these four elements could assess how Salinger uses them symbolically to offer information on the characters, their relationships, and the overall situation of deception.

2. **Body parts and their colors:** How do the colors that are associated with various body parts of the characters provide additional information about the psychology of the characters? How does Salinger use the motif of eyes throughout the story?

Are Joanie's eyes violet, blue, green, or the color of seashells? The eyes are said to be the window to the soul. If that window is described differently by different observers, this implies that it has a lack of transparency to the people who are looking through it. Do men see what they want to see when they look at this woman? Does Joanie have a strong sense of identity? An essay analyzing the symbolic use of body parts and the colors ascribed to them could determine why each character is linked primarily to one bodily feature and one color. Another possible approach is to argue how the use of body parts and their colors helps develop the themes of relationships, deception, and dissimulation. How does the mention of Joanie and Lee's body parts function as commentary on the physical interaction between the two characters?

3. **Animal imagery and references:** Why does Arthur think that his wife is an animal? Why does Lee propose that all humans are essentially animals? Why does Arthur assert that he is not an animal? What do the bedbugs on the hotel sheets represent?

An essay on this topic would likely engage with an analysis of the historical and social context of the story because it interconnects with Salinger's condemnation of the modern urban condition. Individualism and competition may cause some people to treat others in an exploitative manner, but Salinger shows in this story that there will always be a few people who will stand up for what is right. Bedbugs are virtually invisible parasites that feed off human beings' detritus. What comparison is Salinger making between the bedbugs on the sheet and elements of the lawyers' conversation? Another approach to this topic would be to explore the qualities that make someone succumb to bestial behavior. Why has Joanie regressed to behaving like a "dog"? What human qualities are necessary so that a person can withstand losing his or her humanity?

Bibliography

French, Warren. "A Nine Story Cycle." *J. D. Salinger, Revisited.* Boston: Twayne, 1988. 79–80.

Goldstein, Bernice, and Sanford Goldstein. "Zen and *Nine Stories.*" *J. D. Salinger: Modern Critical Views.* Ed. Harold Bloom. New York: Chelsea House, 1987. 81–93.

Wenke, John. "Nine Stories." *J. D. Salinger: A Study of the Short Fiction.* Boston: Twayne, 1991. 53–56.

"DE DAUMIER-SMITH'S BLUE PERIOD"

READING TO WRITE

"**D**E DAUMIER-SMITH'S Blue Period" is the only one of Salinger's *Nine Stories* that is predominantly set in Quebec, Canada, and has a protagonist that is a Francophile. The young man who calls himself Jean de Daumier-Smith grew up in Paris and professes to be more at ease communicating in French than in English. Feeling lonely and uncomfortable in the frenetic New York milieu that his stepfather brought him to following the death of his mother, Jean answers an advertisement for an art instructor. The "Friends of the Old Masters" art school is located in Verdun, a suburb of Montreal, a Canadian city where the majority of the population speaks French. In this city, Daumier-Smith feels able to reinvent himself:

> I had been painting, I said, since early childhood, but that, following the advice of Pablo Picasso, who was one of the oldest and dearest friends of my parents, I had never exhibited. However, a number of my oil paintings and water colors were now hanging in some of the finest, and by no means *nouveau riche*, homes in Paris, where they had *gagné* considerable attention from some of the most formidable critics of our day. Following, I said, my wife's untimely and tragic death, of an *ulcération cancéreuse*, I had earnestly thought I would never again set brush to canvas. But recent financial losses had led me to alter my earnest *résolution*. I said I would be most honored to submit samples of my work to Les

Amis Des Vieux Maîtres, just as soon as they were sent to me by my agent in Paris, to whom I would write, of course, *très pressé*. I remained, most respectfully, *Jean de Daumier-Smith*.

Very little is true in this excerpt from his application letter—not even his name. However, he unwittingly divulges much information about his state of mind. Jean de Daumier-Smith is a character worthy of analysis. An essay examining this fascinating young man would need to touch on the theme of misrepresentation, as his lies are abundant.

First, he claims that his wife has just died of cancer. The truth, of course, is that his mother has recently died. His drastic alteration of the nature of his relationship with his mother is revealing because, earlier in the story, he had admitted that he and his stepfather were "in love with the same deceased woman." This statement alludes to the Freudian Oedipus complex, which describes sexual attraction on the part of a young boy toward the mother and jealousy and antagonism toward the father figure. An essay on this topic could look for instances where Daumier-Smith demonstrates rivalry with his stepfather and covert desire for his mother. Such an analysis could also determine whether the young man resolves his Oedipus complex by the end of the story.

The use of allusion in this excerpt provides additional information about the protagonist and warrants consideration. The primary allusion is to Pablo Picasso, the Spanish painter (1881–1973). The years 1901 to 1904 are known as Picasso's blue period. During these years, his art was suffused with blue tones that established a melancholic mood and stressed the isolation of many of his works' subjects. During his blue period, Picasso was young, had left home, and was struggling economically. He was also depressed by the suicide of a friend. Jean de Daumier-Smith's claim of a link with Picasso becomes more than just a lie; it is symbolic of his own situation. Picasso's blue period was supplanted by the rose period, when his art became lighter and less bleak. Thus, the title's reference to the blue period foreshadows a better time in the young man's life. Salinger's use of the Picasso allusion, perhaps in conjunction with the borrowing of the artist Honoré Daumier's last name and the name's significance to the main character, is a possible essay topic. Furthermore, the themes that the blue period evokes, such as isolation, loneliness, and coming-of-age, could all be explored in essays.

Salinger's wry sense of humor that permeates this short story is also exemplified in the excerpt. The short story is told retrospectively by its narrator, Daumier-Smith, as he looks back on a phase of his life that he now finds faintly ridiculous because of his own youthful pretentiousness. Salinger mocks Jean's affectations through the use of language. Jean asserts that his letter of application was written in French. However, Salinger is obliged to reproduce the letter in English so that his Anglophone readership can understand it. Leaving certain words in French is a droll touch that highlights the letter's pretension. Daumier-Smith's Francophilia, the process of communication, and the progression from immaturity to maturity are ideas that the letter broaches and constitute topics that could become the focus of an essay.

TOPICS AND STRATEGIES

The remainder of this chapter will propose topics for essays on "De Daumier-Smith's Blue Period" and general approaches that could be used to write about those topics. These suggestions might help trigger your own ideas for original essay topics.

Themes

At some stage in life, most people have wished for a different life or to be someone other than who they are. Few people, though, attempt to turn that dream into reality by changing their name and reinventing themselves. As the protagonist of "De Daumier-Smith's Blue Period" finds out, picking a different name and lying do not automatically improve the quality of life. Moreover, misrepresentation does not lead to better human relationships. The web of lies that Jean constructs contributes to his isolation and loneliness as a young foreigner living in an alien city. Immigrants often face problems adapting to a new culture and way of life, but the hardships can also cause a person to mature quickly. Jean's process of maturation entails a shedding of the youthful delusions that have clouded his perception of the world. Redefining the world often leads to new understanding and changed relationships with friends and family. The short story "De Daumier-Smith's Blue Period" incorporates the consideration of a number of themes; however, some of them overlap, and writing an essay on one theme may lead to discussion of a different but associated theme.

Sample Topics:

1. **Misrepresentation:** Why does Jean tell so many lies about himself when he applies for the job as an art instructor? Apart from Jean, who and what else misrepresent themselves in the story?

Jean misrepresents himself in his application letter and continues to compound his lies after he arrives in Montreal. What is he trying to achieve by misrepresenting himself? What motivates his lying? Ironically, the art school is also guilty of misrepresentation, and Jean does not find what he expects at Les Amis Des Vieux Maîtres. What motivates the school to misrepresent itself? In a way, the school and the young man are a good match. How does each party respond to the other party's misrepresentation? An essay could analyze the motivations for, the functions of, and the consequences of misrepresentation and lying.

2. **Isolation:** What events have caused Jean to feel isolated and alone? How does Jean's isolation in Montreal precipitate his reaction to Sister Irma? What images does Salinger use to underscore Jean's sense of isolation?

Many factors contribute to Jean's feelings of "solid loneliness" in New York. At the start of the story, one image that attests to his outsider status is his fantasy of the game of Musical Chairs. How do the Yoshotos and Montreal heighten his isolation? When someone craves human interaction, sometimes he or she gives an incident or a relationship more significance than it really deserves. An essay could examine how Jean falls into the psychological traps created by loneliness and how his setting and situation contribute to his isolation. Another approach would be to analyze the imagery, such as the descriptions of the orthopedic appliances store, that Salinger uses to pinpoint Jean's sense of isolation.

3. **Coming-of-age:** How do we know that Jean views his time in Montreal as a slightly embarrassing and pathetic event from his past? What event causes Jean to mature?

An essay on this topic would probably also consider elements of the Oedipus complex discussed in the "Philosophy and Ideas" section. Jean's crisis is triggered by the death of his mother. At age 19, he is lost and alienated from himself and others. The series of events in Montreal induces him to grow, culminating in an epiphany outside the orthopedic appliances store. What are the differences between Jean the narrator and Jean the art instructor character? What did Jean learn about himself and others during his stay in Montreal?

4. **Delusion:** Many of the characters are deluded in one way or another. What are the different ways in which characters are deluded? Why does Jean want to remain in ignorance in certain situations?

In one of his letters to Sister Irma, Jean states that "at this point in [his] life," he is "willing to stay in the dark." Why does Jean not want to know the truth about Sister Irma's painting? A common cliché states that ignorance is bliss. What other examples in the story indicate Jean's willful choice to remain in ignorance? What does his delusion about the Yoshotos' sexual life imply about Jean's own psychosexual development? The story portrays many of the aspiring painters as deluded about their artistic abilities. An essay could debate the advantages and disadvantages of allowing a degree of self-delusion to moderate potentially painful interaction with the world.

Character

The only character who is adequately developed in this short story to provide enough material for an essay is the main character, Jean de Daumier-Smith. However, the real name of this character is never disclosed. Jean de Daumier-Smith is a carefully chosen pseudonym, which hints at the possibility that his true name may be John Smith. However, this hypothesis cannot be proven. Whatever the case, Jean de Daumier-Smith is a phony who contrasts with the self-reflective "John Smith."

Sample Topics:

1. **Jean de Daumier-Smith:** How does Jean develop throughout the course of the story? What motivates Jean to behave the way he does?

Since Salinger uses a first-person narrative point of view, the reader is able to gather significant insight on the main character. The main character narrates his story retrospectively, providing critical commentary by the mature Jean looking back at the immature Jean. One approach to this essay topic is to trace Jean's development, stressing the changes in his personality that differentiate the mature from the immature Jean. Another approach would be to look at Jean's motivations for behaving the way he does at different points throughout his story.

History and Context

This story's setting is unusual for Salinger because the plot's events mostly transpire in the city of Montreal, Quebec, Canada. Salinger has lived much of his life in the state of New Hampshire, close to the border with Quebec. Quebec is a distinct place in North America because French is the official language and the majority of the population speaks French. It has battled to assert its unique identity and has resisted assimilation into English-speaking Canada. Montreal provides an apt backdrop for someone who is fighting to find his identity and who desires a Francophone environment in which to express himself. When French speakers are obliged to live in English-speaking cities, they might have a sense that something is always lost in translation. Unsurprisingly, Jean is disappointed when Mr. Yoshoto makes him spend his first morning at the art school translating comments from French into English. However, many people, such as the Yoshotos, willingly choose to surrender the chance to live in a place where their first language is spoken because of the economic or political opportunities that a foreign country may offer. Traveling to another country where a person's native tongue is spoken is a rare luxury that facilitates full interaction with the local population. Interacting with people of different backgrounds and living in foreign cities can change a person's perspective on life and help him or her to grow intellectually and emotionally.

Sample Topics:

1. **Verdun, Montreal, in 1939:** How does the French Canadian setting help develop Jean's characterization? How does Jean's Francophilia contribute to the story's plot and themes?

Verdun is a neighborhood of Montreal that is partly characterized by the economic hardships of many of its inhabitants. Immigrants have found their way to this corner of the city because of its low rents. Canada, on the other hand, is a country that has long been viewed as a more liberal neighbor of the United States, where those who have not agreed with some American policies (slavery, the Vietnam War, the Iraq War, etc.) have found refuge. Thus, Jean's escape to Verdun, Montreal, when he is displeased with his life in the United States is imbued with connotations of struggle, freedom, and rejection. An essay on this topic could analyze how Salinger deploys the French Canadian setting and uses French allusions and language to elaborate on some of the story's themes, such as misrepresentation, communication, and isolation.

Philosophy and Ideas

According to Freud's theory of the Oedipus complex, a heterosexual boy must break his bonds with his mother and relinquish jealousy of the father in order for normal sexual development to occur. Normally, this obsessive love of the mother is renounced around age four or five. In the case of Jean de Daumier-Smith, the typical phases of sexual development have been delayed, possibly because of the end of his mother's marriage to his father and his mother's illness. Whatever the explanation, Jean is able to respect and admire his stepfather only when he narrates his tale and looks back at his own jealous past. Thus, "De Daumier-Smith's Blue Period" can be analyzed as a story that charts the main character's sexual maturation.

A religious or mystical experience compels Jean to view the world from a different perspective and to mature. His epiphany involves the bizarre claim that *"Tout le monde est une nonne."* This sentence has several possible interpretations. One way of understanding this enigmatic statement is that everyone is searching for communion with a higher power to give meaning to his or her life. Critics Gwynn and Blotner suggest the interpretation that everyone lives an isolated life, separated from the rest of humanity by a figurative wall. Since Sister Irma is prevented from pursuing her artistic talents by Father Zimmermann, Jean may recognize that everyone has obstacles and challenges in life that must be overcome. Art is one method that humans use to convey their vision of the world to others. Sometimes that vision is clichéd, but at times an artistic creation can touch the imagination of its audience in a way that the artist may not have anticipated. Jean feels that the destiny of the artist is to be "slightly unhappy constantly." Why is the artist doomed to be miserable?

Sample Topics:

1. **The Oedipus complex:** What is the nature of Jean's relationship with his mother, both when she was alive and now that she is dead? Who are the obstructive father figures in the story with whom Jean has to contend? How does Jean surmount his Oedipal dilemma?

Jean refers to his mother as his wife. See the "Reading to Write" section for a brief discussion of the significance of his wife/mother conflation. He also tells Sister Irma a story laden with Freudian meaning about going to meet his mother and running into a man without a nose. Jean describes another fantasy involving Sister Irma that similarly illustrates anxiety associated with a castration complex because of its allusion to Peter Abelard, a medieval philosopher and theologian who was castrated as a punishment for impregnating his student, Heloise. Several male characters act as repressive and controlling father figures who interfere with Jean's fantasy relationship with his mother/Sister Irma. Who are these male characters and what role do they play in Jean's development? At the end of the story, what sentence indicates that Jean has resolved his Oedipus complex and entered the realm of normative heterosexuality? Papers could analyze the significance of Freudian ideas in this short story. The Gwynn and Blotner analysis of this story will be helpful in getting you started on this topic.

2. **Religion:** What is Jean's attitude toward Sister Irma and her religious painting? What happens to Jean outside the orthopedic appliances store?

An essay could discuss the use of religious ideas and images in the story. As is typical in Salinger's works, the religious ideas that he engages with are culled from a mixture of faiths. Jean's appreciation of Sister Irma and her work is reminiscent of Holden's response to the two nuns he meets in *The Catcher in the Rye*, his acceptance of Christ, and his rejection of organized religion. At the end of the story, Jean has an ineffable, transcendent experience outside the orthopedic appliances store. This experience is depicted by Salinger as an example of Zen Buddhist satori, a flash of sudden spiritual enlightenment.

3. **Art:** How does art influence the lives of the characters in the story? How does the story describe the relationship among artists, their work, and their audience?

Although many people may feel an artistic impulse, the story posits that only a few have true artistic talent. According to the story, what is the difference between successful art and hackneyed art? How does society respond to the artist? Consider Mr. Yoshoto and Jean. Mr. Yoshoto has produced a fine painting of a goose, and Jean is perhaps an artist in the making. Both are obliged to teach because Western society does not provide much financial support to artists. Can good art be taught? Can art be taught by correspondence? The art school students' choice of subject matter in their paintings is varied. What does the subject matter reveal about the relationship between art and the artist? Essays on this topic could take a number of approaches. The role of the artist in society and the nature of art and artistic interpretation, for example, are potential topics.

Form and Genre

Some of Salinger's works describe situations in which a character has seemingly achieved enlightenment of a Buddhist nature. Seymour, for example, is shown in *Seymour: An Introduction* to have reached a point in his life where he is suffused with happiness because he has grasped the oneness of all existence. An experience of enlightenment must, by its very nature, be ineffable because words create a separation from the thing they attempt to describe, thereby destabilizing the concept of unity. Enlightenment is a state that can best be experienced from within, not expressed through words. This limitation is a problem that has beset all authors who have wanted to write about the experience of enlightenment. For Daumier-Smith, there is no less likely place to experience transcendence than in the mundane environment of an orthopedic appliances store. As critic Wenke proposes, the incongruity of realizing unity as a result of a woman falling over a pile of trusses and irrigation basins raises the possibility that Salinger is mocking the human need to attribute importance to minor events in our lives. The reference to Honoré Daumier supports the idea that Salinger is satirizing his society. Besides being a naturalist painter, Daumier was a caricaturist who satirized the foibles of the bourgeoisie in his work.

Sample Topics:

1. **"De Daumier-Smith's Blue Period" as a satire:** Jean describes his favorite cartoon of an open mouth and a dentist. What is the

cartoon satirizing? How could Jean's final epiphany be considered satirical? In what other incidents does Salinger use mockery or humor to laugh at aspects of Jean's world?

An essay could examine how satire is used in this short story. Since Honoré Daumier was a satirist and Jean claims Daumier's name as his own, the first place to look for satire in the short story would be in events and descriptions linked to Jean. What does his cartoon tell us about his view of the world? Where else in the story is art used as satire? Since Jean admits to a penchant for satire, an essay could examine areas of his story where his hyperbolic and droll language hints that he is not taking his subject matter seriously.

Language, Symbols, and Imagery

The orthopedic appliances store is described by Jean in detail on two separate occasions. The field of orthopedics deals with bones, joints, and the physical. However, both times that Jean looks in the window, he has a spiritual awakening or vision. The repetition of details connected to the store and the window display indicates that they are of great importance to an understanding of the story and could be the focus of study for an essay. Another physical object that is mentioned many times, but in different contexts, is the chair. The presence or absence of chairs seems to reflect Jean's state of mind at any moment. His state of mind is also symbolically communicated through the parallels that the story provides to elements of Picasso's blue period.

Sample Topics:

1. **The orthopedic appliances store:** Why does Jean's first vision of being a visitor in the garden of urinals and bedpans depress him so much? Why does his second experience at the store change him?

Jean's first description of the store uses imagery that evokes isolation, degradation, and helplessness. Why does the store have this effect on him? When he finds himself standing in front of the store the second time, the incident with the

woman frees him to reach out to his art students with compassion. What aspects of the store have symbolic meaning?
Consider, for example, the woman, the trusses and the irrigation basins, the glass window that separates the two characters, and the fact that both lose their balance during this
incident. An essay could analyze all the symbolic aspects of
the store and how they relate to some of the story's major
themes and ideas.

2. **Chairs:** What is the significance of Jean's Musical Chairs fantasy? Why does Jean not move a chair into his room at the
   Yoshotos until he is ready to write and apologize to his former
   students?

   Jean's fantasy of the game of Musical Chairs illustrates how
   Jean feels separate from the world around him and how he
   wants the rest of the world to accommodate his needs. Subsequent to this fantasy, there are many references to chairs
   throughout the story, culminating in Jean's final acceptance
   of a chair in his room. An essay could examine the functions
   and meanings of chairs in the story. What do chairs signify to
   Jean? Why did he choose not to have a chair in his room when
   he first arrived in Montreal?

3. **Picasso's blue period:** How is the Picasso allusion used to elucidate Jean's character and development? What elements contribute to a mood in the story that conjures up Picasso's blue
   period?

   The reference to the blue period makes some elements of the
   short story acquire symbolic meaning. For a brief discussion
   on this topic, turn to the "Reading to Write" section of this
   chapter. How does knowledge of Picasso's blue period help us
   understand Jean, his present frame of mind, and his sojourn
   in Montreal? This essay topic could be broadened to include a
   discussion of other artistic references and their significance to

the story's meaning, such as Honoré Daumier, El Greco, and Mr. Yoshoto's goose painting.

Compare and Contrast Essays

This short story deals with several themes and motifs that have appeared in other Salinger works. Jean's epiphany at the orthopedic appliances store is reminiscent of Holden's moment of understanding at the carrousel at the end of *The Catcher in the Rye*. If it is accepted that Holden assents to his entry into the adult world and is able to move on with his life after his moment of truth at the carrousel, then he and Jean are two of Salinger's young male characters who make this transition into adulthood successfully. Jean can also be compared to other Salinger characters who feel alienated from their society but are able to embrace humanity by the end of their respective story.

Within the story itself, much detail is given to the various paintings that Jean comes across throughout the course of the story. The details of each painting reflect on the character and the fantasies of the artist and could become the basis for a comparative essay. Furthermore, the most important painting to Jean is Sister Irma's burial painting. It creates a distinct contrast with the orthopedic appliances store, as the former deals with the spirit while the latter responds to the needs of the body. However, close reading of the text could disclose that they have more in common than might be initially suspected.

Sample Topics:

1. **The different paintings:** Why does Salinger describe each painting in so much detail? What do the different paintings reveal about each artist? Why do Sister Irma's and Mr. Yoshoto's paintings stand out to Jean?

Each painting's description divulges information about the artist. How do the different paintings compare with each other? What determines whether Jean considers an artist to have talent? An essay comparing the different paintings would need a thesis that would extend the analysis beyond just a surface description of the different works of art. This thesis should unify the essay and give the topic significance.

2. **The orthopedic appliances store and Sister Irma's painting:** How do the two objects both symbolize the unification of the body and the spirit?

Sister Irma's painting depicts Christ being carried to his tomb in the garden of Joseph of Arimathea. In both visions involving the orthopedic appliances store, Salinger uses the word *garden* or *flowers*. This establishes a link between the painting and the store. What are the parallels that Salinger creates between the two objects even though they are seemingly so distinct? How does each object evoke a transcendent moment? An essay comparing and contrasting these two objects would need to look closely at all the small details that are used to describe both and determine their significance.

3. **Jean de Daumier-Smith and Holden Caulfield:** Why are these two young men resisting the transition into adulthood? How does each young man resolve his relationships with the world and with others?

One way to approach this essay topic would be to compare the endings of the novel *The Catcher in the Rye* and the short story "De Daumier-Smith's Blue Period." What event triggers each young man's changed perspective on his world? Both young men are also troubled by issues of sexuality. How do their sexual issues complicate the way they behave in the world? What similarities are there in the way they conduct themselves with women? An essay could compare their relationships with women and show how their sexual inexperience affects their interaction with other people, both male and female.

Bibliography

French, Warren. "A Nine Story Cycle." *J. D. Salinger, Revisited.* Boston: Twayne, 1988. 80–83.

Goldstein, Bernice, and Sanford Goldstein. "Zen and *Nine Stories.*" *J. D. Salinger: Modern Critical Views.* Ed. Harold Bloom. New York: Chelsea House, 1987. 81–93.

Gwynn, Frederick L., and Joseph L. Blotner. "De Daumier-Smith's Blue Period." *The Fiction of J. D. Salinger.* Pittsburgh: U of Pittsburgh P, 1958. 33–40.

Wenke, John. "Nine Stories." *J. D. Salinger: A Study of the Short Fiction.* Boston: Twayne, 1991. 56–60.

"TEDDY"

READING TO WRITE

DIARIES FULFILL different functions according to the needs of the diarist. The process of writing can provide clarity on events that have happened or that are scheduled to happen, facilitating reflection. Diaries can also be used simply to keep a record of what should be done throughout a particular day. Whatever its form or function, the privacy of a diary is considered sacrosanct by everyone who keeps one. The stereotype of a child diary writer is a young teenage girl who pours out her heart and soul to her diary's pages; diaries are not typically associated with 10-year-old boys. The fact that Teddy, the eponymous main character of the short story "Teddy," schedules a specific time each day to write in his diary immediately establishes this young boy's difference from the norm. His diary entries show that his diary has two principal purposes: to chart his own activities and to comment on other people's emotions:

I could have asked mother where daddy's dog tags are but she would probably say I don't have to wear them. I know he has them with him because I saw him pack them.

Life is a gift horse in my opinion.

I think it is very tasteless of Professor Walton to criticize my parents. He wants people to be a certain way.

It will either happen today or February 14, 1955 when I am sixteen. It is ridiculous to mention even.

These four entries are dated October 28th, 1952. Teddy's diary indicates that he has a very busy schedule for a 10-year-old boy. Professors and researchers are lining up to interview him all over Europe because of his ability to predict the future. The excerpt obliquely hints at Teddy's own possible demise. Throughout the story, Teddy has been intimating that October 28th may be his last day for this incarnation. Several possible essay topics emerge from the content of his diary, given that he knows that October 28th may be his last entry. If indeed Teddy is aware that he may die on this day, the lack of emotion in his diary is startling. His tone remains flat and neutral, to the point of being dogmatic. A character study on young Teddy could examine why he repudiates emotion and consider the impact on his life of his belief that emotion is futile. Additionally, there is an interplay between life and death that runs throughout this story, tying in to Teddy's assertion of the veracity of Vedantic theories of reincarnation. This could lead to essays analyzing the story's perspective on the duality of life and death or discussing its critique of Western forms of knowledge.

One negative result of Teddy's eschewal of emotion is evidenced in the extract from his diary. He notes that he should ask his mother where his father keeps his military dog tags. This relates back to an earlier diary entry, where Teddy has determined that he should occasionally wear his father's dog tags, as it would please him. Teddy observes that this filial action would not "kill" him. His mother, however, would probably not encourage him to wear the tags. From these comments, the reader learns that Teddy has to force himself to interact on an emotional level with his parents. He is mindful of the effect that their emotions have on them, and he makes notes to himself to respond to those emotions in a way that they would consider normal. However, these notes urging himself to simulate suitable emotions for the benefit of others could be interpreted as emotionally manipulative. His family's dysfunctional relationships could form the basis of an essay. Alternatively, character studies of the McArdle parents or Booper, the younger sister, could examine their contentious behavior and attitudes.

The diary excerpt stresses Teddy's main objection to his family and to human relationships in general. He ascribes Professor Walton's criticism of his parents to a desire to control people by dictating their ways of behaving and thinking. There is also a suggestion that people have preconceived ideas of how another person should feel in a certain situation. Failure to match these expectations is then construed negatively. Teddy feels this in his own relationships with his parents. He claims that they are more attracted by their vision of a parent/child relationship than by the actual child they have created. Teddy is a gifted child, and his parents seem ill-equipped to deal with his unusual modes of interaction with others. They shut down any attempt by Teddy to discuss philosophical ideas. Conversely, any attempt by his parents to treat him like a normal boy is shut down by Teddy. The special child is a recurring Salinger character. The function and presentation of Teddy as a gifted child presents itself as a potential essay topic.

Since Teddy is a gifted child, the excerpt raises another critical question. If Teddy knows he is going to be pushed into an empty swimming pool by his sister later that day, why does he not take steps to avoid this confrontation? His failure to do so makes his choice to go down to the pool a form of suicide. However, his attitude is clear: "Life is a gift horse." The boy has learned the meaning of the term "gift horse" only the day before, and like a student who has been asked to use the term in a sentence to prove comprehension, Teddy deploys it to argue for the uncritical acceptance of everything that life brings, including death. In contrast, his diary reveals an occasionally critical and condescending attitude toward people and their individualistic and controlling ways. Therefore, the diary could be analyzed in an essay exploring the ironies that Teddy unwittingly discloses in the contradictions between what he claims to believe and his actions.

TOPICS AND STRATEGIES

The ideas suggested in the remainder of this chapter will propose a variety of essay topics on "Teddy." These suggestions should be used as a starting point to aid you in generating your own innovative approaches to each topic.

Themes

Parents who constantly bicker, a younger sister who tells him she hates him, and a posse of researchers and professors pursuing him for predictions of their death: This is the life of 10-year-old Teddy McArdle. There is no doubt that his intellectual needs are not being met within the bosom of his dysfunctional family. Teddy's physical appearance also emanates an aura of neglect. He wears baggy shorts, he sports a shirt with a large hole in it, and he is in dire need of a haircut. The narrator claims that Teddy is a beautiful child, but he would not be perceived as "cute." An undercurrent that menaces the interaction of the McArdle family is the pervasive threat of violence. Husband and wife thrive on fantasies of the other's violent death. The father warns his young son of the physical consequences of failing to obey his commands. Booper takes pleasure in informing a toddler she has just met of his stupidity and in suggesting ways that his parents could be murdered. Teddy's universe is not a pleasant or safe one. Is it possible that he would be happy to escape it? One manifestation of his troubled life can be detected in his assertion that emotions are not important. He wonders what emotions are "good for." Clearly, his family life would not cultivate positive emotions in a sensitive and intelligent child, but Teddy has extrapolated his personal experience to the universe at large. Teddy argues that emotion, particularly love, often manifests itself as a form of control, and that there are aspects of the world that are not enhanced by the application of emotion to them. Additionally, succumbing to an emotional reaction does not alter the reality of the universe. The universe simply is. Therefore, there is no point being affected by the weather or getting frustrated with children, for example, because they behave according to their own nature. Nonetheless, a life devoid of passion and love has its constraints, along with the benefits of never suffering from negative emotions. Teddy exhibits limitations in his personality without seeming to be conscious of them as limitations.

Sample Topics:

1. **Dysfunctional families:** How have the McArdle children responded to their unhappy family situation? In what ways are all the relationships within the McArdle family counterproductive?

   The McArdle parents are not good role models for their children. The father's style of parenting reflects the "do as I say, not as I do" school of parenting. Mr. and Mrs. McArdle do not gain the love and respect from the children that most parents would desire. An essay on this topic could analyze how the children have adopted stereotypical roles within a dysfunctional family. Teddy has become the sensible, responsible child. In some respects, he has taken over the parental role. He brings credit to the family because he is being cultivated by leading intellectuals for his wisdom. Although Teddy receives much external validation, he is distanced from his inner emotions. Booper, on the other hand, has assumed the role of the child who acts out. She expresses the pent-up frustrations that the rest of the family members attempt to deny. Another approach to this topic would be to analyze all of the different relationships among the four family members, determining the causes of the tensions and unhappiness.

2. **Violence:** How do the violent natures of the McArdle parents and Booper operate as a critique of the society that has nurtured them? What causes each character to act out with violent language and behavior?

The story shows how violence begets violence. A violent society may produce violent citizens. A violent family may produce violent children. Exceptional people may be able to withstand the pressures of a violent environment, but the average person will vent his or her frustrations on those around them. An essay examining the violence of the characters could analyze their interactions and assess why violent threats have become normalized. How does each character respond to violence? Another approach would be to evaluate which aspects of the characters' society have contributed to their violent and aggressive natures. For example, the description of how the deck chairs have been lined up points to an individualistic and territorial society even in a situation (a transatlantic cruise) that should be pleasurable.

3. **Emotions:** Why does Teddy denounce emotions? How has Teddy's renunciation of emotions affected him and his relationships with others?

What good are emotions? What effect do our emotions have on others? An essay exploring Teddy's attitude toward emotions could consider whether his choice of having no emotional life has affected him negatively or positively. His diary shows constant reminders to himself to respond more humanely to other people. This indicates that he is aware that his lack of feeling is hurtful to others. Why might Teddy want to disengage from the people around him and from his unspiritual society? Does the story show emotions as being beneficial to any character or in any situation?

Character

The members of the McArdle family are all unbalanced in different ways. The story introduces them as they are making a journey across the Atlantic on an ocean liner. For many people, the chance to relax for a few days on a well-equipped ship would be a welcome respite from everyday obligations and responsibilities. Surprisingly, the McArdle family is presented as stressed despite their setting. Their interaction with one another is hostile and aggressive. They have spent some time in Europe. Teddy has been interviewed by various professors who are interested in his unusual clairvoyance. Teddy explains to Bob Nicholson that his father wanted to return to New York on an earlier ship than the one on which they are traveling. However, they were obliged to wait for some people to talk to the young boy. The tension between father and son is palpable from the opening lines of the short story. Teddy's busy schedule dictates the family's movements, providing a reversal from the norm, in which children adapt to their parents' needs. In this sense, a degree of power resides in the 10-year-old boy. His father's impotence is exemplified by his inability to force Teddy to get off an expensive suitcase on which the boy is standing. Teddy's superior position is shown by his standing above them and reflecting on the meaning of existence, while the two parents lie prone, quarreling. Booper is isolated on another part of the ship, acting out her own legacy from the dysfunctional family dynamic.

Sample Topics:

1. **Mr. and Mrs. McArdle:** How do the McArdle parents behave with their children? How do Teddy and Booper respond to their parents?

The ideal American family is usually portrayed as having a loving, hardworking mother and father who would sacrifice themselves for the well-being of their children. An essay examining the strengths and weaknesses of Mr. and Mrs. McArdle could discuss the ways in which they fail to conform to expectations for good parents. Additionally, Salinger uses some of their traits to critique the individualistic, ego-driven, materialistic Western society. These traits could be analyzed, and their impact on their two children could be explored.

2. **Teddy:** Why is Teddy considered a child prodigy? What beliefs does Teddy have that differentiate him from everyone else in his world? How does Teddy behave with family members and strangers?

There are various possible approaches to an essay focusing on Teddy. One would be to analyze his interactions with other characters. What difficulties does he have in relating to other people? Another essay could probe Teddy's role within his family. In what ways is his behavior with his three family members remarkable? Teddy could also be examined through the lens of his attitudes and philosophies to see how they affect his behavior.

3. **Booper:** Why is Booper so aggressive and full of hatred? What are Booper's feelings toward her parents and her brother?

A typical Salinger young girl character would still be innocent even if she displays signs of her eventual corruption by society. Booper, however, has no redeeming characteristics in the story. Writing about Booper could involve analyzing her role within the family dynamic. Why does she hate Teddy? Why is she hostile when talking about her mother? Another approach would be to appraise all her human relationships. For example, why is she so aggressive to the toddler, Myron? What has caused this child to develop such a violent personality? The story suggests a variety of explanations, such as her recent entry into reincarnation cycles, the lack of attention she receives from the world compared with her brother, and Mr. and Mrs. McArdle's contrary attitudes as to how she should be parented.

Philosophy and Ideas

In *Seymour: An Introduction,* the narrator, Buddy, comments that he has "published an exceptionally Haunting, Memorable, unpleasantly controversial, and thoroughly unsuccessful short story about a 'gifted' little boy aboard a transatlantic liner." Published in 1953, "Teddy" generated a strong reaction from its *New Yorker* readership. Used to Salinger's advocacy of children as innocent and pure, the presentation of Teddy with his renunciation of emotion was found shocking. Many readers believed that Teddy murders his younger sister at the end of the story. Since he has no motive and since he probably has premeditated this act because he had foreknowledge of the possibility of a tragedy happening at the pool, he is a brutal child killer who kills just because he can. Even readers who believed that Teddy is killed by Booper were horrified at the prospect of a child embracing his own death with stolid equanimity. How could living in the United States impede a spiritual life, as Teddy claims? Why was Teddy not afraid of death? If it is affirmed that Teddy is the one who dies at the end of the story, the main reason why he accepts his fate is because of his belief in reincarnation. In his conversation with Bob Nicholson, he does not assent to Nicholson's attempt to label Vedantic reincarnation a "theory." Teddy argues for its centrality in life. Consequently, for Teddy, life and death are not polarized, as in the Western way of thinking. They are two sides of the same coin. His (or Booper's) death at the pool is not a tragedy, because it will allow the child to be reborn. Since each instance of rebirth brings with it the knowledge of former lives, a person can grow in wisdom with each incarnation. Ultimately, increased wisdom might lead to "final Illumination."

Sample Topics:

1. **Western forms of knowledge:** Why does Teddy believe that logic and Western intellectualism have prevented children

from perceiving the true nature of the world? How has Teddy's perception of the world harmed him?

Western forms of knowledge contrast significantly with many Eastern approaches to understanding the universe. An essay on this topic could look at Teddy's critique of Western attitudes toward education, reason, and emotion to show the weaknesses and limitations of Western knowledge structures according to Teddy. However, another approach would be to consider how Eastern ideas have eviscerated Teddy, affecting his behavior and his interactions with others.

2. **Life and death:** Why did Teddy not tell the professors of religion and philosophy the full details of how and when they will die? Why does Teddy not find death sad? What is Teddy's approach toward life?

In Western philosophies, death is the end of life for each soul; many Eastern philosophies suggest that death leads to the rebirth of an old soul in a new body. Teddy believes that he carries the knowledge accrued from former lives within his mind. Meditation is the key to accessing this store of information. His belief in reincarnation yields a different perception of both life and death than if he were to believe that life on earth occurs only once. An essay on this topic could examine the different perspectives on life and death that the various characters hold. Emotion, too, adds an extra dimension to ideas of life and death. Teddy avers that emotion, not death itself, creates a sense of tragedy.

Form and Genre

Foreshadowing is a literary device that presents symbolic or descriptive clues to tip the reader off as to what is going to happen later on in the text. This clue can often be understood only retrospectively. In a way, foreshadowing contains elements of prophecy in it. One function of foreshadowing is to create suspense or to prepare a reader covertly for a surprise ending. This is the case in "Teddy." However, one unusual contradiction is that the foreshadowing in "Teddy" sets up a dual interpretation of the story's ending. Additionally, the foreshadowing that Salinger incorporates ties in directly to the characterization of Teddy as a boy who is capable of prophecy. Similarly, one of the story's central ideas is the proposition that Vedantic reincarnation is a facet of human existence. In Vedantic reincarnation, knowledge of one's former lives can be accessed through meditation. This information negates the fear of death, since death is known to be not final. In Salinger, characters who believe in reincarnation, such as Seymour and Teddy, do not fear death and they accept it as a means to return to the world in another body. The idea of reincarnation could be considered an unusual form of foreshadowing, because the possibility of a death and a return are always adumbrated. In "Teddy," foreshadowing has several functions: It structures the short story, it enhances characterization, and it supports some of the story's central ideas.

Sample Topics:

1. **The use of foreshadowing:** How does Salinger's use of foreshadowing create the framework that underpins the short story? How does the use of foreshadowing in "Teddy" unify the story's structure, characterization, and philosophical ideas?

Salinger's use of foreshadowing in this short story is deliberately perplexing. Arguments could be put forward to propose that the story foreshadows Teddy's death at the hands of Booper or, the less likely option, that it foreshadows a surprise ending and makes Teddy overturn fate by murdering Booper. Whichever interpretation is accepted, the implications of the foreshadowing can be charted throughout the story. Another approach would be to show the parallels between the use of foreshadowing and Teddy's ideas on reincarnation, existence, and forms of knowing. For this essay, Teddy's discourse on the existence or otherwise of the orange peel in the ocean becomes key. His final conversation with Bob Nicholson also includes pertinent information.

Language, Symbols, and Imagery

In the 1950s, traveling between Europe and North America was a protracted affair by modern standards. Transatlantic liners were the preferred mode of travel, but a journey across the Atlantic took days. The post–World War II period was a busy one for these behemoths until they were made redundant by the advent of commercial airlines. The ocean liners were usually well outfitted, with facilities and activities to entertain the passengers. The liner that Teddy and his family take has many features that Salinger uses symbolically to critique aspects of his society. In this story, Salinger uses the character Teddy to articulate his frustrations with individualistic and ego-driven Western society. One way that the reader receives insight into Teddy's thoughts on his world is through his diary. A diary often operates as a record of private responses to a person's life, experiences, and world. There can be a perceptible gap between the way someone behaves in public and the thoughts he or she jots down in a diary. In this way, a diary can represent one side of the public/private dichotomy. Some people also use a diary to keep their life organized. Teddy's notebook has lists of duties he must fulfill and tasks he wishes to accomplish. His diary provides another perspective from which to analyze Teddy, because it reveals traits that differ from those suggested by his interactions with other characters. Throughout "Teddy," the description of each character's voice is used by Salinger to complement characterization. Detailed information is provided about the tone and modulation of the voices of Mr. McArdle, Teddy, and Bob Nicholson. Salinger uses adverbs or brief phrases to distinguish the other characters' voices. For example, Booper is described as talking "commandingly," whereas Mrs. McArdle's first words indicate that she "evidently had a little trouble with her sinuses early in the morning."

Sample Topics:

1. **The transatlantic liner:** How does Salinger use the setting of the liner to reproduce the social problems that he felt were rampant in and detrimental to Western society? How do features of the liner symbolically throw into relief Teddy's ambivalent position in his society?

An essay analyzing the symbolism of the transatlantic liner might approach it from the starting point that the liner functions in many respects as a microcosm of Western society. For example, the arrangement of the deckchairs and the way people define their territory around the deckchairs comments on individualism and acquisition. Another angle, though, would be to look at how Teddy's behavior on board the liner highlights his difference from the other passengers. For example, at the start of the story, Teddy is gazing out of the porthole, contemplating the big picture of the ocean and the universe. In contrast, his parents are lying down in bed in the cabin, focusing only on the smaller picture of Teddy standing on Mr. McArdle's luggage.

2. **Teddy's diary:** How do aspects of Teddy's diary highlight the differences between Teddy and the other passengers? How does Teddy's diary emphasize the duality between his private and public lives?

A paper examining the significance of Teddy's diary could analyze each entry to show how it reveals character traits that are kept hidden in his day-to-day interactions with his family and with strangers. Additionally, his choice of notebook, his handwriting, and his insistence on writing at the same time every day pinpoint some of the idiosyncrasies of the young boy. How does his diary identify the conflicts that Teddy must face in his dealings with other people?

3. **The importance of voice:** How does the detailed description of each character's voice aid in characterization? Why does Salinger use the voice to distinguish his different characters?

Vocal tone is one of the primary ways by which humans judge one another. If someone sounds bored, loud, nasal, or bossy, others may distance themselves from that person because they attach negative judgments to that particular voice tone.

An essay discussing Salinger's use of vocal tones could analyze the description of each character's voice and determine how it produces the reader's negative or positive judgment of that character. An extension of this topic would be to analyze other features of the characters' voices. What kind of diction do they use? What inflections do they use? How well do they listen to other characters?

Compare and Contrast Essays

In Buddy Glass's comments on "Teddy" in *Seymour: An Introduction,* he mentions that "somewhere in [the story] there was a detailed description of the boy's eyes." He goes on to explain that his family members had felt that he was attempting to paint Seymour's eyes through his description of Teddy's mildly crossed eyes. Parallels between Teddy and Seymour abound, but it is also interesting to observe that Buddy (Salinger's professed alter ego) contends that the short story was "controversial" and "unsuccessful." One of the short story's controversial messages is the assertion that leading a spiritual life in the United States is "very hard." Both Teddy and Seymour endure the knowledge that their spiritual outlook on life creates a gap between themselves and their family members, at least from the family members' perspective. This is ironic because Teddy's and Seymour's religious views promote the unity of everything in the universe. Both Teddy and Seymour have formulated a worldview from a blend of Eastern religious ideas. Although Teddy is a child and Seymour is a man at the time of their respective deaths, both choose their deaths, albeit in different ways. If the eyes are the window to the soul, then there is a suggestion that Teddy could be viewed as an incarnation of Seymour, although he cannot literally be Seymour reincarnated because of discrepancies in dates and ages. However, Teddy informs Bob Nicholson that, in his previous life, he stopped meditating and his spiritual advancement was stymied because of a relationship with a woman. This reference establishes another possible link with Seymour. Seymour's spiritual crisis is magnified by his marriage to Muriel. The last thing Seymour does before pulling the trigger on his gun and committing suicide is to look at his sleeping wife. Salinger clearly places many clues to convey the idea that Teddy and Seymour have more in common than just their religious views.

Sample Topics:

1. **Teddy and Seymour Glass:** What are the similarities between Teddy's and Seymour's religious outlooks? How has being gifted children resulted in similar experiences for Teddy and Seymour? What images and plot events does Salinger incorporate to emphasize the parallels between Teddy and Seymour?

Seymour's suicide features in the first of the pieces in *Nine Stories*. Teddy's death features in the last story. If Teddy does die at the pool and if he knows that Booper is going to kill him, then walking down to the pool to meet his death can be construed as a form of suicide. An essay comparing these two characters could focus on their beliefs, their childhood experiences, their physical appearance, their relationships with family members, or their search for spiritual enlightenment.

Bibliography

French, Warren. "A Nine Story Cycle." *J. D. Salinger, Revisited.* Boston: Twayne, 1988. 84–87.

Goldstein, Bernice, and Sanford Goldstein. "Zen and *Nine Stories.*" *J. D. Salinger: Modern Critical Views.* Ed. Harold Bloom. New York: Chelsea House, 1987. 81–93.

Wenke, John. "Nine Stories." *J. D. Salinger: A Study of the Short Fiction.* Boston: Twayne, 1991. 60–62.

FRANNY AND ZOOEY

READING TO WRITE

RARELY DOES a narrator inform the reader of a text's purpose and potential problems, but that is exactly what happens at the beginning of the "Zooey" section of *Franny and Zooey*. The narrator of this section is Buddy Glass, Franny and Zooey's older brother, and his introduction of his narrative is crucial for an understanding of how to approach the text in order to start writing about it.

The information that Buddy supplies at the start of "Zooey" is explicit and is conveyed using a first-person narrative point of view, although in the rest of the story he uses third-person omniscience. In the following excerpt, Buddy explains how he came to know all the minutiae of dialogues and dramas in which he did not participate. Additionally, he articulates the main theme of the story, unveils aspects of characterization, and categorizes the genre of the text:

> . . . I know the difference between a mystical story and a love story.
> I say that my current offering isn't a mystical story, or a religiously
> mystifying story, at all. *I* say it's a compound, or multiple, love
> story, pure and complicated.
>
> The plot line itself, to finish up, is largely the result of a rather
> unholy collaborative effort. Almost all the facts to follow (slowly,
> *calmly* to follow) were originally given to me in hideously spaced
> installments, and in, to me, somewhat harrowingly private sit-
> tings, by the three player-characters themselves. Not one of the
> three, I might well add, showed any noticeably soaring talent for
> brevity of detail or compression of incident. A short-coming, I'm

afraid, that will be carried over to this, the final, or shooting, version.

Buddy's knowledge of the events is perhaps not firsthand, but he makes it clear in this passage that his family members were not reticent in giving him all the pertinent information. On the contrary, they regaled him with excessive detail to help re-create the exhaustive account that follows. One essay topic that becomes possible from this narrative structure would be to discuss the function of Buddy as the narrator. Why did Salinger use Buddy as narrator? Why did he not use Zooey or an anonymous third-person narrator who is external to the story? Buddy's tone demonstrates that his relationships with his family members are equivocal. He is sarcastic about the fact that they were long-winded in relating their stories to him. Nonetheless, his concern for them is also apparent. He refers to them as "player-characters," which establishes a sense of distance from them, but he also describes his interviews with them as "harrowing," which implies a personal engagement with their stories. Thus, Buddy is both an involved and uninvolved narrator, character, brother, and son. Since Salinger has deliberately chosen to incorporate Buddy as the narrator and to have him stress the collaborative nature of the narrative, certain key themes start to emerge from this situation that could become the basis for essay papers. One theme is collaboration. How is the idea of collaboration elaborated through the different family relationships and through the different voices we hear in the text?

Buddy's ambivalent role in the text is highlighted further by his description of his story as a "prose home movie." In the extract, he calls the finished story the "shooting version." In response to this assertion, it would be interesting to consider the ways in which Buddy can be seen as the director of this movie/story. An essay on this idea could examine the cinematic techniques that Salinger/Buddy replicates in the story. Another approach would be to evaluate Buddy's role not only as director in the sense of fashioning the mise-en-scène but also in the sense of being the person who is controlling what the actors do and say. How aware is Buddy of the level of control he exerts over the rest of his family despite his physical absence throughout the story? Is Buddy a puppet master or

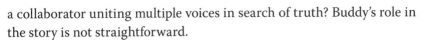
a collaborator uniting multiple voices in search of truth? Buddy's role in the story is not straightforward.

There is a strong sense, however, that he is presenting the truth as he sees it. We get this impression from the honest criticism of his own story when he admits that it lacks "brevity" and "compression." So when Buddy informs the reader that the story's main theme is love, we can be reasonably confident that one goal in his telling the story is to portray the love that his family members feel for one another. This family love is complicated, certainly, but an analysis of the complex relationships among the four main characters could lead to many worthwhile essay topics. However, Buddy also points out that many readers might believe religion and mysticism are important themes of the story. These topics will also merit exploration because Salinger and his characters have a wide range of knowledge of world religions and spiritual practices.

TOPICS AND STRATEGIES

The rest of this chapter will discuss topics for essays on *Franny and Zooey* and general approaches that could be used to write about those topics. This material should help stimulate your own ideas. Every topic discussed in this section could generate a variety of viable essays.

Themes

Franny and Zooey engages with many themes, and the text is often very explicit about its position on some of the themes. For example, when Franny and Zooey debate the nature of acquisition, Franny argues that acquisition of knowledge is as inane as trying to accumulate wealth and property. In fact, the content and tone of the two young adults' conversation is not what might be considered typical chat between people of this age (or any age for that matter). Salinger has Zooey justify the strangeness of the conversation by remarking that their upbringing was not normal. They were educated by their two older brothers in a nontraditional way, and all seven siblings were child stars, appearing regularly on a radio show called "It's a Wise Child." The outcome of this unusual childhood is that Zooey suspects that Franny and he are both "freaks." Their uniqueness notwithstanding, one mundane talent that both siblings possess is acting ability. Zooey works in television as a leading man, and Franny has had stage success, although she has rejected acting as a career at the time the events of the story unfold.

Performance also carries over into other areas of the characters' lives. The ideas of performance as mimicry and as entertainment come together at the end of the story when Zooey enters Buddy's former bedroom. Zooey reaches out to Franny by imitating their brother. In the bedroom, Zooey finds snippets of words and written recollections that convey the positive features of performance. The reader learns how the various family members celebrated Seymour's 21st birthday by entertaining one another through song and dance. A dominant theme that arises from the interaction among the family members, whether they are present or absent in the Manhattan apartment, is that their involvement in one another's life is a consequence of an underlying love they share. The theme of love is critical because the narrator flags it as the primary focus of the novel.

Sample Topics:

1. **Acquisition:** Why does Franny have a negative attitude toward acquisition? Why does Zooey rebuke her for trying to "acquire" the Jesus Prayer? What different forms of acquisition does Salinger discuss in the novel?

Western thinking advocates that the acquisition of wealth and property offers a model of living that facilitates individual fulfillment. However, Salinger, through the characters Franny and Zooey, proposes an insidious side of acquisition when the process of acquisition carries over into realms such as learning and spirituality, which in no way benefit from an acquisitive approach. How does acquisition negatively affect the process of learning? Aside from the dialogue on the topic of acquisition in the "Zooey" section, Salinger's novel displays other examples of acquisition. Look, for example, at the seemingly irrelevant lists of furniture or the contents of the medicine cabinet. Essays on the theme of acquisition might consider the effects of these lists. What is Salinger implying about the nature of acquisition through these lists? Do the lists support or contradict the position on acquisition of either Franny or Zooey?

2. **Normality:** In what ways has their unusual childhood education affected Franny and Zooey? What has been the legacy on Franny and Zooey of having been child stars?

All seven Glass siblings participated in the radio show "It's a Wise Child" over a period of 16 years and as a result were celebrities. Audience reception to their celebrity was a mixture of hostility and admiration. Furthermore, because of the age difference between the oldest Glass siblings (Seymour and Buddy) and the youngest (Franny and Zooey), the older pair were formative in shaping the education of their younger brother and sister. How did this education differ from a traditional one? How has this education shaped who Franny and Zooey are today? Essays on this topic could analyze the effects on the two characters of being "abnormal." The effects could be both positive and negative. At the end of the novel, Zooey delivers an interpretation of Seymour's Fat Lady to Franny that helps her come to terms with her sense of superiority to the average person. Another essay could consider how the symbol of the Fat Lady helps amplify the theme of normality.

3. **Acting and performance:** According to the novel, what are the limitations of acting on stage, in television, and in movies? How is it significant that many of the Glass family members have been, or still are, performers? What positive aspects of performance does the novel mention?

In several places throughout "Zooey," Salinger provides critiques of the limitations of acting in the movies, on television, and in stage productions. However, some Glass family members have made acting and performance their life's work. Essays on performance could examine the reasons why Salinger is critical of the art of acting. Another approach would be to consider the novel's ambivalent attitudes toward acting. Although acting has inherent flaws, there can be positive facets of performance, as evidenced by Seymour's account of his 21st birthday. How is performance a worthwhile activity? How does this fragment of knowledge about Seymour's past help trigger Zooey's decision to phone Franny and pretend to be Buddy?

4. **Love:** Why does Buddy describe his narrative as a "compound, or multiple, love story"? How is the love among the characters made clear? What are the complications that sometimes impede the expression of love between characters?

Essays on the theme of love could approach the topic from one of several angles. An essay could examine Bessie's love for her children and how it manifests itself differently with each child. Another essay could focus on the love that exists between brother and sister. Zooey demonstrates a kind of tough love to Franny that Franny both rejects and accepts. Furthermore, older brother Buddy is involved in the theme of love, but it is complicated by his deliberate physical absence from the family. However, his act of writing the story can be analyzed as an act of love. In addition to familial love, notions of universal love are also broached in "Zooey."

Character

This novel presents three characters in depth, all of whom offer up the possibility for a detailed character study. Franny is the only character who features in both sections of the novel, and one interesting approach would be to chart the development of Franny through the two parts of the novel. How does she develop from a college girl on a date to a girl lying on a couch having a breakdown? Furthermore, she is the central character of the "Franny" section of the novel but is arguably secondary to Zooey in the "Zooey" part. Could this decentralization of her characterization have any connection to some of the philosophical ideas of the novel?

Zooey's presence dominates the novel's second section. Buddy's portrayal of his younger brother is multifaceted, however, since Zooey is shown as both loving and hateful toward other characters. One character Zooey has mixed emotions toward is his mother, Bessie Glass. She flits among her children trying to bring them solace or to find support herself in them. Her importance cannot be underestimated in a house of seven children and a husband who is described as living in the past. Physically, she roams around from one room to another in the apartment, attempting to make sure that everything in her world coheres.

Sample Topics:

1. **Bessie Glass:** What is Bessie's role within her family? What kind of relationship does she have with Franny and Zooey? How do her physical appearance and mannerisms help characterize her?

Bessie is a former vaudeville performer who has given birth to seven children, two of whom are dead by the time the story's events are relayed. Seymour's suicide and Walt's death in World War II still haunt her and affect her relationships with her remaining children. One possible approach for an essay would be to examine her relationships with her children and consider her role in the family. Zooey is often quite patronizing toward her and mocks her interpretation of events. However, she does seem to have a more profound understanding of him than he usually gives her credit for. At times in the novel, Zooey is forced to adjust his attitude toward his mother. Bessie's clothing, her accoutrements, and her manic smoking habits are described in detail by Salinger. Another paper could analyze how these details are used to enhance her characterization. Finally, Zooey frequently calls his mother "fat" or "fatty." An essay could analyze her link with Seymour's Fat Lady. Bessie may be only a static secondary character, but her presentation and function in the novel provide feasible topics for papers.

2. **Zooey:** What is Zooey's attitude toward his own childhood? Why does he criticize his job? What are his dominant character traits? What is the nature of his epiphany in Buddy and Seymour's bedroom?

The characterization of Zooey is complex and, in some respects, contradictory. Some of his traits make him very likable, whereas manifestations of his sense of superiority can be repellent. He has a tendency to pontificate to Franny and can be quite obnoxious to his mother, but at the end of the novel, his desire to help his troubled sister becomes paramount. An essay on Zooey could take one of several approaches: It could analyze his relationship with different family members, it could determine his role within the family, or it could trace his development throughout the novel. Finally, a paper could investigate how Zooey is used by Salinger to articulate and embody central ideas such as the duality between wisdom and knowledge and the conflict between a private and public self.

3. **Franny:** How does Franny develop throughout the novel? Why is she having a nervous breakdown? How has her childhood shaped who she is as an adult?

In the "Franny" section, Franny is going through the motions of living a normal college life, but over a meal, her hostility toward her boyfriend and his values becomes palpable. The scene culminates in her passing out in the restaurant, muttering to herself. Franny spends most of the "Zooey" section lying on the couch but, significantly, gets up at the end to take a phone call and enters a room that is permeated by the smell of fresh paint. An essay could analyze Franny's malaise with society and discuss how she finds the strength to overcome her despondency. Another approach would be to try to understand why Franny clings to the Jesus Prayer as a route out of her despair. The significance of her unusual childhood with its nontraditional education could also be considered for its impact on Franny.

History and Context

The two sections of the novel are very different in terms of the environment in which they are set. The restaurant setting of "Franny" contributes to a scathing indictment of the middle-class culture that promotes conformity, pretentiousness, and self-absorbed individuality. Although Franny's beauty and physical appearance correspond nicely with the requirements of her expected female role in this milieu, her cynical condemnation of her boyfriend, his friends, and their values is uncharacteristic, to say the least. In the "Zooey" part of the novel, however, the setting shifts to the Glasses' Manhattan apartment, which has an insular ambiance. The apartment's location in New York City does not directly add to the major themes and ideas of the novel.

The other elements of the context that play an important role in developing the novel are the multiple references to ideas and figures from various world religions. Ideas derived from Eastern religions and spirituality became popular in the United States at the beginning of the 20th century. The search for alternative perspectives on the world was often prompted by a skepticism toward or rejection of Western ideas. It is interesting in this context that Franny chooses to read a Russian text, *The Way of a Pilgrim*. For Franny, the East articulates a spiritual worldview that could be interpreted as promoting anti-individualistic values and practices. At the same time, overlaps in areas of religious thought and practice around the world could be seen as providing evidence of broad human truths that deserve serious attention from anyone searching for spiritual answers.

Sample Topics:

1. **American bourgeois culture:** What aspects of the college culture that is portrayed in "Franny" does Franny condemn? How does Salinger use the character Lane Coutell to embody the negative qualities of the American middle class?

Franny's boyfriend, Lane Coutell, personifies the self-absorption and arrogance of 1950s white, middle-class America that Salinger found so abhorent. An essay on this topic could look at the incidents where Lane demonstrates his self-preoccupation and his lack of empathy for anyone else. In what ways is he a phony? How does he prove he is only interested in appearances and his own gratification? This essay would consider aspects of the society that Franny critiques, such as conformity and rigid gender roles. Other elements of society, namely mindless television programs and psychoanalysis, are also presented by Salinger as facets of life that promote uniformity.

2. **Eastern religious ideas:** How does Zen Buddhism influence the themes and plot of the novel? What is the nature of Franny's spiritual crisis? What is the significance of the book *The Way of a Pilgrim?* How does embracing Eastern ideas symbolize a rejection of the 1950s Western worldview?

Zen Buddhism asks its adherents to strive for enlightenment, a state of unity with the world in which desire and suffering are no longer experienced. Unity is a condition of no knowledge and pure consciousness, the antithesis of the acquisitive, individualistic outlook of the Western world that Franny deplores. One approach to this topic is to assess how Salinger builds Zen Buddhist ideas into his novel and the effect of those ideas on his characters. The state of enlightenment cannot be taught per se, as unity comes from within each person. Nevertheless, the Zen instructor still plays an important role in guiding his acolytes along their spiritual path. Do any characters seem to be taking on the role of the Zen master? Who are they and how do they teach their "students"? Another approach to this topic would be to consider how the religious ideas posited in the pilgrim books and elsewhere in the novel offer an antidote to Western bourgeois culture. The quotations on the back of Seymour and Buddy's door are culled from thinkers from all over the world. What is the significance of this mélange of ideas?

Philosophy and Ideas

Franny and Zooey could be labeled a philosophical novel. In many respects, it is a novel of ideas as opposed to a novel that is driven by plot. For example, some of Zooey's long speeches seem more like editorials on a particular subject rather than regular conversations between two young people. Salinger justifies this by portraying his two main characters as exceptionally intelligent and unusual in their upbringing. One of the ideas that recurs throughout the story is a questioning of the value of teaching and teachers. As a college student, Franny has firsthand experience of bad teaching. She laments that her professors are force-feeding her knowledge but not aiding her growth toward wisdom. An explanation she suggests for this failure to educate students is that Western society defines education as the acquisition of knowledge. The domain of knowledge consequently becomes a place where people can parade their knowledge and feel superior when their acquisition of knowledge exceeds another person's. Franny argues that teaching and the acquisition of knowledge often disintegrate into a pointless display of ego.

The novel suggests that wisdom can be gained not through competition at college but by turning to the ideas and findings of people from the past. This wisdom can be imparted through teaching (the words of a wise person) or through a person's legacy (memories, books, or words). The novel is haunted by people and ideas from the past that shape who the characters are today. Thus, there is a sense that the dead are still living, whereas ironically some of the living are portrayed as virtually dead in some fundamental respects.

Sample Topics:

1. **Teaching and teachers:** How has bad teaching had an effect on the lives of Franny and Zooey? How has good teaching affected the outlook of Franny and Zooey?

The issue of teaching and teachers is equivocal in the novel as there are examples of both effective and ineffective teachers. Franny criticizes the teachers she has encountered at college. She accuses them of lacking interest in their subject and of being preoccupied with appearance and self-glorification. Zooey reprimands her for her blanket condemnation of teachers, pointing out that he had had one teacher at college who was a wise scholar. Furthermore, Seymour and Buddy have been influential in teaching their younger siblings. Again, it could be argued that the result of that teaching is ambivalent.

The most important book alluded to in the novel, *The Way of a Pilgrim*, recounts the search of one man for a teacher to help him pray incessantly. In this example, he finds such a teacher. Essays on this topic could discuss the effects of bad or good teaching on the lives of the characters in the book.

2. **Wisdom versus knowledge:** How does the novel define wisdom? How does the novel define knowledge? How does the Jesus Prayer connect to the idea of wisdom?

Throughout the novel, there is constant tension between notions of wisdom and knowledge. Although this topic is closely linked to the idea of teaching, essays on this subject can also consider aspects distinct from the teaching process. There are other conduits of wisdom and knowledge that Salinger places in the novel, namely, books, religion and religious practices, and words. Each conduit presents a possible avenue of investigation leading to an essay. How does Salinger convey the importance of books? How does religion lead to wisdom? Whose words guide Franny and Zooey on their path to wisdom? Whose words mislead them in the pursuit of knowledge? Does Salinger always portray knowledge as superfluous, or are there areas of knowledge that can lead to wisdom? Where does wisdom come from, according to the novel?

3. **The ego:** Franny tells Lane that she is "sick of ego, ego, ego." Why does she find it so offensive that people just want to "get somewhere" in their lives? How does her understanding of the ego link to the theme of phoniness?

Franny abandons acting because she feels it is a climate that promotes egotism. Actors crave attention and recognition, and this self-aggrandizement undermines the art of drama. Franny is as repelled by her own ego as by everyone else's. She seeks a Buddhist-like detachment from her own sense of individual selfhood since a separate sense of self pushes people to want to stand out from the crowd. Zooey encourages her to change into a loving and forgiving member of humanity. Essays on this topic could analyze the importance of the symbolic Fat Lady to Franny's journey away from ego. An alternative approach would be to investigate the impact of the ego in acting, teaching, or writing, as argued by the novel. Salinger ridicules ego-driven behavior through his representation of Lane Coutell. What are the dangers to society of everyone being motivated to succeed as an individual?

4. **Life and death:** How do the dead continue to affect the lives of the living? How does the relationship between the living and the dead reveal an intrinsic unity among all humankind?

The novel shows several ways that the dead continue to guide and inform the living. One of the most important voices of the dead is that of Seymour, whose "ghost" functions in the novel as a character. An essay could evaluate the impact of Seymour on the other characters. Another way that the novel presents the continuity between the living and the dead is through books and ideas that have been passed down through the ages but that still shape and instruct the living. A different approach to this topic would be to explore the various means that Salinger uses to establish an active bond between the dead and the living. In the context of Eastern religions, the cyclic nature of life and death stresses the importance of repetition and rebirth. Bessie Glass tells Zooey that he has an uncanny resemblance to Buddy; Zooey calls Franny "buddy" as a term of familiarity. At the end of the novel, Zooey takes on the voice of Buddy, which allows Franny to be "reborn." Another possible approach to the topic of life and death is to analyze the characters who are both living and dead. Although Buddy is not literally dead, he has retreated into an isolated cabin where he eschews most human contact. The Glasses' father, Les, lives "entirely in the past." Why are these characters trapped in a limbo between life and death?

Form and Genre

The form and genre of *Franny and Zooey* are subjects for debate. Although it was published in novel form in 1961, the two sections of the novel originally appeared independently. The short story "Franny" appeared in the *New Yorker* in 1955, and the same magazine included "Zooey" in a 1957 edition. Thus, discussions of the novel's form and genre are complicated by the earlier publications of its component parts. Some critics feel that the two parts of the novel do not cohere. For example, they argue that there is a lack of continuity in the character Franny, who is not recognizable as the same person in the two parts. Furthermore, the styles of the two parts are distinct. The clever dialogue and subtle characterization of "Franny" give way in the second part to painstaking details of setting and character movement that provide a backdrop to Zooey's exposition of ideas. However, there are still viable, albeit nontraditional, ways to write about the form and genre of this novel. One route into this novel is through an analysis of the novel as a "prose home movie." This is how narrator Buddy Glass describes "Zooey." A home movie is made with the intention of screening the end product to family members, who will likely laugh at themselves or cringe with embarrassment at certain segments. Buddy admits that the three principal characters in the home movie have all critiqued the footage. Another approach is to assess the novel as a sermon. A sermon can be understood as a speech that gives religious instruction and encouragement. It usually has a spiritual or moral message. With this approach to the novel, the "Franny" section can be understood as illustrating the deranged social order and values against which the characters struggle. "Zooey" ultimately advocates tolerance and love of the people who are caught up in this deranged world.

Sample Topics:

1. ***Franny and Zooey* as a prose home movie:** What techniques does Buddy employ in the telling of his story that could be considered cinematic? What are the effects of presenting the story as a "movie"?

In many places throughout the novel, Buddy includes passages that describe the effects of lighting on a particular scene. He also alludes to his characters as dramatis personae whose movements are being mediated by a director. Also, the apartment is presented as a stage set where each element has been deliberately placed for effect. An essay could analyze the cinematic techniques used by Buddy with the purpose of determining their effect on the telling of the story. What themes does this cinematic method engage with? Consider, for example, how important the themes of acting and performance are to the novel as a whole. If literature is accepted as a highbrow art form and a home movie is lowbrow, what point is Salinger making about the tension between the two art forms if he makes Buddy present a literary story as a "home movie"? How does the presentation of a story as a home movie destabilize the boundaries between fact and fiction?

2. *Franny and Zooey* **as a sermon:** What is the moral and spiritual thrust of Zooey's sermon? Can the message of Zooey's sermon be understood as Salinger's message?

An essay on this topic would need to determine whether Zooey can be understood as the mouthpiece of Salinger. On the dust jacket of the original 1961 Little Brown and Company publication of the novel, Salinger wrote that Buddy Glass was his "alter-ego and collaborator." At the end of the novel, Zooey is masquerading as Buddy on the phone. Thus, the characters and the author all fuse to a certain degree. The story "Franny" depicts the vain, superficial, ego-driven society that Franny rejects and yearns to transcend through incessant prayer. Zooey, on the other hand, preaches acceptance of this Gomorrah and its undistinguished inhabitants. Essays analyzing the novel as a sermon could decipher the moral and spiritual message of the sermon and show how the sermon is intended to uplift and inspire. Consider, too, how the sermon draws from different religious faiths, not just Christianity.

Language, Symbols, and Imagery

The principal stylistic feature of this novel is dialogue. In literature, dialogue has to simulate real conversations, and writers use special techniques to achieve this mimetic effect. However, dialogue in literature is much more structured, ordered, and complete than real-life speech, but readers accept the literary version because real-life dialogue would be difficult to follow and would not allow the plot to unfold neatly. In *Franny and Zooey*, although the conversation between Franny and Lane Coutell seems authentic, the reader might have difficulty accepting the extraordinary tenor of the conversation between Franny and Zooey. Salinger protects himself from a charge of not being realistic by having Zooey explain that, as a result of being child prodigies, they do not converse like normal people. Instead, they "hold forth." A further consequence of this style is that there are fewer symbols and images than in many other Salinger works. Nonetheless, there are still a few symbolic elements that contribute to the text's deeper meaning.

The Jesus Prayer is one element that glues the two parts of the novel together. At the end of "Franny," Franny has already started muttering incessantly. It is to Lane Coutell that Franny first explains the importance of the little book bound in pea-green cloth. The prayer forms part of subsequent discussion within the Glass apartment. In the apartment, the conversation moves among the bathroom, the living room, and the bedrooms. Each room represents either a public or a private space. Most people expect privacy in a bathroom, while a living room can be shared by everyone. Issues of privacy are critical to the novel and affect all the characters to different extents. Whether they are in a private or a public space, the Glass family all smoke excessively. Although attitudes toward smoking were different in the 1950s than they are today, none of the characters seem to be able to do anything without a cigarette in hand. The details that Salinger provides for each character's smoking habits can be analyzed to determine how their method of smoking reveals their character.

Sample Topics:

1. **The Jesus Prayer:** What does the Jesus Prayer represent to Franny? Why does Zooey criticize her for fixating on the prayer?

At the end of the "Franny" section of the novel, Franny is seen lying on a couch with her lips "forming soundless words." In her explanation to Lane Coutell, she describes how repetition eventually allows the prayer to move from the lips to the heart, where it becomes synchronized with the heartbeat. This prayer technique has been promulgated by various world religions as a way to get closer to God and find humility. One approach to writing about this topic is to analyze the reasons that Franny has resorted to incessant prayer. Zooey criticizes her praying and labels it egotistical because it causes her to focus on herself. What is she trying to achieve? This essay would connect with the character study of Franny and the critique of American bourgeois culture.

2. **The bathroom, the living room, and the bedrooms:** How is the theme of privacy elaborated through the different rooms? How do the rooms concretize the dichotomy of public versus private?

A restaurant washroom is more private than the dining area. An apartment is more private than a restaurant. A bathroom is more private than a living room, and a bedroom can be a shared space but is nevertheless more private than a living room. In the novel, there are a variety of public and private spaces. The Glass children have grown up in the public spotlight, and Zooey continues to perform in a public arena. Yet in the Glass apartment, he seems unable to find any privacy. Bessie barges in on him in the bathroom and ignores his requests to leave. Why does she stay where she is not wanted? Franny has taken up residence in the living room, which should be a shared space, but her presence prevents the room from fulfilling its true purpose. Both bedrooms in the story are negotiated spaces where people who ostensibly do not belong there can venture. An essay on this topic could analyze the different rooms on the basis of the interplay between private and public. The theme of privacy could be the focus of another essay, and analysis of the various rooms would provide the textual support for the argument.

3. **The motif of smoking:** How do each character's smoking mannerisms aid in their characterization? Under what circumstances do the characters smoke?

The novel is full of references to the characters lighting up a cigarette, exhaling the smoke in a particular way, or stubbing out a cigarette. The three main characters' smoking habits, however, are distinct. Bessie smokes right down to the stub and is continually brushing imaginary tobacco flakes off parts of her body. She carries king-size cigarettes in her kimono and is ready to share them with her children. Zooey's cigarettes are often described as having gone dead. He tends to abandon them in odd places and sometimes cannot seem to make up his mind whether to smoke or not. When he enters the living room to talk to Franny, he starts to smoke cigars—a shift that is significant. Franny is not associated so much with smoking until she enters her mother's bedroom for the final conversation with Buddy/Zooey. Salinger's use of smoking to enhance characterization is an essay topic with potential. Another approach would be to show how smoking mannerisms reflect the dynamics of the relationships between the characters at any given moment.

Compare and Contrast Essays

There are two main ways that a comparative essay on *Franny and Zooey* can be handled. The first way is to compare aspects of the novel with other works. Other Salinger works provide fertile ground for comparison because many characteristic Salinger themes recur in the various texts. The second way is to find elements within the novel itself whose comparison will offer insight on theme, ideas, form, style, or characterization.

On the basis of the first method, Franny has many similarities with another of Salinger's infamous young protagonists, Holden Caulfield. Although they differ in gender and age, Franny and Holden are both appalled by the values of their society and are seeking a way to reconnect with a society that leaves them feeling alienated. Another Salinger character who shares commonalities with both Franny and Zooey is the young, eponymous protagonist of the short story "Teddy" in *Nine Stories*. Franny and Teddy are gifted young people who deplore Western intellectualism and find hope in Eastern mysticism. Within the novel itself, one comparison that is an option would be between Franny and her brother Zooey. They have experienced a similar childhood, yet they are responding to their current situations in divergent manners. As both characters are substantially developed in the novel, various angles can be adopted when comparing them.

Sample Topics:

1. **Franny and Holden:** Why do both Franny and Holden have a psychological breakdown? How does each character respond to her or his mental fragility? How does each character resolve her or his psychological estrangement from society?

Both Franny and Holden are adrift in New York City, yet Franny is holed up in her family's Manhattan apartment whereas Holden is running amok all over the city trying to avoid going back to his parents. An essay could compare the situations and values that have provoked the two characters to reject their respective societies. Both characters are also implicated in the values against which they are rebelling. Zooey points this out to Franny, whereas Holden is in denial about his own contamination by hypocrisy. Comparing the two characters through the prism of the theme of hypocrisy would be another approach to this topic. Each character reaches a different resolution on his or her estrangement from society, although both resolutions involve a degree of acceptance. A comparison of the resolutions of the two novels would also be a feasible paper topic.

2. **Franny and Teddy—a critique of Western intellectualism:** Why do Franny and Teddy rail against Western modes of knowledge? What do Eastern ideas offer these characters that Western intellectualism and knowledge structures do not?

An essay on this topic would need to engage with the history and context of the works to understand why Salinger keeps revisiting Eastern beliefs and suggesting that they offer a superior approach to life than Western ideas. Although interest in the East had been prevalent since the early 20th century, in the 1950s and 1960s Eastern philosophies and spirituality were associated with the counterculture rather than with mainstream culture. An essay on this topic could discuss the values in the Western tradition that Salinger was attacking through his characters' attitudes. Both Teddy and Franny have been damaged by Western approaches to knowledge.

3. **Franny and Zooey—the gifted young:** How have Franny and Zooey reacted to their "star" status? How has their unusual childhood influenced who they are as young adults?

Despite their similar childhoods, Franny and Zooey have distinctive personalities and respond to the same stimuli differently. For example, their respective relationships with their mother bear little similarity. Their attitude toward acting has culminated in different outcomes. An essay comparing these two characters could select any combination of their traits or attitudes as its starting point. An extension of this topic would be to compare the young boy Teddy (another of Salinger's gifted child characters) on the basis of being special in a society that tends to worship celebrity in an unhealthy way.

Bibliography

Alsen, Eberhard. *A Reader's Guide to J. D. Salinger.* Westport, CT.: Greenwood Press, 2002.

———. *Salinger's Glass Stories as a Composite Novel.* Troy, NY: Whitston, 1983.

French, Warren. "The House of Glass." *J. D. Salinger, Revisited.* Boston: Twayne, 1988. 89–98.

Kazin, Alfred. "J. D. Salinger: 'Everybody's Favorite.'" *J. D. Salinger: Modern Critical Views.* Ed. Harold Bloom. New York: Chelsea House, 1987. 19–27.

Lundquist, James. "A Cloister of Reality: The Glass Family." *J. D. Salinger.* New York: Ungar, 1979. 115–50.

Wenke, John. "The Glass Family." *J. D. Salinger: A Study of the Short Fiction.* Boston: Twayne, 1991. 63–89.

RAISE HIGH THE ROOF BEAM, CARPENTERS AND SEYMOUR: AN INTRODUCTION

READING TO WRITE

THE NOVEL *Raise High the Roof Beam, Carpenters and Seymour: An Introduction* presents a challenge to write about because the two component novellas were not originally conceived of as a cohesive narrative unit. When Salinger decided to publish them together, he justified his choice by asserting that the two stories' compatibility was accomplished by their mutual focus on Seymour Glass. However, he admitted in an editorial note that the two novellas would likely be perceived as differing in mood and effect.

Despite their incongruity, there are still overlaps in the characters, themes, and ideas of the two novellas that provide material for potential essay topics. Both stories are narrated by Buddy Glass, and both deal with a retrospective elucidation of aspects of his older brother Seymour, who committed suicide in 1948. Both novellas explore the complex, symbiotic relationship the two Glass brothers shared. Buddy's admiration for his older sibling is clarified by details in both tales about Seymour's extraordinary intelligence and his spiritual search. Both novellas broach the themes of communication, the search for truth, and family relationships. Any of these themes could be the starting point for writing an essay. The two novellas engage with the idea of the doppelgänger, or double. In literature, the double may manifest itself as an alter ego of a particular character, the author may portray the two opposing sides of one person by means of two different characters, or the author may conflate himself with one of his characters. Salinger deploys all of these doppelgänger techniques in *Raise High the Roof Beam, Carpenters and Seymour: An Introduction.*

Salinger's use of doppelgängers could be missed unless the reader pays careful attention to the fine details of the text. In fact, the interrelatedness of the two novellas is accentuated by Salinger's characteristic inclusion of small details that may initially seem puzzling and abstruse. The complexity of the text's details are exemplified in the following excerpt, the final paragraph of *Raise High the Roof Beam, Carpenters.* In this passage, Buddy wakes up in his own apartment (after having passed out drunk) and finds that a nameless old deaf mute, whom he met earlier that day at Seymour's wedding, has gone:

> My last guest had evidently let himself out of the apartment. Only his empty glass, and his cigar end in the pewter ashtray, indicated that he had ever existed. I still rather think his cigar end should have been forwarded on to Seymour, the usual run of wedding gifts being what it is. Just the cigar, in a small, nice box. Possibly with a blank sheet of paper enclosed, by way of explanation.

In this paragraph, Salinger makes a connection between the old man and Seymour Glass. Three items prove baffling but are clearly important in understanding the old man's role in the story and his ghostly doubling of Seymour: the empty glass, the cigar end, and the blank sheet of paper. Analysis of small textual details can initiate topics for papers. For example, references to glass recur throughout the novel.

Buddy feels kinship with the old man throughout the story because the old man is his sole ally against the bride's friends, who are hostile toward the Glass family because of Seymour's failure to attend his own wedding. The old man serves as an uncanny replacement for the missing Seymour. The empty glass is immediately suggestive of Seymour. Glass is Seymour's last name, and even though the story is professedly about

Seymour's wedding, Seymour was missing ("empty") from his own wedding. The old man, too, although present in the wedding party, was effectively absent because he could not participate in the discussions and is described throughout as existing in his own world.

The link between Seymour and the deaf mute is solidified when Buddy contemplates sending Seymour the old man's cigar end. A cigar is often smoked in celebration of something important but, in this case, the cigar is finished and extinguished, connoting that the important event is over. The cigar seems to foreshadow ending and termination, not only of the wedding but also of Seymour himself. The blank sheet of paper reinforces this sense of foreboding. Its emptiness suggests that there is no story or explanation. An unmarked sheet of paper is a blank slate, or a tabula rasa, suggesting the ancient philosophical proposition that argues that the human mind is empty and unformed until experience shapes it. Thus, this reference to a blank piece of paper provides a clear link to the discussion of Seymour as a young boy that follows in the second novella and to the problems that Buddy has in putting words to paper when writing about Seymour. (See Dennis L. O'Connor's article for an interpretation of these three items from a Buddhist perspective.)

A close reading of this excerpt shows that many potential essay topics can be created for this novel despite its division into two distinct novellas. One approach to writing about this novel is to look for other "doubles" to investigate or to analyze one part of a doubled pair (such as the old deaf mute) to determine his or her function and significance in the text. Many themes are suggested by the passage, such as relationships, different types of communication, and the duality of life and death. All of these topics could provide the basis for viable papers that draw on both stories for supporting textual evidence.

TOPICS AND STRATEGIES

This section of the chapter will discuss possible topics for essays on *Raise High the Roof Beam, Carpenters and Seymour: An Introduction* and various approaches that could be used to write about those topics. This material should help you produce your own ideas for essays.

Themes

Raise High the Roof Beam, Carpenters and Seymour: An Introduction engages with many themes even though both novellas have limited plot and action. Some of these themes are quintessential Salinger concerns that he had explored in earlier works; others reveal a developing interest in new areas of philosophy and religion. One theme that features in several of his works is the dynamics of family relationships. Any time one brother writes about another brother, the theme of relationships is touched upon. In this case, the theme is more poignant because Seymour has committed suicide many years before the stories are written by Buddy, whose professed goal in writing about his brother is to try to formulate the truth about him. This truth proves elusive and difficult to communicate. Buddy cannot separate his own ego from his representation of his brother, and he realizes that there are multiple truths that could fittingly characterize his brother. Seymour was involved in his own search for truth in the arena of spirituality. When Buddy reads Seymour's description of himself in his diary as being suffused with happiness, Buddy discerns that his brother found spiritual enlightenment. Many of the themes the novel advances intersect with philosophical ideas that are discussed in the "Philosophy and Ideas" section.

Sample Topics:

1. **Communication:** What different forms of communication, written or otherwise, does Salinger describe in the novel? What effects do the different types of communication have on Buddy?

The second part of the novel novel starts with an influential act of communication: Seymour reads his infant sister a Taoist tale. The tale encapsulates the didactic purpose of communication. What is Seymour trying to teach his sister through this tale? How does this tale connect with other forms of communication that are presented throughout the novel? In his apartment, Buddy observes that Seymour's wedding day was a day of "wildly extensive communication via the written word." He is referring primarily to the deaf mute's note, Boo Boo's message on the mirror, and Seymour's diary. Essays on this topic could discuss the effects of these types of communication on Buddy. Why is he struggling to communicate with the reader? Another approach would be to analyze the different forms of communication and determine how the message is related to the medium.

2. **Brotherly love:** Why do the two brothers have such a close bond? How has Seymour's suicide marked Buddy? Why does Buddy admire Seymour so deeply?

This type of essay would need to evaluate the strengths and weaknesses of the relationship that the two brothers shared and continue to share despite Seymour's death. Clearly, they have an extraordinarily close relationship, but an essay could analyze whether Salinger presents this as beneficial or detrimental to Buddy. Often, a middle child feels overlooked within a family's dynamics. Has Seymour's brilliance affected Buddy?

3. **The search for truth:** What are the different truths that Buddy is trying to grasp? What truths was Seymour searching for?

The two brothers are both preoccupied with a search for truth, but the nature of that truth differs enormously. Essays could focus on either brother's search for the truth. Seymour's search was for a way to live in the world that would enable him to embrace the good in humanity. Buddy, on the other hand, is searching for multiple truths through the process of writing about his brother. Why did Seymour marry such a seemingly incompatible wife? Why did he spend time with Muriel's family when they failed to understand or appreciate him? Who was Seymour? Why did he kill himself? How do the Taoist tale and the description of his marble-playing strategy shed light on the truth of Seymour?

Character

With this novel, the opportunity for papers on character studies is reduced because of the limited number of well-developed characters that

Salinger incorporates. Nevertheless, there are still a few possible topics. Since one focus of the novel is Seymour, an obvious starting place for a character analysis is the title character himself. A curious facet of Salinger's representation of Seymour is that the character is always absent. In *Raise High the Roof Beam, Carpenters,* he is absent from his own wedding and the plot's events. The reader only has access to Seymour's thoughts through his written communication that Buddy reproduces. In *Seymour: An Introduction,* he is absent in the sense that Buddy finds it difficult to capture him in writing. Regardless, through inference and the details that Buddy does provide, Seymour would make an interesting character for study.

One of the more unusual characters is the Matron of Honor in *Raise High the Roof Beam, Carpenters.* It is rare for Salinger to depict an adult female character in a positive light. His stock female characters, such as Muriel and her mother, are uniformly superficial and conformist. Only Glass female characters, specifically Franny and Boo Boo, are spared this stain of female banality and self-absorption. In many ways, the Matron of Honor satisfies all the expected negative qualities of a Salinger 1950s woman caught up in a world of image and no substance. However, Buddy responds to her differently than might be predicted, as he finds some of her qualities admirable. This female character would make an intriguing character study because of her nontraditional forthright attitude as she attempts to defend her friend's honor.

Sample Topics:

1. **The Matron of Honor:** Why is this character referred to by her title rather than by her name? What is her function in the story? Why does Buddy respond to her with a combination of admiration and trepidation?

   The Matron of Honor (Edie Burwick) dominates the conversation in the car. She is a character who makes decisions and acts while the other characters tend to follow her lead. What makes her such a strong character? Salinger presents this woman ambivalently. Her hostility to Seymour and Buddy (because of Seymour's betrayal of her friend Muriel) causes

Buddy to depict her critically, focusing on her affectations and superficialities. On the other hand, her character commands respect. Which of her qualities are admirable? What kind of honor is she upholding? An essay on the Matron of Honor would need to analyze the ambivalence in her representation to determine her function in the novel.

2. **Seymour—Sick Man, mystic, poet, or saint?** According to Buddy, how is Seymour a "Sick Man," a mystic, a poet, and a saint? What kind of an older brother was Seymour to the other Glass siblings?

Seymour has had a profound and lasting effect on Buddy and the other Glass brothers and sisters. He has been instrumental in shaping their outlook on the world and guiding their spiritual and philosophical development. One approach to a study of Seymour would be to analyze him in his role as an older brother and to discuss his influence on and relationship with Buddy and perhaps the other Glass siblings. Another approach would be to examine Seymour as a Sick Man, mystic, poet, and saint, as Buddy labels him. How successfully does he fulfill each of these epithets?

Philosophy and Ideas

Many of the philosophical ideas contemplated in this novel overlap with possible topics in the areas of theme, character, and symbolism, because the novel is essentially a novel of ideas rather than a novel driven by plot. Many of the ideas in the novel are quite esoteric but, if approached carefully, could become the basis for some thought-provoking essays. One of the main concerns of the novel is the process of writing, whether it is creative writing that culminates in poetry and fiction or academic writing that searches to understand the life of an artist and his or her work. Salinger adopts different stances toward the various domains of writing. This novel charts the process of writing from Salinger's perspective, although he expresses that process through his alter ego, Buddy. Through Buddy, Salinger explores the relationship between the writer and his reader, the writer and his subject, and the writer and the selection of material. Through this process, Salinger uses the device of doppelgängers (doubles and doubling) since the boundaries between himself and Buddy and between Buddy and Seymour become blurred. A work of art can exist simply for its own sake, as the vision of the "artist-seer." However, according to Buddy, the artist suffers throughout the process of bringing an artistic creation to fruition. The end product of the artistic process is an artifact that actualizes the artist's pain, a pain that academic or professional readers are unable to fully comprehend because they lack creative spirit.

Sample Topics:

1. **The writing process:** What is the significance of the two epigraphs that Salinger inserts at the beginning of *Seymour: An Introduction?* What are the difficulties that Buddy encounters when writing about his brother? Why does Seymour say that writing is a religion, not a profession?

   Raise High the Roof Beam, Carpenters and Seymour: An Introduction can be analyzed as a novel about the writing process. One approach to this topic would be to examine the problems that Salinger/Buddy identifies in the process of putting ideas onto paper. Another approach to this topic is to consider what qualities are necessary for a human to become a true artist. The two opening quotations provide critical information on Salinger/Buddy's perspective on the relationship between the writer and his creation. The second novella starts with a consideration of the relationship between writer and reader and upsets the expected hierarchy and symbiosis of this relationship. The novel is dedicated to the "amateur reader." How does Salinger/Buddy differentiate between an amateur reader and a professional reader? How does the nature of the relationship between writer and reader affect the writing process?

2. **Poetry:** According to Buddy, what makes Seymour an exceptional poet? Why is it meaningful that Seymour favored Chinese and Japanese forms of poetry?

Although the topic of poetry is closely linked to the process of writing, there is sufficient detail in the novel to make it a topic in its own right, even though there are areas of overlap with the idea of the creative process and the theme of communication. Buddy narrates an anecdote in which Seymour was able to select the correct coats for his parents' party guests based on intuition rather than prior knowledge. How does Buddy use this incident to argue for Seymour's intrinsic bond with Eastern poetic forms? How does Chinese and Japanese poetry differ from Western poetry? Buddy never reproduces any of Seymour's poems, although he does paraphrase a few. What seem to be the foci of Seymour's poetry? Why has Buddy chosen not to have Seymour's poems published?

3. **Doppelgängers:** Why does Buddy have problems distinguishing himself from Seymour? Why does Salinger use Buddy as his alter ego? Why do so many of the characters have significant similarities with other characters?

In *Raise High the Roof Beam, Carpenters*, the characters observe that Charlotte Mayhew resembles Muriel. As was discussed in the "Reading to Write" section, the old deaf mute mirrors Seymour in some respects. Buddy claims to have written some stories that sound suspiciously like Salinger's texts. What is the purpose of all this identity confusion? An essay could analyze the various instances of doubling and discuss their effects.

Form and Genre

As with *Franny and Zooey*, essays on form and genre for *Raise High the Roof Beam, Carpenters and Seymour: An Introduction* are complicated by the fact that the two novellas were put together as a novel somewhat arbitrarily. Nevertheless, this arbitrariness can become the focus of an essay, as the novel includes many components that could be described as postmodern. The postmodern novel is a very broad concept but, in this context, can be defined as a novel that gives an impression of discontinuity. Postmodern writing can be reflexive; in other words, it is fiction that is conscious of itself as fiction and that may address the construction of, or the nature of, the fictional world. Whether considering each novella separately or the novel as a whole, there is a feeling of discontinuity in *Raise High the Roof Beam, Carpenters and Seymour: An Introduction.* There is no plot per se, giving the work a chaotic feeling. The doppelgängers discussed in the "Philosophy and Ideas" section confound the traditional form of a novel in which author and character and author and narrator are distinct. In this novel, boundaries are deliberately blurred. An essay could argue that the novel challenges many novelistic conventions and breaks free from normal standards of both form and genre. There is another way, moreover, of analyzing the unusual and unconventional form of the novel. One potential approach to this novel is to think of it as a Taoist novel. The Taoist tale that Seymour tells Franny is critical in conveying the main message of the novel. It can be argued that the form of the novel parallels the tale's main message of elevating essence over appearance and of promoting "not-aiming."

Another way of approaching the form and genre of this novel is to think of it as a eulogy about Seymour written in a "semi-diary" form. A eulogy is a text written to celebrate the life of someone who has died. Since the title of *Raise High the Roof Beam, Carpenters* is taken from the first line of an epithalamium (a marriage song that incorporates predictions of happiness) by the Greek poet Sappho (born circa 630 B.C.E.), the eulogy merges life and death in its telling of the dead Seymour's marriage and life.

Sample Topics:

1. *Raise High the Roof Beam, Carpenters and Seymour: An Introduction* as a semi-diary eulogy: Why does Buddy describe his story as being in "semi-diary" form? In what way can the novel be described as a eulogy?

The function of a diary is to express one's personal and private thoughts about a particular subject or event. The function of a eulogy is to celebrate publicly the life of a dead person. It should not include excessive detail about the person who has written the eulogy. Therefore, the two forms of diary and eulogy are not really compatible. However, an essay could show how Buddy attempts to merge the two forms in writing the stories about his brother. How does Salinger use verb tenses to differentiate the diary elements from the eulogic elements? Does Buddy resolve the tension between the public nature of a eulogy and the private nature of a diary? Why does Buddy describe his work only as a semi-diary and not just a diary? How is it possible for a eulogy about Seymour to become a story about Buddy?

2. *Raise High the Roof Beam, Carpenters and Seymour: An Introduction* **as a postmodern novel:** How does this novel challenge novelistic conventions? What techniques does Salinger use to thwart reader expectations of traditional plot and character development?

Salinger deploys many techniques, such as doubling, "literary cubism," and stream of consciousness, that make this novel disrupt typical reader expectations of what constitutes a novel. Essays on this topic could analyze any number of the unconventional stylistic techniques Salinger uses or show how the disruption of novelistic conventions links to the themes of the search for truth and communication.

3. *Seymour: An Introduction* **as a Taoist novella:** How does the form of the novella correspond with the main message of the Taoist tale? How does the novella's discursive style reproduce the lesson of the curb marble game anecdote?

At first glance, *Seymour: An Introduction* seems to have no logical development plan as Buddy wanders from topic to anecdote to digression. However, the Taoist tale's placement at the start of the novel and the marble game's inclusion toward the end serve the purpose of framing the main ideas conveyed in the novella. Why is it important that Kao overlooks the appearance of the horse and focuses on the animal's inward qualities? How does the prioritization of essence over appearance carry over into the sequence of details that Buddy includes in his portrayal of Seymour?

Language, Symbols, and Imagery

Salinger incorporates many situations, characters, and images that carry symbolic meaning and add to the depth of the novel. Many of the symbolic elements associated with Seymour are linked to religious ideas since he sought spiritual peace. The significance of the Taoist tale to the rest of the novel is flagged by its strategic placement in the opening pages of the novel. The meanings of this tale are manifold. Linked to this tale is the account of how Seymour played marbles as a boy, which is recorded toward the end of the novel. These two tales impart a similar message, and both help elaborate the relationship between Seymour and Buddy. As discussed in the "Reading to Write" section, the old deaf mute (Muriel's uncle) plays a symbolic role in the novel, and this bizarre figure shoulders layers of meaning that could be discussed in an essay. Buddy meets the deaf mute in a wedding car on a stifling day. The car gets trapped by a parade celebrating American values. The occupants of the car relocate to Buddy's apartment, where they again come together in a strange blend of unity and disharmony. The foreboding mood of *Raise High the Roof Beam, Carpenters* is partially conveyed by the sense that the main players are immobile and trapped.

Sample Topics:

1. **The marbles game and the Taoist tale:** What does Seymour want to teach Franny when he reads her the Taoist tale? What does Seymour want to teach Buddy when he instructs him how to play marbles?

Seymour is acknowledged by his siblings as their spiritual teacher. Buddy states that Seymour's religious foundation is fashioned from an amalgam of "New and Old testaments, Advaita Vedanta and classical Taoism." The Taoist tale elevates intuition over reason and essence over external appearance. Similarly, the marbles game explains that not-aiming will bring greater success than consciously aiming. How do these two anecdotes told by Buddy help make sense of Seymour's search for spiritual enlightenment and his improbable marriage? Essays on this topic could show the relevance of the two symbols to the novel as a whole or to Buddy's search for truth.

2. **The old deaf mute:** Why does Buddy feel a bond with the old deaf mute? How does the old deaf mute provide insight into Seymour?

Salinger presents the nameless old man as a surreal and cryptic character. Analysis of his symbolic meaning provides a possible essay topic. Although he is sitting in the car with the other frustrated and angry wedding guests, he is immune from emotion. He stares unflappably ahead as if he is on a different plane. His difference is continually stressed in terms of not only his behavior but also his physical appearance. His link to Seymour is made clear when his brief note is interpreted by Buddy as "poetry," given that Seymour is a poet. Everything about the old man seems to have symbolic meaning, from his deathlike appearance to the items he leaves behind in the apartment. See the "Reading to Write" section for a discussion of these items.

3. **Imagery of entrapment:** Most of *Raise High the Roof Beam, Carpenters* takes place in enclosed spaces. What is the effect of this? How does the enclosed setting enhance some of the novel's main themes?

Most of *Raise High the Roof Beam, Carpenters* is set in a cramped, stifling, and stationary car. The lack of escape torments everyone except the old deaf mute, who seems imperturbable. The setting assists in the characterization of the passengers in the car. How does the cramped car help develop the plot? Other parts of the novella also describe enclosed spaces where strangers are forced to cooperate with one another. Analyzing the reciprocity of setting, theme, and characterization could be the focus of an essay.

Compare and Contrast Essays

Although the novel is ostensibly about Seymour, exploring the truth about his older brother results in an epiphany for Buddy. The two brothers are shown to have areas of affinity that extend beyond just a physical likeness. They both share a comparable knowledge of Eastern philosophy, but whereas Seymour apparently reached the Zen Buddhist state of enlightenment, Buddy is unable to achieve the necessary detachment from his ego that allows the type of spiritual happiness that Seymour found. The two brothers can be compared on the basis of many elements.

The novel has many similarities with *Franny and Zooey*. Since they were written in the same period (the mid- to late 1950s), their parallel themes and concerns are not surprising. In terms of structure, the two novels are remarkably consonant. The first part of each novel comprises a story where one character is engaged in a dialogue that provides a loose link to the second part of the novel. The second part of each novel is more didactic, aiming to convince its audience of various spiritual ideas. More specifically, the endings of both novels follow a comparable pattern and could become the focus of an essay.

Sample Topics:

1. **Seymour and Buddy:** How are the two brothers similar? How do the two brothers differ? What impels Buddy to continue living whereas Seymour commits suicide?

The two brothers can be compared in terms of their character traits and personalities. An analysis of the two brothers will almost certainly touch on the themes of the search for truth, communication, and spiritual happiness. Their different styles of writing offer critical information about the differences between the two men; Seymour's diary does not demonstrate the lack of cohesion that troubles Buddy's narrative. If Seymour had found spiritual happiness, why did he commit suicide? Why does Buddy live as a recluse?

2. **Comparison of the resolutions and denouements of *Franny and Zooey* and *Raise High the Roof Beam, Carpenters and Seymour: An Introduction*:** What is the religious idea that Salinger articulates through Zooey in *Franny and Zooey* and through Buddy and Seymour in *Raise High the Roof Beam, Carpenters and Seymour: An Introduction*?

The two novels finish in comparable ways that deliver essentially the same global message and an epiphany for the characters who comprehend that message. The novels argue for the acceptance, love, and importance of all humanity. In the different novels, how is Zooey akin to Buddy? Are there any differences between the two characters? In what ways is Zooey's relationship with Franny at the end of *Franny and Zooey* parallel to Seymour's relationship with Buddy in *Raise High the Roof Beam, Carpenters and Seymour: An Introduction*?

Bibliography

Alsen, Eberhard. *A Reader's Guide to J. D. Salinger.* Westport, CT.: Greenwood Press, 2002.

———. *Salinger's Glass Stories as a Composite Novel.* Troy, NY: Whitston, 1983.

French, Warren. "The Search for the Seer." *J. D. Salinger, Revisited.* Boston: Twayne, 1988. 99–116.

Lundquist, James. "A Cloister of Reality: The Glass Family." *J. D. Salinger.* New York: Ungar, 1979. 115–50.

O'Connor, Dennis L. "J. D. Salinger's Religious Pluralism: The Example of "Raise High the Roof Beam, Carpenters." *J. D. Salinger: Modern Critical Views.* Ed. Harold Bloom, New York: Chelsea House, 1987. 119–34.

Wenke, John. "The Seymour Narratives." *J. D. Salinger: A Study of the Short Fiction.* Boston: Twayne, 1991. 90–108.

INDEX